TRUE CRIME WRITINGS IN COLONIAL INDIA

The emergent culture of crime writings in late nineteenth-century colonial Bengal (India) is an interesting testimony to how literature is shaped by various material forces including the market. This book deals with true crime writings of the late 1800s published by 'lowbrow publishing houses'—infamous for publishing 'sensational' and the 'vulgar' literature—that had an avid bhadralok (genteel) readership.

The volume contains the author's translations of selected true crime writings by Bakaullah and Priyanath Mukhopadhyay who worked as darogas (Detective Inspectors) in the police department in mid- to late nineteenth-century colonised Bengal. These published accounts of cases (in Bangla) investigated by them are among the very first manifestations of the crime genre in India. The writings reflect their understandings of criminality and guilt, as well as negotiations with colonial law and policing. Further, through a selection of cases in which women make an appearance either as victims or offenders (or sometimes as both), this book sheds light on the hidden gendered experiences of the time, often missing in mainstream Bangla literature.

Combining a love for suspense with critical readings of a cultural phenomenon, this book will be of much interest to scholars and researchers of comparative literature, translation studies, gender studies, literary theory, cultural studies, modern history, and lovers of crime fiction from all disciplines.

Shampa Roy is Associate Professor at the Department of English, Miranda House, University of Delhi, India. Her recent publications include *Gender and Criminality in Bangla Crime Narratives in Late Nineteenth and Early Twentieth Centuries* (2017), *In Zenanas and Beyond: Representations of Indian Women in British Colonial Texts, 1800–1935* (2011), and *"Bad" Women of Bombay Films: Studies in Desire and Anxiety* (2019, co-edited with Saswati Sengupta and Sharmila Purkayastha). Dr Roy's articles on topics ranging from Victorian *memsahibs*' writings to postcolonial pedagogy have appeared in international journals like *Feminist Review*, *Interventions*, and *Studies in Travel Writing*. Her areas of research interest include the nineteenth-century and early twentieth-century English novel, popular literature, and crime fiction (in English and translations into English as well as Bangla).

TRUE CRIME WRITINGS IN COLONIAL INDIA

Offending Bodies and Darogas in Nineteenth-Century Bengal

Shampa Roy

LONDON AND NEW YORK

First published 2021
by Routledge
2 Park Square, Milton Park, Abingdon, Oxon OX14 4RN

and by Routledge
52 Vanderbilt Avenue, New York, NY 10017

Routledge is an imprint of the Taylor & Francis Group, an informa business

British Library Cataloguing-in-Publication Data
A catalogue record for this book is available from the British Library

Library of Congress Cataloging-in-Publication Data
A catalog record has been requested for this book

ISBN: 978-0-8153-6050-6 (hbk)
ISBN: 978-0-367-54099-9 (pbk)
ISBN: 978-1-003-08762-5 (ebk)

Typeset in Sabon
by MPS Limited, Dehradun

For all those readers who like to have their spines chilled and their blood curdled by a good mystery!

CONTENTS

A NOTE ON SPELLING AND TRANSLITERATION

Here are some of the rules that I have followed while transliterating Bengali terms into English.

All non-English terms, except proper nouns and names of people, are italicized wherever they appear in the text, without exception. Hence, *thhana*, *chaukidar*, *babu* and so on. Caste and community names have not been italicized, but they have been capitalized; for example, Dom, Sadgop, Brahmin, Bagdi and so on.

Words like Boishnobi have been transliterated keeping in mind the Bengali pronunciation even though many readers might be familiar with the word being Romanized as Vaishnavi.

Names of places—cities, towns, villages and districts—have been transcribed using the more popular or recognizable spellings of these places in English. Certain key places that appear in the book and have numerous pronunciations and spellings both in scholarly writing as well as administrative documents are spelled across the book like this: Medinipur/Midnapore as Medinipur, Navadvipa/Nabadvipa/Nabadwip/Naboddip as Nabadwip and Kolkata/Calcutta/Kolikata as Kolkata.

ACKNOWLEDGEMENTS

The greatest debt that I owe is to the *darogas* whose case accounts opened my eyes to the possibilities of crime writings in the late nineteenth century beyond the ubiquitous Holmesian model. Their meticulously recorded accounts of criminal investigation in Bangla take their readers on journeys that are very different from the ones envisioned by Doyle's fictions. Unlike Doyle's hero who sets out to dazzle with his ratiocinative powers, the *daroga* narrators give us investigative processes that are protracted and often riddled with errors of judgement and missteps that make the investigator hero far more fallible and realistic. As such, the experience of reading these contemporaries of Holmes, who had actually worked as detectives in the police department in colonial Bengal, was a novel one that pushed me to translate these writings for a wider audience.

A huge thanks to Routledge and to Aakash Chakrabarty in particular for expressing interest in this translation project, extending every possible support to facilitate the journey and answering all queries with a great deal of patience and understanding. Without Aakash, Brinda, Sophie and Cathy this book would not have seen the light of day.

As Visiting Research Fellow in the School of Law, Politics and Sociology (27 May to 7 June, 2019) at the University of Sussex, I was able to focus on my work without any worries. I am extremely grateful to Prof. Elizabeth Seal for all her help and for making me feel at home on the bewilderingly large campus. I'll always treasure my memories of discussing the fascinatingly diverse area of crime studies with her.

Being chosen for The Charles Wallace India Trust (CWIT) Visiting Fellowship 2019–2020 allowed me to work at the British Centre for Literary Translation (BCLT) in the University of East Anglia, UK for nearly two and half months, and helped my research and the final putting together of the manuscript in immensely fruitful ways. I am extremely grateful to Dr. Bijaylakshmi Nanda for granting me leave from college so I could visit UEA and focus on completing my book. To Anna Goode I'll always be thankful for all her help and encouragement while I was working at UEA. I learnt a great deal about the histories, theories and politics of translation from

Prof. Duncan Large, the Director of BCLT. Both Duncan and Anna made sure I was able to work in an amenable environment at the UEA campus. The seminars related to Translation Studies as well as Crime Fiction at UEA were enriching in terms of yielding both scholarly insights as well as valuable friendships. The papers that I presented at the University of Sussex and at UEA were based on early drafts of my book and the warm response that they received assured me that macabre mysteries always find an interested audience. A huge thank you to Stuart and his family for making my stay in Norwich so wonderfully comfortable.

My friends and colleagues, Saswati Sengupta and Sharmila Purkayastha, implicitly understand and support the importance of research-based work, especially on 'bad' women. Even while working on separate projects, we always have enough to share, argue and laugh about. My sister Sangeeta is the other crime genre aficionado in the family and my reading of an interesting crime novel is never complete without animated discussions with her. As always, Rajarshi was dragged willy-nilly into sharing this journey of birthing a book with all its woes and joys, excitement and worries. Without his unstinting help, the book would not have been possible.

1

INTRODUCTION

Writings centred on crime and detection emerged in the 1890s in Bangla, when *darogas* (Detective Inspectors in the colonial Police Dept. in Bengal) began to write and publish what were supposed to be true accounts of cases that they had investigated. Accounts of investigation by *daroga*s like Bakaullah and Priyanath Mukhopadhyay are, for all intents and purposes, the earliest manifestations of a dedicated crime genre in Bangla. They are the earliest cultural consequences of the newly introduced legal processes and protocols of investigation which werealso of popular interest in imported European crime fictions in colonial Bengal. Such is the iconic stature of Saradindu Bandopadhyay's Byomkesh Bakshi (who made his appearance on the horizon of Bangla crime writing in the 1930s), fuelled by the spectacular renaissance the fictional detective has enjoyed in recent cinema and tv, that it has led to an unfortunate eclipsing of the importance of his predecessors like *darogas* Bakaullah and Mukhopadhyay, who pioneered the field of crime writings in Bangla. Emerging as they did in the late nineteenth century, the *daroga*s' crime-centred writings were new forms of cultural articulation and reflected a response to transformations in the domain of criminal investigation, policing and law in Bengal under colonial rule.[1] Immensely popular amongst contemporary readers of late nineteenth century Bengal, these writings deserve greater attention from modern readers, especially crime genre enthusiasts, and to be read as meticulously crafted accounts of crimes and criminal investigation of the time. They also yield rich insights into the social formation within which they were produced. This volume, with its ten translated case accounts—three of Bakaullah and seven of Priyanath Mukhopadhyay—from their original Bangla, hopes to make these non-canonical writings available to a wider spectrum of readers who are unable to read them in their original language (Dasgupta and Pal, 2013; Mukhopadhyay, 2004).

II

Crime-centred writings can often yield rich insights into the social experience of the historical moment in which they were produced. The fascinating enterprise of pursuing clues and leads and investigating mysteries also inevitably lead to engagements with questions about why and how crime and criminality were understood, defined and dealt with in their contemporary contexts. And since questions related to criminality cannot be fully understood without delving into several social and ideological issues that cluster around the ever-changing boundaries between legitimate and illegitimate behaviour within specific social locations, the pursuit of such questions becomes an exploration of the historical moment in all its varied complexity. As such, crime-centred writings like the *daroga* accounts not only enhance and refine our understanding of what was constructed as crime, culpability and notions of justice and redress within their contexts, they also provide a window into many aspects of life and law in the late nineteenth century period in Bengal.

The accounts selected for translation are of cases in which women make an appearance either as victims or offenders, or, more interestingly, as both. Many of the investigations described in the accounts bring to light female acts of resisting and undermining of normative gendered roles and duties. These female transgressions and assertions of agency took place within a context which is associated with the relentless debating of the so-called "woman question" as it took shape in colonial Bengal. The education of 'upper'-class/caste women (its extent, nature and ill-effects), their attire, mobility, roles and duties within the familial space, the age of consent, their lives as widows—all these issues and more, related largely to the construction of emulation-worthy models of upper caste Hindu/Bengali/Indian femininity, generated reams of hortatory and prescriptive writings in mid-late nineteenth-century Bengal. A considerable amount of discursive labour in the field of Bangla writings at that time was expended on describing the duties and virtues of the putatively quintessential Hindu *ramani* (woman) and her body, "a locus of unconquered purity … moulded from infancy by a *shastric* regimen" (Sarkar, 2013: 143). Epithets like *sati-lakshmi* and *griha-lakshmi* were popularly deployed to consolidate highly restrictive ideals of femininity that were linked to an inviolable and monolithic Hindu identity, as well as to the sanctity of the *hindu griha* (hindu household).[2] These ideas were further strengthened when tied to ideas of the nation.

Colonial law was largely complicit with brahmanical patriarchy in denying women any personhood outside of roles governed by the strictest of familial and caste-bound codes. It helped reinforce patriarchal regulations and controls to curb any possibility of female expression of desires for socially unsanctioned intimacy. Young widows, for instance, could be punished with a death penalty if found guilty of attempting to abort/having aborted unwanted pregnancies. Within the caste-patriarchal system, a widowed woman's sexual life was seen as ending with the death of her husband and she was then subjected to extremely rigid codes of enforced celibacy and austerity. Fear of harsh social and familial reprisals left widows with no choice but to abort pregnancies that resulted from either consensual liaisons or rapes. Besides strengthening the excruciating proscriptions that bound upper-caste widows' lives and sexuality, the criminalizing of abortion made them vulnerable to potential harassment and intimidation by local authorities and police officials.[3] Similarly, Sections 366 and 498 of the newly codified laws framed women exclusively as potential victims of "enticement" and "abduction" and refused to grant them any sexual agency or to view them as capable of making choices in cases of elopement. The framing of elopement as "abduction" also made it easier for families to forcibly bring back those women who had chosen to elope with their lovers.[4]

At the same time, colonial laws chose not to intervene in the various forms of violence that women were subjected to within the domestic space. Investigation began only when the violence turned homicidal. Most of the investigated homicides described by the *daroga* narrators in the translated accounts, for instance, are the consequence of wrathful men "punishing" wayward female relatives for imagined/real sexual infractions. Buried in the accounts are fascinating tales of women who, despite the severity and all-pervasive nature of controls, found the courage to act in ways that threatened the patriarchal system. These are real life stories of ordinary women who were not passive upholders of the oppressive ideals of patriarchy, but resourceful and strong individuals who desired better/different worlds of social and sexual relationships and opportunities, and were often unafraid to escape familial ties and homes in search of them. Battered, brutalized, killed, humiliated, threatened and exiled from home, the difficult daughters, wives and widows in these accounts draw our attention to hidden gendered experiences of the time that have not always found their way into mainstream literatures in colonial Bengal.[5] Embedded in these popular texts and refracted through the patriarchal prejudices and paranoia that shape these writings, there are women's voices and stories which can be retrieved and read not as evidence of "culpable" behaviour, but of rebellious assertion of female agency and desire.[6] Given the paucity of nineteenth-century material in Bangla that record ordinary women's voices, the reported dialogue between the *daroga* and potential witnesses, or women's statements/*ejahar*, are undeniably valuable for helping us recuperate some lost tales of resistant femininity.

III

Undeniably, as a crime-centred genre, the *daroga* accounts were a legatee of the colonial encounter. For one, their emergence was tied to the ways in which crime and criminality were defined and dealt with in a context shaped by the formation of modern institutions and procedures related to crime – the momentous codification of criminal law, the formation of a police dept. and the development of "scientific" techniques of investigation such as anthropometry, fingerprinting and forensic post-mortems.

It was in 1861, following the Indian Rebellion of 1857 and the assumption of direct rule by the British Government, that the provincial police forces of British India were unified and a "modem" police organization was established.[7] The 'new police' idea was formulated within a broader context of establishing British administrative, legal and civil hegemony within India, and the evolution of the police continued to support these purposes. With Act V of 1861, which still governs India's present-day provincial police forces, the Police Code was devised for the first time and the system of regular town patrol was introduced. It made a number of changes in the police organisation, and marked the increased importance of the police as an institution of colonial control in India. As Peter Robb has noted:

> placing the developing police force in a broader context of imperial purposes in India, it is seen that it long remained a largely symbolic representation of power and order.
>
> (Robb, 1991: 129)

The highest-ranking positions of Superintendent and above were monopolized by European officers, while the lower ranks of the police—the positions of Inspector, Sub-Inspector, Head Constable and Constable—were the province of Indians, although there were some European Constables, Head Constables and Inspectors, particularly in cities and ports. In 1868, a dedicated Detective Dept. was set up in Kolkata by the Commissioner of Police, Stuart Hogg, almost a decade before the emergence of the same in Scotland Yard. Special rules were framed regarding investigation and for the first time culpable homicide, burglary and grievous hurt were termed "special report cases".

The image of the *daroga* as constructed in the accounts of Bakaullah and Mukhopadhyay—as that of a dexterous and dogged pursuer of leads and criminals—militated against popular contemporary stereotypes of local police officers and *darogas* as corrupt, boorish, venal and inefficient. Trenchant criticism of the police was published with great regularity in Bangla newspapers and periodicals like *Sadharani*, *Som Prakash*, *Hindu Sanskarak* and *Hindu Ranjika*.[8] In these writings, police officials, especially the *darogas* of villages and *muffosil* areas were described as insensitive, ignorant, greedy, oafish and overweening bullies. They were also represented as being complicit with wealthy landlords and only interested in lining their own pockets. Quite often, however, the critique of the police would also become a scathing expression of class snobbery mingled with religious and casteist prejudices. The deplorable state of the police department, in such writings, is ascribed to the fact that "men of low caste" and "uneducated *mussalman*s" enjoyed a monopoly of the offices of *darogas* and *jamadars*. Throughout the nineteenth century, the colonial administration also bemoaned its inability to attract "educated" or "respectable" Indians in sufficient numbers for the positions of Inspector and Sub-inspector.

> The number of Bengalees have fallen from 330 in 1875 and 311 in 1876 to 274 in 1877. The difficulty of finding Bengalees of intelligence and education who are content to enter in the lower grades and earn promotion by good service, is very great; but it is thoroughly understood that men of this stamp are essential for detective purposes and when good men can be obtained, they are readily accepted. C. T. Metcalfe, Annual Administrative Report, April 30, 1878.
>
> (Chattopadhyay, 1982: 137)

Critics of the system however pointed out that the dropping numbers could be linked to the government's refusal to increase salaries of Indian police officers and its obstreperousness about keeping administrative expenses at the lowest level possible.[9]

IV

Based on Bakaullah's preface to his case accounts, in which he briefly talks of the circumstances in which he became a *daroga*, it is possible to conclude that he was recruited in the 1840s when the East India Company was obsessively focused on stamping out *thuggee* and Commissioner Sleeman was searching for courageous and intelligent young Indian men to help him in his mission.[10] Not much is known about Bakaullah, except that he was born into a well-to-do family in a village in the Hooghly district of Bengal and subsequently moved to either Kolkata or some other town to complete his education in a *madrassa*. In his preface, Bakaullah talks proudly of the *daroga*'s post as one that was associated with prestige, power and wealth, and describes being thrilled when the post was offered to him while he was a young student. His name surfaces in a letter dated 2nd July, 1868, written by Special Duty Inspector General of Police, J.H. Reilly, to the Personal Assistant to the Inspector General of Police, where he draws the Inspector General's attentions to Detective Inspector Munshi Bakaullah's (spelt Bakaoollah in his letter) "successful exertions" and talks of him as deserving "great credit for the zeal and intelligence he has displayed" in arresting a gang of poisoners that ran their operations between Gaya and Ranigunge (Bengal Judicial Proceedings, 1868).[11]

Priyanath Mukhopadhyay (1855–1917) joined the Kolkata police department in 1878 and retired in 1911 after working as a *daroga* for 33 years. He started publishing his case accounts in a journal called *Anusandhaan* (Investigation) from 1889, but soon after began serializing the accounts in a monthly magazine called *Darogar Daftar*.[12] *Darogar Daftar* was devoted entirely and exclusively to Mukhopadhyay's eagerly-awaited narratives about crimes and their investigation anchored, for the most part, in real events, people and experiences.[13] In the 1898 *Baishakh*/April edition of *Darogar Daftar*, its editor/publisher Baninath Nandi asserts about the novelty of this enterprise:

> We do not include anything that has been embellished by our imagination in these books. Only real incidents have been written about … *Darogar Daftar* is an absolutely new kind of a book in every possible way. This kind of writing has never before been published in the Bangla language. Even though it is often written in the narrative form, it can definitely not be called a novel full of imagined things.
>
> (Nandi, 1898: 4)

Darogar Daftar was the longest running serialized journal largely devoted to true accounts (*prokrito ghhotona*) of crime-solving. It ran for nearly twelve years and described to its readers what was meant to be read as an arduous and objective investigative process—*anusandhaan*—which would consolidate their faith in the infallible workings of the law. The *anusandhaan* is described in these accounts in terms of viewing corpses with forensic acumen, interrogating suspects, gathering information, pursuing possible leads in search of evidence, deciding what might constitute relevant evidence after sifting through the collected information, analysing it and arriving at conclusions leading to the final uncovering of the "truth" about the crime.

V

There is no gainsaying that, generated by colonial forms of policing, the *daroga* writings also owed their existence to a context shaped by the multiple and complex cultural consequences of colonial education, the burgeoning of print culture and the formation of an avid middle-class readership. They debuted in a colonial Bengal in which the print industry had expanded exponentially over the nineteenth century thanks to fast-growing indigenous presses clustered largely in what was the *battala* area of North Kolkata.[14]

Furthermore, it was a context where Vidocq's memoirs, Eugene Sue's *Mysteries of Paris*, Reynolds' *Mysteries of London*, the novels of Wilkie Collins and Mary Braddon and the adventures of fictional detectives like Sexton Blake and Sherlock Holmes were all extremely popular amongst Bengali readers.[15] Some read them in English, others when they were translated or adapted into Bangla.[16] Annual reports of libraries, like the Kolkata Public Library in the late nineteenth century, suggest that fiction (both English and Bangla) circulated the most and that writers like Doyle, Collins, Reynolds and Eugene Sue were never short of readers. Their overwhelming popularity, for instance, is satirically represented in Tagore's short story called *Detective* through the protagonist, a police detective and a crime genre afficionado whose passion for the genre is indistinguishable from anglophilia. Such unquestioning enchantment with the English language and literatures and wistful admiration for the unfamiliar urban landscapes of Paris and London are mocked and shown as resulting in a skewed perspective on reality and self-destructively delusional behaviour (Tagore, 1899/2001: 307–312).

Anglophilia of this kind was also clearly evident amongst some of the Bangla writers of crime fiction who privileged the Eurocentric vision and appeased their readers by producing "*chhayabalambans*" (De, 1905: 1) of European crime writings.[17] This was especially the case when, in the wake of the phenomenal popularity of Conan Doyle's fictions, many Bangla writers of crime fiction turned invariably to the Holmesian model for inspiration. But equally there were readers, writers and publishers of Bangla crime who critiqued and eschewed indigenous writings that attempted little other than obvious and crude regurgitation of their western sources. As one reader of Bangla crime writing asserts, the need of the hour was not "incompetent translations of English or French crime writings", but texts written in ways "entirely the writers' own" (*Bangabashi*, 1906, in Ghosh, 2011: 7). The *daroga* writings, especially Mukhopadhyay's *Darogar Daftar* series, which were contemporaneous to the Holmes fictions, garnered immense popularity amongst Bangla readers of the time without being mimicries or reproductions of western models. Readers of the *daroga* series were also repeatedly reassured by Baninath Nandi that they were authentic records of crime-solving by an actual police detective and nothing like the salacious *kechhas* or sensational descriptions of scandalous liaisons associated with the *battala* presses.[18] Plied with assurances that the series would "specially make every effort ... to enhance and strengthen the Bangla language", readers of Mukhopadhyay's accounts grew in numbers and by the seventh year of its publication, Nandi could proclaim with justifiable pride:

> Today *Darogar Daftar* has entered its seventh year. In this country rarely does a journal retain its popularity in a consistent manner for so long. Undoubtedly this is a matter of great pride. The life and success of such journals depends entirely on their readers. It is because we have such kind readers that we are able to feel proud today.[19]
>
> (Nandi, 1898: 3)

In Mukhopadhyay's own words, *Darogar Daftar* were based on "Those various cases that (I had) solved or at times, failed to solve, during the long period spent working as a police officer" (Dasgupta, 1958: 4). Inhabiting a space that overlaps with some of the recognized categories of crime writing in which "detection" of crime is the pre-eminent generic trope—police procedural, detective, true crime, mystery, police memoir—the accounts are difficult to tie down in terms of any prescribed typologies and remain separate and distinctive in their representation of the investigative process. As Nandi goes on to say,

> *Darogar Daftar* is a completely new kind of book. Never before this has anything like it been published. Which is why many readers haven't yet been able to decide what category of writing it fits into and whether to call it fiction or poetry. But even though its written in the form of a narrative, it cannot be called a novel full of imagined events. Nor can its writer be called a novelist.
>
> (Nandi, 1898: 4)

Shaped by colonial policing and legal systems, the *daroga* writings that mediate "*prokrito ghotona*"—real events—of investigation and bring to light many buried tales and voices, also ended up as supplements to "the institutionalised stories told in courts and police stations" as well as "the culturally authoritative texts of the law" (Rowland, 2001: 17). Furthermore, unlike in most conventional English crime fictions of the time where the "solving" of the case by the triumphant detective becomes synonymous with a reassuring, social order-affirming denouement, the *daroga* narratives often offer less-than-reassuring closures. They don't end with the detective's triumphant identification of the criminal but afford glimpses of what happens in the trials that follow. And in doing so, they often leave readers with a sense of unease and uncertainty about the inequities and contradictions in the judicial system.

As such, these writings are testament to the mutable and fluid nature of the crime genre and to the need to look beyond generic conventions and formulae tied to the Anglo-American "grand tradition".[20] Their meandering plots and uncertain endings draw our attention to discrete evolutions of the genre in different historical contexts and push for the importance of reading them in terms of the social/political context in which they have been produced.[21] Thus despite being contemporaries of Holmes, for instance, the two *darogas* do not describe their investigations as spectacular feats of case-solving achieved through dazzlingly individualistic acts of ratiocination and clue-reading. Their writings display long-drawn, meticulously-undertaken investigations that often involve misreading of evidence as well as tedious pursuit of leads and of obstreperous, tight-lipped witnesses who refuse to trust the police.[22] In the accounts of both *darogas*, frustrating failures and bitter disappointments are often what characterize the investigative process. Their hardships are also compounded by the fact that, unlike Holmes who can simply dismiss the authority of doltish police officials like Lestrade, the *darogas* are only too aware of being colonized subjects and *chakurijibis* (employees) bound by the requirements that their positions impose on them. Their fraught relationship with colonial authority is laid bare when they refer bitterly to themselves as beleaguered employees of the colonial govt., duty-bound to fulfil every arbitrary order and every oppressive demand of their superior officers.

> While the local police has been asked to assist in every possible way, the primary responsibility of looking into this case has been assigned to me. Given that in this job we have to keep a record of even the number of times we go out to urinate, do I have a choice but to follow orders?
>
> (Bakaullah, *Ray Mahashay*, 1890 (approx.)/2013: 65)

> It is so very easy for a superior officer, to issue orders of this kind to his junior officer. But what never ceases to surprise me is why our superiors are unable to give us any suggestions as to how such orders are to be followed. At any rate, once I get my orders, I have no choice but to follow them, to the best of my abilities whether I succeed or fail in my mission.
>
> (Mukhopadhyay, *E Ki Khoon*, Vol. 1, 1894/2004: 156)

> We are a colonized race. We have no choice but to obey orders.
>
> (Mukhopadhyay, *Girijashundori*, Vol. 1, 1895/2004: 220)

When *daroga* Mukhopadhyay narrates his negotiations of colonial authority, what becomes clear is that he wants his readers to view him sympathetically not only as a disenfranchised colonized struggling to fulfil the demands of his profession, but also as one whose anxieties and dilemmas stem equally from his deep investment in the normative hierarchies and social codes related to caste/class/gender associated with conservative constructions of a Hindu *bhadralok* identity. The references to his anxious struggles to uphold such beliefs and ideals at any cost, even when they become incompatible with his professional commitments, help consolidate his credentials as a diligent professional, a put-upon colonized subject and most importantly, a Hindu *bhadralok* acutely aware of his caste/class status.[23]

> Hindus of this country never (especially in the evenings) touch a corpse or even objects related to the corpse. But despite being Hindus, we police officers are never able to observe such rules. Despite knowing that I would have to take a bath later that night after touching the things of a dead person, I fulfilled the demands of my duty.
>
> (Mukhopadhyay, *Balihari Buddhi*, Vol. 1, 1894/2004: 193)

Predicaments arising out of such simultaneous commitments become especially evident in accounts of cases where women across caste and class surface as witnesses, perpetrators or victims of crimes that disrupt patriarchal ideals of social coherence. And interestingly, while patriarchal censure shapes both *darogas*' responses to female transgressors, their tacit complicity in caste/class hierarchies is evident in their extreme caution when investigating possible infractions by upper caste/class women and their concern about the potential social disgrace and ruined reputations of affluent households that come under the scanner during the investigation. In *Ray Mahashay*, *daroga* Bakaullah talks of his anxieties while traveling to investigate the alleged abortion by a powerful *zamindar*'s sister.

> The case involved a high-born young woman of an affluent family; she was a *zamindar*'s sister and she lived in the inner quarters of the household. How was I going to investigate her? How was I going to go around collecting facts about the case? I became frantic with worry as I wondered about these things.
>
> (Bakaullah, *Ray Mahashay*, 66)

His subsequent musings about the case suggest that he sees himself as working within a social system where inequalities of wealth and privilege often decide the nature and extent of the investigative process. *Daroga* Mukhopadhyay, in fact, freely admits to undermining and subverting the law, in order to preserve the reputation of upper caste/class women and their families in his accounts of cases titled *Aashmani Laash* (Aerial Corpse) and *Kubudhhi* (Imprudence). In contrast, when interrogating women who either belong to poor families or survive in the metropolis by working as domestics, he has no qualms about resorting to high-handedness and intimidation or even representing their victimhood as well-deserved comeuppance for their sinful acts.

VI

The translating of these records poses several challenges, many of which have to do with the fact that the word order in Bangla is often quite different from that of English. As such, despite Venuti's assertions about the dangers of "domesticating" the source text by minimizing its foreignness in the target text, and Spivak's critique of "translatease", the absurdity of a literal translation has been avoided (Venuti, 1998: 241, Spivak, 2012: 314–16). Bangla seems to be a more dense language, and often retaining the integrity of the original means having to break up the lines in English. In Bangla, many prepositional relations are created by inflecting nouns, definite articles are simply understood and plural or singular nouns are perceived from the context. Also, at times certain words are so saturated with cultural meanings that the pedantry of footnoting becomes unavoidable. Despite such problems and conundrums, my translation has remained as faithful as possible to the *darogas*' painstaking record of the tortuous process of investigation, so different from narratives devoted to displaying the virtuoso performances of fictional detectives likes Holmes. The fastidiously described minutiae of the investigative process also throws up the multiple and conflicting perspectives and voices that intersect with the omniscient narrative and help produce a heteroglossia of responses to gendered questions of guilt and justice. For it is these that make it relevant within our context, which continues to be haunted by some of these questions.

Note: The exact publication dates of Bakaullah's writings not being known, they could not be mentioned along with the case accounts. However, since Bakaullah joined the police in the 1840s, almost three decades before Priyanath Mukhopadhyay, his cases have been placed before those of Mukhopadhyay.

Notes

1 Girish Chandra Basu's *Sheykaaler Daroga r Kahini* (The Tales of a *Daroga* Those Days) published in 1885 is also a *daroga* account of the time. Basu's account is mostly focused on his experiences and adventures as a *thug*/ dacoit chaser.

2 Both words gesture at the ideal wife of Hindu brahmanical patriarchy. "*Sati* recalls the goddess as the sacrificing wife whose myths ideologically sanctioned the horrific practice of widow immolation in parts of India while *Lakshmi* is the golden deity of happy conjugality" (Roy and Sengupta, 2019: 46).

3 In the account titled *Ray Mahashay*, it is Bakaullah's investigation that saves the *zamindar*'s sister Saudamini from punishment and disgrace. But it is clear that the silencing of her voice and sexual agency by colonial law makes Saudamini's body an even more vulnerable site for the playing out of male conflicts and battles for power. However, in the account titled *Can of Worms*, Bakaullah has no sympathy for the young upper caste widow Premada who had eloped with her lover Haridas, and even plans to arrest Haridas' poor aunt for helping Premada abort her foetus.

4 The most commonly applied section with regard to abduction was Section 366, which runs thus:whoever kidnaps or abducts any woman with the intent that she may be compelled to marry any person against her will, or in order that she may be forced or seduced to illicit intercourse, or knowing it to be likely that she will be forced or seduced to illicit intercourse, shall be punished with imprisonment of either description for a term which may extend to ten years and shall be liable to fines (IPC, 1860).

5 The *Amritabazar Patrika* on 20 February, 1868 talked of conducting interviews with prostitutes, of whom eight admitted they had engaged in adultery, got caught and had to leave home to escape punishment or had eloped with their lovers to escape the trials of widowhood and had been subsequently deserted (Basu, 2003: 602–604). In 1872–3, Bankim Chatterjee, Deputy Magistrate of Murshidabad, along with other magistrates, was asked to write reports on the

causes of prostitution. The novelist wrote that since "Hindu society tolerated no compromises and shut its door forever against those who broke through these restraints even once", women had no other means of survival (Chatterjee, Judicial File, Oct. 1872).

6 I am fully aware of the fact that the female "voices" heard in these writings cannot be read as being unproblematically authentic. But awareness of their being mediated does not have to lead necessarily to an invariable dismissal or repudiation of these writings as offering nothing but distorted and manipulated versions of women that only served the prevalent structures of power. As Carlo Ginzburg says in his renowned work on early modern witch trials, "The voices of the accused reach us strangled, altered, distorted; in many cases, they haven't reached us at all. Hence-for anyone unresigned to writing history for the nth time from the standpoint of the victors-the importance of the anomalies, the cracks that occasionally (albeit very rarely) appear in the documentation, undermining its coherence" (Ginzburg, 1990: 10).

7 In 1793, Governor General Cornwallis had transferred police powers from local landlords to magistrates appointed by the East India Company. Although the intention was to establish a network of *thhana*s or police stations presided by the *daroga* or police inspector, as representatives of Company power, the reality remained far more complex. For although the *zamindars* were stripped of their authority over local law and order, they were still relied upon to provide names for appointments to police and they also retained control over the village watch (*chaukidar*), as well as the power to punish their tenants through their own private *lathiyal*s (retainers trained in wielding clouts and truncheons).

8 In his long critique of the prevalent police system in Bengal, *Pulish o Lokrakhbh*a, Ramakkhoy Chattopadhyay writes about the police in Bengal, "Arrogance, corruption and nasty behaviour seem to be requirements of their rank. They thrive on harassing people. Neither *bhadralok* nor *abbhadralok* can hope to preserve their self-respect when they approach the police. When the police arrive in villages for inspection, the *bhadralok* of that area go into hiding. Magistrates of many districts have complained about the police officers not getting the support of local villagers during inspection tours, but none of these Magistrates have tried to get to the bottom of this matter to find out the real reasons for this" (Chattopadhyay, 1892: 35).

9 As early as in 1798 a Circuit Judge had stated that "the salary annexed to the situation (of the daroga) which hardly exceeds the wages of a respectable menial servant, is so very inadequate to the nature and responsibility of the trust, and so very inconsiderable that it deterred men of rank and character from accepting the office". Analysing the flaws of the system, Frederick Shore linked the miserable pay of the *daroga*s to their vulnerability to corruption and said, "Sense of duty etc are all very fine words but the feelings of human nature will have their sway; if good service be wanted, the proper price must be paid for it. For it will not be obtained without" (Chattopadhyay, 2000: 67).

10 The assumption that Bakaullah was recruited at some point in the 1840s is based on the fact that William Sleeman—under whom he talks of having been appointed—became *Commissioner for the Suppression of Thuggee and Dacoity* in 1839.

11 The exact date of the publication of Bakaullah's accounts is not known. According to Sukumar Sen they were published before 1896, but he fails to give a specific date (Dasgupta and Pal, 2013: 12).

12 The words of scholar and librarian at Bengal Library Haraprasad Shastri (who wrote brief summaries of the Bangla texts collected in the erstwhile Bengal Library) introducing the writings of Priyanath Mukhopadhyay can be found in

the 1892 Bengal Library Catalogues (India Office Collections): "The most noticeable feature of the literature of the year in fiction is the appearance of a large number of detective stories in Bengali, entitled Darogar Daftar, by Babu Priyanath Mukharji, an officer of the Detective Department of the Kolkata Police. The stories are clever and smart ... They show the usefulness of native talent in detecting crimes in native society." Haraprasad Shastri, Catalogue of Bengali Printed Books (London: J.F. Blumhardt, 1892). Subsequently in 1894 he writes: "Babu Priyanath Mukharji continues to write his experiences as a detective officer, and has published nearly a dozen short stories during the course of the year. His stories, which appear in monthly parts, are exceedingly popular" (Ibid., 1894).

13 To ensure that his readers were not misled about the truth status of the accounts, Mukhopadhyay says that while his first person narratives are meant to be read as documenting "*prokrito ghhotonaa*" (actual incidents/cases) investigated by him, accounts not written in the first person were meant to be seen as fictions (Mukhopadhyay, Vol. 1., 2004: 6).

14 The field of popular writings in the late nineteenth century, though inseparable from the phenomenon of the *battala*, was also a contradiction-riddled and complex field because of what the *battala* often came to signify for *bhadralok* readers. *Battala*, which began by simply being a geographical space, gradually also accreted other meanings and came to be seen in terms of cheap, even insalubrious texts that the *bhadralok* was not entirely comfortable being associated with. "*Battala* which lasted for almost a hundred years had to fight the so-called custodians of 'high' culture continually for its survival. Many such people used to think of *battala* as 'bad' stuff. They would not even allow what they judged as unclean, obscene, low, trivial and unreadable *battala* books to enter their houses" (trans. mine) (Biswas and Acharya, 2013: 6).

15 In the decades following the onset of formal English education, an increasing number of English publications (histories, grammars, schoolbooks, poetry, novels, biographies) became available in the Indian market. Between 1850 and 1863–4, the export of books and printed matter from Britain to India doubled in value from 148, 563 pounds to 313, 772 pounds (Joshi, 1995: 39). The vast bulk of print arrived in the ports of Kolkata and Bombay.

16 Dickens' *Bleak House*, which, among other things, is about a crime and its investigation by a police official, was translated several times into Bangla. Wilkie Collins' novels, *The Woman in White* and *The Moonstone* were also very popular among Bengali readers and the former was translated as *Shuklabasana Sundari* (*The Beautiful Woman in White*) in the last decade of the nineteenth century.

17 The word *chhayabalamban* hints at a slippage between an exact reflection and an adaptation of the original.

18 While writings like *Darogar Daftar* (published for more than a decade from *Bandhab Pustakalay* and *Sadharan Pustakagar* presses in the *Battala* area) could not deny their *battala* association, they strove to construct their identity in terms of a vehemently insisted-upon difference from "other" more quintessential *battala* writings which were assumed to be "low" forms of writing in their use of non-*bhadra* language and vulgarity of content. *Kechha* (Scandal) were writings that were primarily centred on sexual scandals or homicides that had created a scandalous furore. Several *Kechhas*, like *Mama Bhhaagini r Paanchaali* (The Tale of an Uncle and his Niece) and *Uhh! Mama r ki Bichaar* (Uhh! What shocking justice meted out by an Uncle) for instance, centred around the *mama-bhhaagni* liaison (incestuous relationship between a young girl and her

maternal uncle) were printed from the *battala* press in the late 1870s, which were about a contemporary case involving one Upendra Basu and his niece Khhetramani Dasi. In 1884 a case of murder, this time that of a prostitute Kusum Kumari by a churlish male client Tinkari Pal who was subsequently hanged, also gave rise to a slew of *kechhaas*.

19 According to renowned scholar and critic of Bangla literary studies, Sukumar Sen, "Many people used to buy *Darogar Daftar*. In villages as well as in cities the houses of educated and *bhadra* Bengalis were bound to have a few copies of *Darogar Daftar*" (Sen, 1988: 151).

20 By the "grand tradition" of crime fiction, I am referring to the standard narratives of Anglo-American crime writing that privilege and reproduce Anglocentric perspectives and literary traditions while tracing the history of the genre. They begin with Edgar Allan Poe's *The Murders in the Rue Morgue* and then move through a selection of English 'classics' such as Wilkie Collins' *The Moonstone* (1868), followed by Holmes and Christie, and completely ignore its transnational emergence and growth.

21 Referring to the development of crime fictions in India, Stephen Knight talks of the earliest manifestations of the genre as "pulp fiction in indigenous languages relocating British models usually Sherlock Holmes" (Knight, 2015: 179). The *daroga* accounts however prove that not all "indigenous" crime writings were simplistic and crude derivations of the Holmesian model.

22 In the account titled *Promoda*, the *daroga* narrator draws attention to the problems faced by *daroga* Bansiram in getting witness accounts from the villagers. Talking of this as a problem faced by many police officers he says, "Most people in this country have very little faith in the workings of the police and as such are extremely reluctant to open up to them. What if the truth leads to their getting dragged into unnecessary police-related complications? Hence, what better adage to live by than 'the dumb has no enemies'?" (Mukhopadhyay, *Promoda*, Vol. 1, 1896/2004: 237).

23 In Bengal the castes are divided into two main groups: 1) Brahmin and 2) Shudra. The second group is further divided into four sub groups: a) the Sat-Shudra (or "clean" shudras) includes such castes as the Kayastha and Nabasakh b) then came the Jalacharaniya Shudras who were those castes that were technically of the Nabasakh group from whom Brahmins and others of "high" castes could take water, like Goala, Sadgop/Gop, Kamar etc. c) the Jalabharaya Shudras from whose hands a Brahmin could not take water and d) the Asprishya Shudras whose touch is considered utterly impure and with whom all contact must be avoided like the Dom, Dhopa, Chamar, Kaivartya, Bagdi etc.

Bibliography

Basu, Swapan. (ed.) (2003) *Sambad-Samayikpatre Unish Shataker Bangali Samaj* (Nineteenth Century Bengali Society in Newspapers and Periodicals), Kolkata: Pashchimbanga Bangla Academy.

Biswas. A. and Acharya, A. (2013) *Bangalir Battala*, Kolkata: Anushtup.

Chatterjee, Bankim. (1872) Judicial File, Letter no. 149/27 and no. 13:252:335. (Letter from Baboo Bankim Chatterjee, Deputy Magistrate to the Deputy Magistrate of Murshidabad, West Bengal Archives).

Chattopadhyay, Basudeb. (2000) *Crime and Control in Early Colonial Bengal, 1770–1860*, Kolkata: K.P. Bagchi & Co.

Chattopadhyay, Ramakhhoy. (1892) *Pulish o Lokrakhhaa (Police and the Protection of People)*, Kolkata: Nobin Chandra Pal Publishers.

Dasgupta, Arindam. (ed.) (1958) *Phire Daikha (Looking Back), The Memoirs of Priyanath Mukhopadhyay and Girish Chandra Basu*, Kolkata: Subarnarekha Publications.

Dasgupta, S. and Pal, P. (ed.) (2013) *Bakaullah r Daftar*, Kolkata: Charchapada.

De, Pachkari. (1905) *Govindram*, Kolkata: Bengal Medical Library.

Ghosh, Baridbaran. (ed.) (2011) *Pachkari De Rachnabali*, vol. 1. Kolkata: Karuna Prakashani.

Ginzburg, Carlo. (1990). *Ecstasies: Deciphering the Witches' Sabbath*, London: Hutchindon Radius.

Joshi, Priya. (1995) *In Another Country: Colonialism, Culture, and the English Novel in India*, New York: Columbia University Press.

Knight, Stephen. (2015) "The Postcolonial Crime Novel" in Ato Quayson (ed.) *The Cambridge Companion to the Postcolonial Novel*, Cambridge: Cambridge University Press, pp. 166–187.

Metcalfe, C.T. (1982) "Annual Administrative Report, April 30, 1878" in Tapan Chattopadhyay (ed.) *The Story of Lalbazar: Its Origin and Growth*, Kolkata: Firma KLM Pvt. Ltd.

Mukhopadhyay, Arun. (ed.) (2004) *Mukhopadhyay, Priyanath. (1892–1903) Darogar Daftar*, Vols. I and II, Kolkata: Punashcha.

Nandi, Baninath. (1898) "Prakashaker Mantabya (Publisher's Comments)" in *Darogar Daftar*, year 7, no. 73, Kolkata: Sikdarbagan Bandhab Pustakalay.

Robb, Peter. (1991) "The Ordering of Rural India" in David M. Anderson and David Killingray (eds) *Policing the Empire: Government, Authority and Control, 1830–1940*, Manchester: Manchester University Press, pp. 126–150.

Rowland, Susan. (2001) *From Agatha Christie to Ruth Rendell: British Women Writers in Detective and Crime Fiction*, Basingstoke, UK: Palgrave Macmillan.

Roy, S. and Sengupta, S. (2019) "'haan haan mein alaida hoon!' (Yes, Yes, I am Different!): The Disorderly Bibi in *Sahib, Bibi aur Ghulam* (1962)" in S. Sengupta, S. Roy and S. Purkayastha (eds.) *'Bad' Women of Bombay Films: Studies in Desire and Anxiety*, Switzerland: Palgrave Macmillan.

Sarkar, Tanika. (2001/2013) *Hindu Wife, Hindu Nation: Community, Religion and Cultural Nationalism*, Delhi: Permanent Black.

Sen, Sukumar. (1988) *Crime Kahini r Kaal Kranti* (The Changes in the Crime Novel), Kolkata: Ananda Publishers.

Spivak, Gayatri, C. (2012) "The Politics of Translation" in Lawrence Venuti (ed.) *The Translation Studies Reader*, London & New York: Routledge.

Tagore, Rabindranath. (2001) *Galpaguchha*, Vol. II, Kolkata: Viswabharati.

Venuti, L. (1998) *The Scandals of Translation: Towards an Ethics of Difference*, London & New York: Routledge.

2

BAKAULLAH'S PREFACE

Ever since the East India Company acquired the *Dewani* (civil) and *Foujdari* (criminal) rights, from Lord Hastings to Hardinge have tried to establish peace in Bengal but have failed in their efforts.[1] People living in this well-governed, modern state today cannot even imagine the condition that the country was in. Those were terrible times. It looked like the proverb—"Might is right"—had been absorbed by everyone into their very bones and proof of it could be found all around. Theft, dacoity, fraud, assault and murder were par for the course. In those days, a man hesitated less before killing a fellow human than he did before swatting a mosquito. Men had extremely strong bodies and that strength was also often accompanied with boldness; equipped with boldness and strength, low-born men of no morals would loot everything in sight. Quite a few upper caste men also adopted this horrible form of earning a livelihood and even led gangs of criminals involved in killing and looting.

All such things have become the stuff of fictions now. Some of the things that have occurred in my own life and others that I have heard from my contemporaries, are indeed very interesting. Once I retired, quite a few renowned people from far-off places would actually pay a hefty travel fare to visit my humble abode and listen to some of those tales. Many of the accounts left them dumbfounded. Let alone ordinary civilians, even modern-day detective police officers can learn a thing or two from such accounts.

It was from Lord Bentinck's time that laws became very strict. The *Thuggee* Commissioner of that time began traveling to various towns and even started scouring all the *madrassas*.[2] He had his ear to the ground and the plan was that as soon as he got information about intelligent young men from well-to-do families, he would offer them the job of a *daroga*.

Under the Company's reign, the position of *daroga* was greater than some great positions. In terms of reputation, power, stature or prestige, there were few officials higher than the *daroga* of a *thhana*. And the Commissioner *sahib* was searching for clever young men for this lucrative post. It really was a golden opportunity for capable youths!

In our district, there was a *madrassa* run by an Urdu scholar and teacher (*Munshi*). Every morning and evening, he would give lessons to about ten to twelve young men and I was one of them. I was twenty-one or twenty-two at the time.

I still remember quite clearly, the month was *Maagh* (mid-January–mid-February in the *Saka* calendar). It was very cold and we—a group of students—were sitting in the sun and prattling away when *Munshi sahib* appeared and said with a smile, "Would you like to be a *daroga*?"

Every child knew that in terms of prestige or power that the position had to offer, it was second to none. The money was good as well. It's true that the police have always been tainted as bribe-takers but there would be no dearth of money for those who wanted to earn it in an honest manner. The department generously rewarded those officers who could resolve cases of theft, dacoity, fraud, murder and assault. Indeed, *darogas* who had done the primary investigation of major cases, were known to have been given as much as five hundred or a thousand rupees for their work. I was aware of all this. As such I was thrilled by the offer and said, "If an offer is being made, I would be only too happy to do it." *Munshi sahib* said, "Go meet the Commissioner at 1 o'clock tomorrow. You will be given a suitable job."

I went and met him the next day and was duly appointed. With some broad instructions I set off for work the following day. The post I got was that of a *daroga* in the detective department. The area of operation was the whole of Bengal. If the need arose, I would even have to travel outside Bengal. Incidents of theft and dacoity were rife everywhere in the country; my main job was to move around and investigate such incidents and to follow the orders of my superior officers to the best of my abilities. Without further ado, I joined duty.

Notes

1 Warren Hastings (1732–1818) was Governor-General of India from 1773 to 1785. Charles Hardinge (1858–1944) was Viceroy from 1910 to 1916.

2 Bentinck (1778–1839) was Governor-General from 1828 to 1835. *Thuggee* Commissioner refers to Major William Sleeman, who assumed charge of the office of *Commissioner for the Suppression of Thuggee and Dacoity* in early 1839. During the operations that he supervised, more than 1400 Thugs were hanged or transported for life.

3

'HANDLESS HARISH'

'Horrible homicide, three murders'

After cogitating for an entire night, I finally began my journey dressed as a traveller. I stuffed everything—official documents, appointment letter, a letter signed by the Commissioner—in a big gunny bag and set off for Nabadwip early in the morning.[1] There are so many lies and half-truths that are used in police work and are admired as our "dexterousness". As soon as I reached Nabadwip, I procured the symbols of the right caste. There was not much time left for the full moon night of *Magh*. The devotees of *Gourango/Gauranga*—the Vaishnavas—along with many other Hindu men and women, young and old, had arrived in hordes to be in Nabadwip. Spending the seventh night of the *Maagh* month (mid-January to mid-February according to the *Saka* calendar) in Nabadwip is considered particularly auspicious.

I took a room on rent in the *aakhra* of Shri Gourango Das Babaji. The *aakhra* had walls along its entire perimeter and flush with the boundary wall was a long shed. Beside this there were three rooms.[2] Babaji had three maids in his service who stayed together in one of these rooms. I took the smallest room on rent. The third was kept locked. In the shed, there were some tiny recesses that were occupied by near-destitute travellers. In the evening, a day after I reached Nabadwip, a thirty-year-old Brahmin, in long robes and fur shoes, carrying a massive stick in his hand, arrived there accompanied by his servant. The servant, who hailed from somewhere in the hills, was extremely dark and had a robust moustache. It was thick, long and turned upwards. His eyes were bloodshot and round like a discus, his gaze was cold and fierce and he was at least six feet tall. Upon arrival, the Brahmin opened up the locked door of the third room and his servant started keeping all their stuff in it. I realised they had taken it on rent. When the Brahmin came and sat outside, the *aakhra* owner asked, "Are you here to fulfil the wishes of the Lord?" The Brahmin said with a grim face, "I am here to fulfill the wishes of the great *Sri Gourango*." The servant then elaborated, "The *babu* wants to travel to Shrichandranath so he had gone to retrieve some of the interest money that he has kept with a merchant."[3]

Later I went and sat on the verandah which was right outside *Babaji*'s (the *aakhra* owner) room. And then, as we got chatting, I learnt a few things. *Babaji* knew the Brahmin quite well and said he was wont to visit Nabadwip on most festivals and special occasions. He then went on to say this about him: "He used to be a fairly wealthy man but now he has renounced the world and become a mendicant. Earlier he had *zamindari* lands in Dhaka. There was even a grandiose two-storeyed mansion. Now there is nothing. There's only some cash which is kept in the custody of a merchant and it is with the interest accumulated on that money that the Brahmin manages to travel around. He has acquired a treasure trove of experiences as a result of his travels into diverse lands. And his name is Harish Bhatt."

During my years as a student, I had read Suleiman's *Duniya Hadishi* and that's when my love of learning about different lands and cultures had begun. Soon after our meal, I befriended Bhatt *babu* and found him delightful. Impressively erudite to boot. He was amicable, warm and polite, and I felt very pleased at having made his acquaintance. He had a glowing face and seemed to belong to a wealthy family. Unfortunately, however, he seemed to have lost his right hand. In fact the entire arm was completely missing. The empty right-hand sleeve of his *kurta* would simply hang uselessly by his side. Driven by curiosity, I even asked him about it; he said, "It's a long story; I'll tell you some other time." After that I didn't pester him any further that day.

What an impressive face and yet an arm missing! He didn't have the most hard-working part of his body. It was just so very sad. But along with sadness I also felt terrible curiosity. Failing to control this curiosity, I raised the matter yet again with him the following day. What I learnt was that on his way back from visiting Pashupatinath, he had been robbed blind by a gang of ferocious dacoits in the jungles of Nepal and it was while fighting with them and defending himself that Bhatt *babu* had lost his arm.

He was quite a shy and retiring person. All his activities, whether it was cooking, eating or changing his clothes, would happen away from prying eyes. He was averse to people seeing how he used his left hand to complete the tasks of the right. That was absolutely fine by me for I didn't really care a fig about that! Within four or five days I became extremely friendly with the man and I heard several tales about various lands and pilgrim spots, near and far.

One day as I was entering the *aakhra*, I noticed that the Brahmin's servant was carrying two or three letters with him to the post office. When I happened to glance at the letters, the writing appeared quite firm and unbroken. Who could have written these, I wondered. Suddenly my mind was jolted. There was no one in the *aakhra* who could have written like this. For Harish was handless!

I had definitely not forgotten the work for which I was being given a salary by the Company. I had even visited the local *thhana* and met everyone and that day I had been invited for a meal there.[4] Since I had gone elsewhere, I had returned to the *aakhra* to change my clothes. And on my way in, almost at the gate of the *aakhhra*, I had met the hill-born man with the letters in his hand. Upon entering, I heard that Harish *babu* was leaving Nabadwip that very night. He would be setting off for Srichandranath. I went to meet him and he greeted me with his usual graciousness; I said to him that perhaps we would never get to see each other again in this lifetime and expressing sadness, I bid him farewell.

That night, it was fairly late by the time I finished with dinner at the *thhana*. And the *aakhra* was at a fair distance from the *thhana*. Even so, when the local *daroga babu* offered to send a man with a lantern to escort me on my way back, I demurred. We were employees of the police department after all. It would hardly behove us to have fears and anxieties of any kind, would it? It was a full moon night and there was intermittent play of darkness and light as I started on my way back on the Boichora Road.[5] As I was walking, suddenly a man pushed past me and rushed off in the other direction. He seemed to be covered from head to toe and had a large turban on his head. Only a pair of eyes were visible and my own eyes couldn't help being drawn to his. They seemed familiar. I couldn't quite remember where I had seen them and yet I felt fairly certain that the owner of those eyes was known to me. But why did the owner of those eyes brush past an acquaintance and then dart away like that? I brooded over this the entire way back, but failed to place those eyes. On returning I heard that Harish *babu* had left.

I have always been an early riser. The next morning I was up early as usual and completed my ablutions. Then, as I softly hummed one of Hafeez's *ghazal*s and strolled about near the gate of the *aakhra*, I got to know that a murder had taken place on the Boichora Road. Someone had killed Ramtarak Bhattacharya's daughter, Bidhumukhi. As soon as I heard this, I set off to look into it. Ramtarak is the son of the well-known *dewan* Ramtanu Bhattacharya, a prosperous gentleman.[6] The aged *dewan* is still alive and it was his granddaughter who had been killed. I saw that she was extremely beautiful. Her age would have been somewhere between twenty and twenty-two. She had never had children. Really, she was quite unusually attractive. The scene of crime was the garden adjoining the house; more specifically, a platform built next to the lake in the middle of the garden. The question that immediately arose in my mind was regarding Bidhumukhi's character. Had she been virtuous, would she have died in a place like this? The police arrived and investigated to the best of their abilities, but to no avail. As such, the verdict was down to the usual compromise—perpetrator unknown and on the run.

The pilgrims who had gathered in Nabadwip for a holy dip on the night of the full moon were all beginning to disperse and preparing to return home, once the full moon was over. I too set off from Nabadwip.

Bidhumukhi had been murdered but no proper investigation had taken place. I was there but I could do little. I felt terribly guilty and it was the burden of this guilt that drove me out of Nabadwip and I reached Shantipur.

In Shantipur also I rented a room. It was after I'd spent a week in that room, that one day I suddenly spotted that handless man, Harish. We came face-to-face and our eyes met but he didn't say anything. I too kept my counsel. I thought I would meet him some other time and decided that meanwhile I would simply identify the place where he lived. With this in mind, I followed him at some distance and returned after seeing the house where he was staying. But I kept wondering why the Srichandranath-bound Harish was here in Shantipur, why he had appeared so preoccupied and indeed why he had hastened off without uttering a single word.

The very next morning I was at the gate of Harish *babu*'s house. That same servant was guarding the gate. When I looked at the man, I noticed his eyes and then something clicked in my mind, as it were, and I remembered the pair of eyes on the Boichura Road. Waves of suspicion rose in my mind. My mind then placed Harish as well on the scales of suspicion and the more I thought about it, the more convinced I became that something was amiss. And it was with such suspicions taking firm root in my mind that I met Harish *babu*.

As I chatted with him about this and that, I observed Harish *babu* closely and realised that he actually didn't lack an arm. I felt quite certain that both his arms were intact. For as he spoke, that arm seemed to move a little within his robe.

Harish *babu* said to me of his own accord, "The visit to Srichandranath didn't happen. I have come to meet a relative here. That's taken care of, so I'll make a move tonight. My carriage is ready."

We sat and talked in the veranda while the servant was inside, making preparations for their departure and tying up their luggage. Suddenly there was a loud clanging noise and we both looked inside. I saw that a large tin box had probably slipped and fallen out of the servant's hands. And it had dropped open to reveal all its contents which had spilled outside. There were false moustaches and beards, wigs, tubs of colour, brushes and a number of neckpieces. The box seemed to be the kind of thing that would belong to a showman who thrived on disguises. Why would anyone carry all this while going on pilgrimages? Harish *babu* looked like the wrathful god of fire! I didn't follow the native languages of the hill areas and the servant didn't follow any Hindi, Bangla or Urdu. Harish *babu* shouted at him in his language and he sheepishly began gathering everything together and putting it all back in the box. Harish *babu* then explained, "When I travel I just have to carry all that stuff. There are many places where you can't get any peace if you don't conceal your caste and religion.

In fact it is even impossible to find accommodation in many such places." After chatting about many other things, I took my leave.

I knew that Harish babu would be leaving in the evening so I didn't go to meet him again. But I just couldn't shake off my misgivings about that man. His words, facial expressions and the disguise-related stuff that I had seen made me certain that he was a human chameleon. Why, I wondered, did he need multiple disguises and what on earth were his reasons for keeping his right arm concealed? Was he someone that I needed to follow?

In the morning, I heard that a murder had taken place. A woman—a young woman of a respectable household had been killed in the middle of a road. I immediately went rushing to Harish *babu*'s abode. Why did I go there? I don't know what prompted me to go, but I did. On making inquiries I learnt that Harish *babu* was no longer there. He had hired a cart and had set off for Kalna some time ago. Feeling rather downcast, I finally started wending my way to the neighbourhood where the murder had taken place. It was quite a scene! The corpse was still lying in the middle of the road. It was drenched in blood. The beautiful colour of the dead woman's skin seemed to have been heightened by the redness that stained her body. For she was beautiful indeed. On looking carefully, I found the manner of the killing very similar to the murder in Nabadwip. The throat had been slit from left to right in one long stroke. The murdered woman was a widow. I got to know from the widowed girl's father-in-law that she had just turned nineteen. During the investigation by the local police, all the neighbours said, "It would be hard to find a more virtuous daughter-in-law. She had been widowed at fifteen and till date she has never even lifted her eyes and looked at anyone. But look at her terrible misfortune—her sister and brother-in-law have also died in a similar manner." I learnt that the widow, Shashimukhi, was the sister of the murdered Bidhumukhi of Nabadwip.

Shashimukhi's rooms were searched in a thorough manner. When the large tin trunk containing her possessions was opened with the key that had been tied to the end of her sari, a few love letters were found. The writer of the letters had not given his name. He had signed it in an oblique manner as "Your very own Bhanu". Thanks to the police investigation it was revealed within hours that there was no writer or indeed person named "Bhanu" in Shantipur. The only Bhanu in the neighbourhood was a milkman and he was illiterate. It became clear that "Bhanu" was a pseudonym and soon the police got busy trying to find this "Bhanu".

A gentleman in the neighbourhood said, "I was returning home after two at night after finishing a game of cards downtown. Right here, by the wayside, I noticed a man who seemed to be in a tearing hurry to go somewhere. He was covered from head to toe, had a huge turban on his head and only bits of his face were visible. He had enormous eyes, and a massive moustache and beard. A tall, strapping young fellow!"

A woman also said similar things. Soon I started getting suspicious. I was reminded of Harish *babu*'s servant when I heard about the round eyes but he didn't have a beard.

After completing his investigations for that day, the *daroga babu* left for the *thbana* and I returned to my rooms. On the way back, I even went to the house of the carriage driver but found that he hadn't yet returned.

In the evening, a visit was paid to the scene of crime yet again. And the search for "Bhanu" continued across several neighbourhoods. But it all came a cropper! Not a single living being uttered a bad word against Shashimukhi's character. As such, eventually the *daroga babu* was compelled to write a closing report for the investigation.

The carriage driver's house was on my way back. When I went to his house, I found he had just returned at that time. The bullocks had been tethered near the trough and the straw spread inside the cart, had not yet been removed. I immediately went and sat in the cart and announced that I wanted to visit Kalna. The fare was decided. The carriage driver said, "I have just returned from Kalna after dropping off a *babu*. I have another good pair of bullocks so I'll be able to take you today."

Even as I talked to him, my eyes were on the cart. The moon was out and the rays of the moon fell on the inside of the cart as well. In that dim light I could make out that there was something black lying in one corner of the cart. When the cart-driver went inside the house to prepare his tobacco, I seized the opportunity and pulled out that black object; it was a beard. Eureka! Everything started to become clear to me. I began recalling things at such speed that I could barely collect my thoughts. Meanwhile the cart-driver had arrived. Since I planned to set off that very night, I went to my house at first. I switched on the light and examined the beard carefully. I was overjoyed. I quickly finished my meal and set off for Kalna.

On the way, I collected some more information. Harish *babu* had spent last night at Guptipara. The cart had been parked in a garden in Guptipara and he had had his meal there. He had even shared some of his food with the cart-driver. Meal over, they had spent the night in the garden. The cart-driver couldn't recall anything more. The *babu* had woken him at the crack of dawn and they had continued their journey.

I asked the cart-driver about the beard as well. He said the *babu*'s servant did have a beard but he hadn't seen it when they had reached Kalna. There he worn a turban which seemed to cover most of his face. In my mind I became more and more certain that the neighbour had been right. The servant who hailed from the hills, was the architect of these crimes.

Next morning, I reached Kalna at ten. I had assumed I would be able to find them soon after reaching but that's not what happened. I roamed around the whole day without even stopping to eat and by the time I reached the *thbana*, it was nearly evening. After finishing my meal, I felt dreadfully exhausted and decided to rest for a while. Later at night, I woke up and went outside to pee. As I climbed down the stairs, my eyes were suddenly drawn to the main road that lay to eastern side of the *thhana*. I saw a figure—about the same build as Harish *babu*'s servant—covered all over with a cloth, darting across hurriedly yet silently. It was as if some divine force propelled me downstairs; it didn't give me much time to think. Sandals in hand, I began following the figure in the clothes that I was wearing.

The man seemed to be quite clever; he realised soon enough that he was being shadowed. He walked down the Southern Road and then reached an area in the west. I was right behind him. On our left was a shrubbery and to the south was a bridge. Right at this point, the man suddenly ground to a halt. I stopped too. And then like a comet, he hurtled towards me and shoved me as hard as he could. I managed to break my fall, but I staggered back a few feet. And yet I recognised him. It was him! Without paying any attention to the injuries caused by his push, I ran forward and grabbed the hill-born man. He was a large, well-built young fellow. Despite my youth I didn't have the strength to keep holding him. He soon freed himself quite easily and started running in the western direction. I ran after him.

When he came in front of an old Shiva temple, he suddenly disappeared. The man who had been running right before me at great speed, had vanished completely. I searched high and low, looked in the same place repeatedly, but there was no sign of him. Where did the man go?!

While I was searching the area surrounding the temple, I suddenly heard a commotion in one of the neighbourhoods nearby. It seemed that Durgadas Bhattacharya's daughter-in-law had been killed. The commotion put paid to all the confusion in my mind. I realised that the armless Harish was behind all three murders. I saw a *chaukidar* rushing towards the neighbourhood from where all the loud noises were coming. I told him, "If there is any genuine desire to catch the culprit, your *daroga babu* should drop the writing of reports of the crime and come here with his team. The culprit is hidden somewhere here."

The *chaukidar* ran like the wind. Within an hour, the premises of the temple filled up with all kinds of police officials. The entire area was cordoned off and was searched in the manner reminiscent of the way fish are netted. On both sides of that particular Shiva temple there are many other older temples. Finally we found our culprits in a decrepit temple nearby. Both master and servant were arrested and they silently went to the *thhana*. The writing of the report of the crime then began. I entrusted the arrested men to the *daroga*, along with the responsibility of taking their statements and then continued with the rest of the investigation. Since the guilty had been arrested and all my suspicions had been proved right, I began investigating the matter accordingly. The investigation took time. I gave my superiors the news about the arrest and then took the two men with me to Shantipur and Nabadwip. Almost a week was spent in all this.

I found out that Durgadas Bhattacharya, Bishwaroop Bhattachrya of Shantipur and Ramtaarok Bhattacharya of Nabadwip were all related. Ramtarak's daughters were married into the families of the other men. Ramtarak had four daughters—Bidhumukhi, Shashimukhi, Sudhamukhi amd Sonamukhi. Bidhumukhi had been married in a village not very far from Nabadweep. Bidhumukhi, being her father's beloved daughter, didn't spend too much time in her marital home. Shashimukhi was the widowed daughter-in-law of Bishwaroop Bhattacharya, an inhabitant of Shantipur. The unfortunate girl had been widowed when she was merely fifteen. Her husband Ramroop used to work for Rani Bhavani and he had died in the town where he worked. Rumour had it that he had been caught in the midst of a peasant uprising in that place, and was murdered. Eight rebels were punished with deportation for this crime. Sudhamukhi was Durgadas Bhattacharya's daughter-in-law. Sonamukhi was unmarried.

When *daroga* babu had tried to take Harish's *ejahar* he refused to utter a word. And the man from the hills didn't follow our language. Finally, I decided to take Harish's *ejahar* myself and with that in mind I took him to a secluded spot. Harish said, "You people can keep beating your heads, but you'll still not be able to prove my guilt. I know I ought to be punished. But all this secrecy has been because of my fear of being exposed. How else would I have managed to commit four murders? I thought and planned this carefully over the last five years. And only then did I take the vow to fulfil my mission. And you think you can suddenly prove my guilt?"

There was however some repentance that had started entering Harish's mind, which is why I thought he might not lie any longer. I sympathised with him and requested that he tell me the truth. He said, "Ok, I'll tell you. I have no kin. Perhaps there are distant relatives but I don't know about them. After Ramtanu retired as *dewan*, his son Ramtarak also became *dewan* for a while. It was at around that time that I had sought refuge at his place. I knew how to read and write. Ramtarak used to take care of my food and clothing. I used to do a great deal of work for him and he used to take good care of me. He wasn't very skilled with the pen, which is why I was of great value to him. His wife (*Ma-thhakurani*) also treated me with respect and affection. I became more or less like a member of their household. Shashimukhi was around thirteen years old at the time. A bridegroom was being sought for her, but till then no one suitable had been found. As such, the wedding was getting delayed. Shashi used to love me a lot and I used to love her even more. We would sit together in secluded spots and talk about many things. We were both of the opinion that we would be very happy if we could marry each other. Our minds were already married; the ritualistic wedding alone was left. I conveyed my wishes to Ramtarak *babu* through Ram Sarkar, his favourite cook. Shashi had also obliquely indicated her wishes to her mother. My master and mistress had a heated exchange over this matter but nothing came of it. I was poor, I had no family, I was a Brahmin of an inferior sub-caste and besides, I was dependant on their family for food and shelter. How dare I come up with such an audacious suggestion? My master was infuriated and kicked me out of the house after humiliating me. I was deeply wounded by this and suffered a great deal. I lost my sole refuge, became a penniless beggar and was in a great deal of pain. And yet I couldn't go anywhere else. I would sit in the forest that ran alongside the boundary wall of that house, wait for Shashi and even get to meet her from time to time. We would talk about our sufferings. I would also get some financial help from her. Ten months passed in this manner. When she was fourteen, Shashi was married into a family in Shantipur. It was as though a thunderbolt fell on my head and turned my dreams to ashes.

Once Shashi went to her marital home, all financial help dried up. There was no hope of any kind left either. What was the point of my staying on in that place? But I decided that I would not let the man who had destroyed my desires, kicked and smashed to pieces the castle of my dreams and made our lives unbearable, have any joy as far as his daughters were concerned. Just as I had loved and lost, I would make sure no one would find happiness in love either. At least not in Ramtarak's family. This then became my life's mission. After taking a vow of this kind, I set off for Radhanagar. I went there and gathered information about the *zamindari*. Shashi's husband had yet to join his office there.

I spent some time there figuring out how I would accomplish my mission and then went to Natore. There I spent a week. I would manage my meals and everything else in temples. Then I got the news that Ramroop had arrived. Why delay any further? I set off that very day and on that night everyone in Radhanagar heard that the *naayeb* had been killed.[7] The rumour spread that rebellious peasants had killed him. That very night I went off to Baidyanath.

I travelled to very many places. Lest I be found and arrested, I started keeping one of my arms concealed. I would keep the right arm hanging in a cotton-stuffed robe in such a manner, that people who saw me assumed I didn't have an arm. I led an itinerant life and thought relentlessly about how I would succeed in my goal. I finally reached Parshwanath and spent four years there. My servant's house was somewhere up in the hills about thirty kilometres away from the Pashunath temple.

These men from the hills are both loyal and trustworthy. They consider giving up their lives in the service of their masters a very small matter. I decided to seek his help for the rest of my mission. We first came to Nabadwip. After that you know all that happened. In short, I am guilty of all four murders—of Ramrup, Bidhumukhi, Sudhamukhi and Shashimukhi. I am Bhanu. In my childhood that used to be my name. Shashi used to know that name alone; that's the name I used when I wrote to her. Shashi never forgot her childhood sweetheart. She had therefore come to see me and we had met. But she was uncertain about leaving that place with me. I became infuriated and didn't let her leave. I protected her virtue by sending her off to the house of death. The subsequent events are all known to you. After I'd successfully completed my mission and fulfilled my vow, I decided to kill myself. But now that I've been arrested, I admit I should be punished for my sins."

I was still a little suspicious. Ramroop had definitely been murdered by Harish but the other three murders, at least the murders in Nabadwip and Kalna, did not seem to have been committed by Harish himself. I remembered quite clearly. I had also come to trust what my eyes had seen. I had seen him on the road in both places so I could assume easily that it was the servant who had committed the murders in both those places. I asked Harish about this in an artful manner. Harish said, "He is innocent. He merely acted out of loyalty. How can I betray his trust? He's innocent."

I had seen the man on the road in Kalna and Nabadwip and in both places he had seemed to me as though he was returning after committing murders. So how could he be innocent? My suspicions weren't allayed. I remained silent. When he saw my silence, Harish said, "Please don't question me any more. If I start denying things you will never be able to reach the end of your investigation of these murders. Just accept whatever I am telling you." I didn't question him any further. The false beard that I had found in the cart had belonged to Harish. The large chest containing the various disguises had also been located in the Shiv temple and it was then searched thoroughly in front of everyone. The beard could not be found. Since the beard owner had identified the beard as his, the question now was why it was lying in the cart. The cart-driver had said that he remembered seeing the servant as having a big beard. I remembered the servant as not having a beard. So we had proof that the hill-man had committed the murders. It was while he was on his way to kill that he had appeared with a beard before the cart-driver. He was concealing his identity with that fake beard. He had come to Guptipara with that fake beard and killed Shashimukhi, returned to the cart with the beard and had taken it off in the cart. Out of carelessness, he had left it there and had assumed that he had dropped it somewhere on his way back. That's the reason why he wore that turban which covered his chin entirely. All this I decided partly on the basis of proof and partly through conjecture. The murder had been committed by the hill–born man and Harish was taking the blame on himself. I thought a great deal about it. Maybe it was better this way. Harish confessed to his guilt even before the Magistrate. The servant was charged with and arrested for being an accessory; he went to prison. Harish had thought he would expiate for his sins by killing himself. In a way his aim was fulfilled. My first job, my first investigation and I won a lot of recognition for it. I was even given a reward for it. My enthusiasm for this job grew tremendously after this success.

Bakaullah

Notes

1 Nabadwip, along with such other provincial towns as Bishnupur, Shantipur, Katwa and Shrikhanda, were key Vaishnava sacred sites in nineteenth century Bengal that claimed a rich legacy of Chaitanya/Gauranga/Sri Gourango, the "founder" of Vaishnavism. These places were populated by *gosvamis, mahants* and *babajis,* all practitioners of *sahajiya* devotion (for more information on Vaishnavism see footnote 2 of *Promoda*).

2 *Aakhra* refer to places where Vaishnava mendicants or even pilgrims could stay at extremely nominal rates.

3 Srichandranath is a hill-based pilgrim spot for Hindu and Budhhist devotees (presently in Bangladesh) with a Shiva temple.

4 Refer to footnote 7 of the Introduction for *thhana.*

5 The word used in the Bangla original to describe the moonlight is *kakjyotsna.* The word is used to describe the kind of bright moonlight that gives the illusion of dawn and fools crows into cawing.

6 The *dewan* was the financial steward in a *zamindar*'s/landowner's estate.

7 A *naayeb* was a rent collecting officer and administrator in a landlord's estate.

4

'A CAN OF WORMS'

'A wily woman and the terrible wages of sin'

On the day that I am going to talk about, I didn't have any work and so, after having my lunch, I walked across to the court and sat down to watch the proceedings of a criminal case. The Defending Counsel was known to me. Shri Pranballabh Sen was a renowned attorney in the area. His practice was well-established and his earnings immense. Mr. Sen had settled here with his entire family.

Mr. Sen did not maintain any books for his daily income and expenditure. From his daily earnings, he would give two rupees to his wife for domestic expenses and the rest of the money he was in the habit of keeping in labelled packets. There were packets with denominations of ten, five, twenty, twenty-five and hundred and each packet had labels with an amount and date written. There were twenty-one such packets that had been made over twenty-one days.

The date of the incident was the twenty-second of the month. The previous month's cash amount had come to four hundred and fifteen rupees. That had gone to the goldsmith's house for making jewelry for Mrs. Sen. But the earnings of the past twenty-one days of the present month, kept in labelled packets in a box, were all missing. The key to the box used to be with Mrs. Sen, but she knew nothing of what had happened to the money. Theft, it was soon concluded, was what had happened.

The Sen household consisted of Mr. Sen and his wife, their maid Premada, their cook Mukherji and an orphaned nephew. The nephew, who was distantly related to the Sens, was staying with them in order to continue his studies, with his uncle's generous help. His name was Probodh and he was about seventeen or eighteen.

In the trial that I was watching, it was this Probodh who was the accused. Although the entire amount was yet to be recovered, a packet dated the nineteenth with fifteen rupees and eight *annas* in it had been found in one of Probodh's books. The packet had the amount written in Mr. Sen's own hand. As such, Probodh had been declared guilty.

In court Probodh was sobbing and saying repeatedly, "Please *huzoor*! I know nothing of this money *huzoor*! I haven't stolen anything."

No one had seen him stealing the money. When the *daroga* had gone and investigated, he had found the packet inside Probodh's papers. All the witnesses gathered there corroborated the *daroga*'s claim about finding the money. The cook Mukherji, as well as Premada the maid, confirmed this. Premada also said that Probodh would often steal food and eat. Mr. Sen further corroborated their statements as witnesses and as a result of all this, Probodh was sentenced to three months' imprisonment.

In those days, postal messengers would carry the post from Chakda to Jessore. There would be three armed postal messengers who would gather at a point, and then set off together. All of them would be on stilts. One day, some dacoits looted the post in a field not far from Chuyadanga. For nearly one and half months after that, investigations had been carried out but none of the dacoits could be arrested. The dacoits had dropped a bag containing letters and the police had managed to retrieve it. Our bosses got duplicate copies made of each of those letters and sent them to all the detective-police of that area in the hope that someone might find a clue in one of them. I had also got a bundle of such letters. As soon as I received them, I started going over each of them. There was one letter that I read four or five times. Here's what it said:

> My derling sweetheart Hari,
>
> Please accept my respect ... tell me how do i keep getting money all the time you are hiding after braking Companys jail ... where i get money ... now i have got some money ... about a hundred rupis ... you come and take after i inform you that it is safe for you and chaos is over. Weather you keep money or give aunt you be careful. the cook here is so good he write all this for me all fine Shrimati Premada Dasi, Maid of Pranballab Sen of Baddaman [*sic*].

I realised that this was the maid Premada from the Sen household. And the writer of the letter must have been that Brahmin cook Mukherji. How did Premada get hold of a hundred rupees? And even if she did find the money, what's the chaos that she refers to? I understood perfectly that the person responsible for that theft was—Premada! The cook knew about the theft and perhaps had even got a share of the stolen money. In any case, Probodh was innocent. Before anything else, it was imperative that he be released. At that very moment I took the letter and showed it to my superior. He said, "Arrest them immediately. Do whatever you need to do in order to get the money from them."

Hari had escaped out of prison. If Premada's letter was true then Hari was a fugitive from law and the aunt would also be a tough nut to crack. All of them seemed to be fairly dangerous. They had to be arrested. But if we began harassing Premada, then the two other criminals would get wary.

When I conveyed this thought to my superior, he agreed. I then took pains to ensure that Probodh was kept in a well-appointed room within the prison without any rigorous labour and got a guard to keep watch secretly over the Sen household. I then took off in search of Hari. The address was given on Premada's letter.

I began my journey. I reached Katwa after some time. After a lot of asking around I finally reached the gate of the aunt's house. I started calling her "*Pishima*" (aunt) in very loud tones but got no response. I could sense that there were people inside the house but they weren't answering my call. After a lot of calling, the door was finally opened and I entered. I couldn't see who had opened the door. When I entered, I found a woman making preparations for evening prayers and lighting lamps; besides her, no one else was visible. There was a blanket spread out on the veranda and I sat down on it.

After lighting the lamps and completing her prayers and chanting "*Hari Bol*" in indistinct tones she came to the veranda and I touched her feet. I asked after her health as if I was more closely related to her than her closest kin. After a great deal of such talk, finally I came to the real matter. Premada wanted to see her aunt. That's why she had sent me and even given me money for the entire journey. There was some other person as well—Premada had not mentioned that person's name—who she said *Pishima* would recognise as soon as she was told. That person was also meant to go with us. As for money, she had sent twenty rupees with me and had told me that she had around a hundred rupees with her. You would get that money as soon as you visit her. Saying this, I put twenty rupees in front of *Pishi* (*Pishima*). As soon as there was the sound of money being kept, a dark and well-built man of about thirty or so emerged from within one of the rooms. He said, "Is she alright?" I realized that the man must be Hari. I replied, "Yes she's fine. She has asked for you specially to visit her. Even sent money." It was indeed Hari and he agreed to go. When *Pishi* went inside with the money, Hari also went in with her and I heard some whispered bickering over Hari taking some of the money for his journey. Neither of them suspected me.

Thanks to *Pishima*, I had a good meal. Then I lay down on that veranda. After hiring a cart, Haridas (Hari) too ate his meal. Then he went off somewhere. I chatted with *Pishi* for a while and then fell asleep. In the early hours of the morning, Haridas came with two carts that had been hired for the journey. On one *Pishi* travelled by herself while in the other Haridas and I sat together and chatted about many things. I talked to him as though there was little that I didn't know about Premada. As we talked, I got to know quite a few things about Premada from Haridas. He was quite a lover. When the subject of love came up, I related an imaginary incident of love from my life. It was because of that love, I told him I had gotten to know Premada. For that love affair had led to an unwanted pregnancy and Premada had rescued us from that disaster. Haridas was assured that he and I were kindred spirits. To strengthen our bond, he began describing his own life story.

Premada, he said, was a Kayastha girl.[1] She had been widowed as a child. Who didn't know the Boses of Haripur? Premada was the widowed daughter of that family. Hari, or Haridas, had been a cook employed by Premada's father. It was at that time that the two of them had fallen in love with each other. It was as a result of this affair that Premada became pregnant. Soon, news spread in the neighbourhood. The sinful act didn't remain hidden for very long and it caused quite a furore! Unable to bear the public humiliation, both Premada and Haridas fled from Haripur. It was after they came to Katwa that with *Pishi*'s kind help, Premada managed to get rid of the signs of her disgrace. She gave *Pishi* all the valuables that she had carried with her. When her health improved, she heard that there was no money left. She was in a real fix. *Pishi* advised her that since she had a body that was fit to do manual labour, there was no need to worry about how she was going to feed herself. Haridas was also relieved to hear this.

After a while, Hari took up opium smoking. Soon he also became friendly with a group of opium-smokers. Almost every day he would go out in the evenings to smoke opium with them. It was a member of that group of men who noticed that the impoverished Haridas appeared more and more emaciated with each passing day and assured him that he would help him find a way to make money. That opium-addict also happened to be a member of a gang of dacoits. Haridas had the required physique, strength and brains and so the dacoit helped him become a member of their gang. But on the day that the gang went out on its very first journey after praying to goddess Kali, Haridas was arrested. No one else in the gang got caught; Haridas alone managed to get himself arrested. He alone went to jail and remained imprisoned thereafter.

Once Haridas was incarcerated, Premada's ordeal was even greater than before. Unable to think of anything else, she pretended to be a girl of the Gop caste and started working as a maid in Pranballabh *babu*'s house.[2] She has been working there ever since.

Haridas said repeatedly to everyone that he was innocent, that he hadn't done anything. He had not been part of any actual act of dacoity, nor did he have a single *paisa* that had come to him as a result of any theft. And yet it was he who was in jail. Before long, Haridas began to look for opportunities to escape from the prison. And when he got the chance, he broke out of prison and then immediately rushed to Bardhaman to meet Premada.

Premada felt that his hanging around in that district might be fraught with perils. So after a great deal of confabulation, they decided that Hari would seek refuge with *Pishi* and hide in her house. Ever since, Premada had been sending money to *Pishi* whenever she could and that's how they managed to eke out a living. Every now and then, Haridas also travelled to Bardhaman under cover of darkness. While he was there, he would remain hidden for a day or two and, after meeting Premada secretly and exchanging sweet nothings with her, he would return to *Pishi*'s house. This had been going on for the past seven or eight months.

Haridas forced Premada out of her *kula*, aided dacoits, helped with a murder and then escaped from prison and was a fugitive till date.[3] His crimes were of an extremely grave nature. *Pishi* had helped in the "killing of a foetus" and was knowingly providing shelter to a fugitive from law. Her crimes were not light either.[4] I had not really hoped that I would be able to nab them. But there I was, just waiting to attain my goal. My chest was all puffed up with pride.

In the afternoon, we reached the bazaar of Taranagar. After asking the cart to stop at some distance from the bazaar, I went in search of puffed rice and curd. I didn't want to take any more risks. I was going to make a formal arrest.

I went through the bazaar and reached the *thhana*. However, after making all the necessary arrangements, when I went back to the cart, I found neither *Pishi* nor Hari was there. The cart-driver told me they had gone near the river. For a while I was stunned. By then some men from the *thhana* had also arrived and soon they spread out in various directions and began looking for the two of them. All our efforts were in vain. It looked like Haridas had managed to disappear into thin air along with *Pishi*. My bag—the one that had all my clothes, official documents, order letters and even my police badge – had also gone along with him. Everything was in it and the entire bag had vanished. I sat on the ground, clutching my head in despair.

That day I stayed in the *thhana*. I did not have a *paisa* with me and all I had was the *kurti* and *dhoti* that I was wearing at that time. There was no shawl that I could wrap around myself. A local *daroga babu* gave me a shawl and then I walked all the way home.

I bathed and had my meal at an unearthly hour and after that, feeling utterly exhausted, I rested for a while. In the evening I sat down to study the papers that had arrived in my absence. I found a letter in that pile of documents. I was told that a man had come and hand-delivered the letter in the evening. When I heard his description, it sounded like the letter-bearer was none other than Harish. Indeed it turned out that Harish, Premada's sinful lover had written the letter. This was what was written in it:

> Khan-sahib, salaam! Dont be angry we ran away. you also not a good man I saw your police badge peeping out of your bag. In any case, you definitely definitely [*sic*] come meet me next Monday in the evening in the Dharmapur fields under the *Mahabrahma* and do it alone otherwise you will not only not see me but also get into more trouble.

I realised that while I had gone to visit the Taranagar *thhana*, Harish had opened and gone through my bag, found my badge and that's why they had fled from there. But why did he want to meet me now? Undoubtedly, he could wreak havoc if I ignored his instructions and did not go alone, and yet how could I go to meet a criminal like him completely on my own? After a great deal of cogitation, I decided to go meet him by myself.

I rode a horse in the evening and reached the spot under the banyan tree on the field in Dharmapur. I scanned the place but as far as my gaze could reach, I could not see any other living being. After a while I saw Haridas. He was riding an expensive horse and soon he approached the banyan tree. He got off his horse and greeted me with a *salaam*. Then he said, "Please don't mind all this. If we hadn't left without informing you, you would have got us into trouble. You would have got even the woman in trouble. Surely I couldn't have let that happen? As for what I want to say to you now, it is this: you are a gentleman. Why are you involved in work of this kind? Leave all this. If it's money that you need, you are welcome to take some *salaami* from me.[5] Why do you want to get into the business of nabbing and arresting? What do you think you'll get out of it?"

"Look Hari, I know I would have led you to a messy situation but then what else could I do? I follow orders. Anyway, let's forget all this. Take your money back; all I want from you is my bag. I don't want to carry on investigating this case."

"I don't need your bag. All the papers inside your bag are exactly as you had left them. You'll get that bag while you are at home. But how do I trust you when you say that you won't keep an eye on us?"

"Whether you wish to believe me or not is entirely up to you. Look Haridas, you might be able to escape. But does Premada have any choices? She was involved in foetus-killing and has stolen money from Pranballabh Sen. How will you prevent her imprisonment?"

"There you go! People like you make a habit of trying to scare us. How can you harm Premada? Probodh was fated to serve the sentence and that's what's happened. The sentence was for three months of which he has completed two and a half months already. Only a fortnight is left. Tell me what good will arresting Premada do? Moreover, where will you find her? I have removed her from here. I have even managed to pull the wool over the eyes of the two police detectives who had started keeping an eye on her. You won't find Premada. Okay, listen to me, you will get your bag soon. All of us will disappear for a while now. In the meanwhile, if you try to raise any sort of an alarm, I'm warning you that you'll be in a lot of trouble. And now I take your leave. *Salaam*!"

Haridas then leapt on to his horse. It was a strong horse and in a flash, it disappeared into the darkness with Haridas on its back. I stood there dumbfounded for a while and then returned home. I had stationed a few men on different points outside the field to see where Haridas would go.

They informed me that the horse rider had not left for the village; he had gone into Bardhaman. They also told me that the rider had stolen Shyama Charan *babu*'s horse. I sent some men to the *thhana* for more information but Shyama charan *babu* had not reported any theft of this kind at the *thhana*. Then I went to meet Shyama Charan *babu* in person. I saw the horse there and was convinced it was the same horse. Shyama *babu* is a respected gentleman of this area. Surely he could not have given shelter and support to a despised criminal like Haridas?

I didn't mention any of this to the *sahib*, my superior officer. I merely said that the investigation was on. He had instructed me to arrest Premada right then, which I had failed to do. And now Premada was a fugitive. The following day, I did receive my bag. Everything inside it was intact.

There was no doubt left that Premada was the one to steal Mrs. Sen's envelope containing money, for we got the letter in order to match it with the cook Mukherji's signature. The two were a match. Mukherji was unable to deny anything. The cook had known that it was Premada who had shrewdly kept the envelope inside one of Probodh's books; he had followed her instructions and kept silent about it. However, Premada was missing, so what could be done? The two wretched men who had been told to keep an eye on her movements lost their jobs. It was because of my failure to grasp things properly that Probodh had to suffer unnecessarily and have his reputation in tatters. My heart was so full of regret! Whether it was *Pishi*, Premada or Haridas, all had vanished without a trace and none got arrested; only Probodh had to suffer. If only I had arrested Premada at that time I wouldn't have felt so guilty.

Gradually a year passed and I investigated another case. But I failed to resolve the earlier case. I travelled to so many places but I found no traces of those three. Over time the investigation ground to a halt. I felt extremely downcast and just couldn't put the episode behind me.

Bakaullah

Notes

1 Kayastha is a caste category. Refer to footnote 23 of the Introduction for more details.
2 A caste category of a 'clean' shudra. Refer to footnote 23 of the Introduction.
3 The Bangla and Sanskrit word *kula* refers to a generic collectivity. The term was used more specifically in combination with the names of specific men to refer to units which would be designated as "clans", "lineages" or "families" in English. Ghosh-*kula*, for instance, would refer to the clan of persons who had a particular Ghosh as their "first ancestral male." *Kulatyag* (abandoning one's *kula*) was the word often used to refer to elopement. Even though it is clear that Premada and Hari had eloped together, the *daroga* at this point refers to the elopement

as a crime committed by Hari. He "forced Premada to abandon her *kula*". As discussed in footnote 4 of the Introduction, the insistence on referring to women's elopement as "being forced out of the *kula*" 1) helped rob women of their agency and framed their action as passive subjection and 2) helped punish the male partner for having "enticed" and "abducted" her.

4 For criminalizing of abortion see Introduction and footnote 3 of the Introduction.

5 *Salaami* refers to a gift of money.

5

'RAY MAHASHAY'

'A great conspiracy and warring factions'

> Saudamini, the widowed sister of *zamindar* Ramtaran *babu* of Krishnapur village has aborted her foetus. Ramtaran *babu* himself, along with his loyal retainer Shridam Ghosh, took the seven-month-old foetus to the tamarind tree next to the pond inside his estate and buried it there. Two fishermen had been catching fish in that pond a few days ago, on the *babu*'s orders, and had seen a heavily pregnant Saudamini. The wife of Kawra Harish is the midwife attached to the *babu*'s family; but she was not summoned this time because of the fear of scandal. Instead the wife of Rupchand Haari of Tarapur was called for the birthing. The baby boy had apparently cried out once after being born. The *chaukidar* at the gate had been passing that way at the time and had heard the baby's wails. Everything will come to light when the police come to investigate the matter.

These were the contents of a letter that someone had sent to the highest police official of the district and signed it "*Osposhto* (Unclear) Das". The *sahib* believed what the letter said. He believed that it was not in the least bit impossible for *zamindar*s to resort to such actions, in order to hide their disgrace. The act was a serious crime and the news-giver was clearly too afraid of the *zamindar* to reveal his actual identity in the letter. While the local police had been asked to assist in every possible way, the primary responsibility of looking into this case was assigned to me. Given that in this job we have to keep a record of even the number of times we go out to urinate, did I have a choice but to follow orders? Soon after receiving the orders, I recorded the relevant information in my diary and, after informing the *sahib*, I set off to begin my investigations into the matter.

I felt quite anxious on the way. The case involved a high-born young woman of an affluent family; she was a *zamindar*'s sister and she lived in the inner quarters of the household. How was I going to investigate her?

How was I going to go around collecting facts about the case? I became frantic with worry as I wondered about these things. I felt a great deal of trepidation. After all, *zamindars* are extremely powerful men; even the most minor of perceived lapses could lead to bodily harm for me. Such incidents are not uncommon. As such, my fears and my worries increased at a steady pace. I entered Krishnapur with all this going through my mind.

It's not as if disgraceful acts of this kind don't occur in well-to-do households. But when have the wealthy ever wanted to suffer the consequences of such actions? In many places what one gets to hear is that after such an unfortunate incident, wealthy families send the wretched woman to Gaya or Kashi in a boat. The poor are not able to afford such solutions that require money and hence they have to bear the shame that follows such affairs in silence. Ramtaran *babu* is a *zamindar*; so why did he fail to take the necessary steps that he could easily afford? Since there was no dearth of money, why did he choose to take on this calumny? This was the first point to ponder.

When I reached Ramtaran *babu*'s house, the local *daroga* was sitting in the drawing room of his house and while several important men from the village had been summoned and were giving their statements, quite a few useless hangers-on had also gathered there. Many other police officers were also sitting at various points in the house. I stopped my vehicle right outside the main gate of the house. I showed my papers to the local *daroga* and then had a brief and preliminary exchange of courtesies with Ramtaran *babu*.

After resting for a while I looked at what had been recorded of the investigation till that point. It seemed as though all the necessary proof had been gathered for the case.

I carefully read the *daroga*'s documents, witness statements and the accounts given by the neighbours. It seemed the case had been solved and that the proof gathered was unquestionable, with every nitty-gritty taken care of. The dismembered body of a baby had been found in the exact spot that had been mentioned in the anonymous letter signed "Osposhto (Unclear) Das". Ramtaran *babu*'s chief cook, Shridam Ghosh, claimed that he had walked to that very spot with a lantern and a spade while the *babu* had followed him with his widowed sister's dead child in his arms. Shridam had dug a hole in the ground and Ramtaran *babu* had placed the corpse of the child in the grave and then filled it up with soil. Two fishermen who had earlier visited the pond to catch fish had also seen their mistress sister with a bloated stomach. After going back home, they had even mentioned this to their wives. All three witness statements were pointing to the same thing and then a dead body had been found; what more proof did one need? The local *daroga* was keen to take Saudamani to the *thhana*. Ramtaran *babu* was saying, "Please spare her and do whatever you need to do, to me. If a crime deserving of death penalty has been committed, then I committed it. I beg you not to drag a girl of a good family to the *thhana*. Please don't shame my glorious lineage in this manner!"

Since it was getting quite late in the day I asked the local *daroga* to pause the investigative proceedings for a while. I broke up the meeting and requested all the gathered villagers to return in the evening. Arrangements for the evening meal began after that.

I felt there were enough reasons to distrust what was before me. Why did Ramtaran *babu* bury the dead child next to the pond? Surely there was enough space for burial within the house. The distance from the main gate, where the *chaukidar* was positioned, to the inner quarters would be half a mile or so. Could the feeble cries of a premature newborn be heard that far? Why didn't any of the villagers who had come to the gathering appear to be sympathetic to Ramtaran *babu* in his terrible crisis? Why was the statement of Kawra Harish's wife not taken? Above all, I felt it was imperative that I first meet Saudamini. I drew Ramtaran *babu* aside for a private chat and said to him, "Look Sir, even though we are police officials, we do know how to respect the status of someone as respectable as you. Your sister is like a sister to me. I do not wish to take her statement. But I would like to meet her once. I need to inspect her limbs in order to dispel a few doubts that I have. Perhaps this'll be beneficial for you. You may be present when I meet her. The three of us could have a meeting that no one else need know about."

After agreeing to this, Ramtaran *babu* went into the inner quarters of the house and made arrangements for our meeting. I met her soon after. The daughter of a wealthy and well respected household, she was a beautiful, twenty-two year old child widow. I felt extremely sad when I saw her. She hadn't had a morsel of food or a drop of water since all this began. Her sole benefactor and protector, her own brother, was about to lose his reputation and his place in society. How could she possibly bring herself to eat? Saudamini looked deathly pale and devastated. I forgot about shame and scrutinised her quite intently. All my suspicions were put to rest. A woman who had just aborted a seven month foetus could never look the way that she did. I could say with complete certainty that she knew nothing of the disgraceful thing that she had been accused of.

She was pure and virtuous but how was I going to prove it? I didn't have adequate evidence to prove this.

Meanwhile the local *daroga* was becoming more and more enraged. Since all the proof was there and the case was nothing if not cut-and-dried, why this delay in making the necessary arrests? He began to insinuate very many things, out of my earshot. Since it was such an important case he was becoming increasingly resentful of the possibility of my taking credit for solving it all by myself. I bore the brunt of all this in silence. I had begun to feel that there was a greater mystery at the root of all that had happened. But how was I going to prevent a respectable young woman of a good family from being arrested?

My investigations soon led to the discovery that there were hostile factions in the village. Both Brahmins and Kayasthas of the village owned *brahmatra* tax-free tracts of land and there was bitter discord between them over matters related to ownership.[1] Both factions had militiamen. Already a few serious cases of violence had happened over these matters. The two fishermen who had given their statements depended on one of the factions. I summoned them and asked them to give a statement all over again. They repeated what they had said earlier. I asked them what the mistress' age was. One of them said fifteen or sixteen while the other said she was around thirty. I asked them what she looked like. One said she was dark while the other said, "very fair-complexioned". On which side of the pond had she gone to take a bath? One claimed she had gone on the eastern side while the other said west. I was beginning to get to the bottom of this mystery. It was evident that the fishermen had neither seen Saudamini nor did they know what she looked like. To confirm my suspicions, when I got five women from within the household and divided them into two groups with Saudamini as part of one group, the fishermen failed to recognise her. I kept them under observation.

Subsequently, when Shridam was summoned, he became untraceable. Earlier Shridam had stated that he had helped dig a hole with a spade. But when I went to inspect the hole it was evident to me that a small spud had been used. There were even a few marks near the hole that were clearly made by a spud. When using a spud to dig a hole, people quite often insert it near the hole and leave marks on the left side. This is because most people used their left hand to operate the spud and the right to scoop out the soil. That's what had happened in this case as well. It became quite clear to me that Saudamini had not aborted her foetus and that now there was enough proof of that as well.

Whenever a meeting breaks up and the participants begin to disperse, they are bound to discuss all that's occurred in the meeting. This is like an immutable law of nature. In order to find out the views of those who had gathered in Ramtaran *babu*'s house, I followed them soon after they left the house. At some distance, where I thought I might overhear them talk freely and fearlessly, I hid behind a tree and waited. It was fairly dark by then.

After a while, four or five men went past. However, I couldn't hear anything worthwhile in their conversation. Then there were two men who walked past but they were silent. Soon after that, when I saw a group of three men engaged in an animated discussion and walking in this direction, I decided to pay special attention to what they were saying. One of them said, "This is a fatal blow! There's no way the wretched little man will find a way to escape this time. Let's see how he exerts his power as a *zamindar* after this! Shameful silence is all that's left for him."

The second person:	"Yes that's how it should have ended! But I'm beginning to have my doubts about this case. Looks like that mongrel from outside might tilt everything the other way."
The first person:	"To hell with that bloody mongrel! The case is ironclad since a body has been found."
The third person:	"But I feel this new fellow is not to be messed with. His very gaze turns my insides into water. Have you seen the way he's dragging everything out into the open? Those two fishermen have more or less folded. Who knows what lies in store for the rest of us."
The first person:	"I am sick of your fears! Who can touch us, if everything's taken care of? Since the body has been found, not even Lord Shiva can come and rescue Ramtaran."
Third person:	"Whatever you might say, I'm not able to get rid of my jitters. I'm going to go off to my son-in-law's house tomorrow."
First person:	"You make me sick! Did you feel any of this fear while stealing the corpse from a Mussalman's grave in the dead of night?"
Third person:	"I was full of courage at that time. All of you were there around me to give me support. Ray Mahashay had also given me a great deal of assurance. But what happens now?"
First person:	"Forget about it. Let the arrests happen tomorrow. Once the brother and sister rot in prison, we'll move on to other things."

I followed all three and made a note of their houses. Listening to the man who talked about stealing a corpse out of a Mussalman's grave, I'd got the feeling that he had become extremely nervous. Lest he run away to his son-in-law's house, I got a policeman to secretly keep an eye on his house in the night.

Early in the morning I knocked on his door. His name was Adwaita Ghosh. As soon as he opened the door, rubbing his eyes sleepily, I handcuffed him and placed him under arrest. Without giving Adwaita any time to gather his wits or change his clothes, we took him to Ramtaran *babu*'s house. I then looked at the record of the cases that Ramtaran *babu* had fought till then and I could see that Adwaita was involved in all of them. His two friends had also appeared as witnesses in these previous cases.

Kept under strict surveillance and tempted with the possibility of freedom if he were to become a state witness and tell the truth, Adwaita relented after a while and showed us the grave from where he had stolen the baby's corpse. About a week ago, the wife of a man named Khodabuksh had given birth to a stillborn child and Khodabuksh had then buried the body in that very grave.

It was soon proved that some people in the village had framed the entirely false case in order to teach Ramtaran a lesson. Since the fishermen depended on the *brahmatra* lands for their livelihood, they had said whatever the landowners had tutored them to say. The fact was that they had never even seen what the pond inside the *zamindar*'s estate looked like. Since Shridam had absconded from the village, it could be safely assumed that all that he had said was untrue. Harish's wife was completely clueless about the entire thing and Rupchand Hanri's wife became utterly confused when she was questioned and began ranting and raving after a while.

The entire plan was hatched by Brajaballabh Ray, and the executors of the plan were Adwaita Ghosh, Ramlochan Ray and Deenbandhu Bagchi. All four were arrested and sent to prison. An absconding notice was issued against Shridam. The remaining four could not escape their punishment.

Saudamini used to call Shridam "uncle". She would look upon him as though he were her father's own brother and respected him immensely. That same Shridam had conspired to disgrace Saudamini! He had given false statements to get his own employer and benefactor into trouble! Everywhere in the village people condemned and censured his actions. Within a week, news reached the police station that Shridam had hanged himself from a tamarind tree in the northern side of the village.

I had called Saudamini my sister. After the case got over, Ramataran *babu* invited me to his house for a meal. For some reason I couldn't visit him at that time. But after leaving the job and nearly three decades of the case being over, I went to the estate at my sister Saudamini's invitation. By then we were all quite old and the meeting was a deeply joyous one. This spiritual bond that was established between the families continued for some generations.

Bakaullah

Note

1 Land gifted to a Brahmin was called *brahmatra*. The owners did not have to pay a tax for the gifted land.

6

'WHAT'S THIS! A MURDER?'

'(The sensational mystery of a man caught with his stabbed wife)' Darogar Daftar, Poush (mid-December–mid-January), 1894

I

Quite often the job of solving of all those complicated cases of homicide in which the identity of the protagonist has remained elusive or where the arrested murderer has either escaped or hidden himself somewhere falls into my hands. I also inevitably get sent to places where cases of theft and fraud have remained unsolved after the initial investigation. But this particular investigation, the burden of which had fallen on my shoulders that day, was of a somewhat different nature. Even though it was a case of homicide, the killer was neither unknown nor a fugitive; in fact, he was apprehended soon after the murder. The police had completed their investigation and he had been presented before the Magistrate *sahib*. The Magistrate took statements from witnesses against him and only after being completely certain in his mind that the murder had indeed been committed by the arrested person did he eventually send him to the Sessions Court for the final trial.

Before I talk about those elements of this case which I needed to work on, I feel it's my duty to place those details that I was already aware of before my readers.

One afternoon in the month of *Maagh* (mid-January to mid-February of the *Saka* calendar) this year, in Gopal Bose Lane a man started shouting loudly, "Murder, murder." A policeman, who was on guard duty on the main road nearby, heard the uproar and rushed to the lane. Some people also ran after him to that spot. When the policeman reached that place, he found a small crowd of people standing around a second-class carriage and a Muslim carriage driver perched on top of it. The door of the carriage stood open. Inside the carriage, a young woman of around twenty, who appeared to be dead, was lying on the floor; there was a terrible wound visible on her chest and her entire body was soaked in blood. In fact, the inside of the carriage seemed to have turned crimson with blood. What's more, some of the blood had even seeped out of the carriage so that the road underneath was also turning red. In front of that dead woman sat a young man of not more than twenty-five, covered in blood and holding a long and fierce-looking knife which was also blood-stained. Many people were throwing questions at him, but the youth was refusing to give any answers. The policeman, after taking all this in, was utterly shocked and addressing the youth, asked him in Hindi, "Who are you? And why have you killed this woman?"

Till that moment, the young man hadn't uttered a word. But upon hearing these words from the policeman, he looked up him and their eyes met. The policeman baulked a little with surprise. I didn't see what the young man's eyes were like at that moment. As such, I can't describe exactly what they had been like. But from what I heard later, it seems that right after committing the murder, the killer's eyes looked like they were brimming with tears. I have seen many killers with my own eyes and have also heard of many from others, but I have neither heard of nor seen murderers whose eyes have filled with tears immediately after committing the crime.

Upon hearing the policeman's question, the youth said, "What does it matter who I am? Why do you need to know that? I have committed this murder. You can now take me wherever you please."

The policeman didn't say anything after this but instructed the coachman to drive the carriage slowly towards the *thhana*. As instructed, the coachman then began steering the carriage slowly towards the *thhana* while the policeman followed it on foot. The crowd that had gathered at the scene of crime was in no mood to be left behind and so went along with them. In due course, all of them reached the *thhana*.

The chief officer of the *thhana* was present in his office at that time and as soon as he heard the news, he rushed to the carriage. When he saw the gruesome scene inside it, he recoiled with horror. The sight of the young man clutching the long, blood-stained knife also caused him great anxiety, for he wondered how he was going to prise it out of his hand.

But it soon became evident that the officer needn't have worried at all, for the youth surrendered the knife into the hands of one of the policemen as soon as he was asked for it. The knife was then handed over to another officer who carried it inside the *thhana* very carefully. When the young man was asked to alight from the carriage, he did so without any demur and then entered the *thhana*. Following the instructions of their superior officer, two policemen then placed the man under arrest and put sturdy handcuffs on his wrists.

And from that very moment, the investigation of this murder began. The corpse was sent for post-mortem. Statements were also taken from all those witnesses who could be gathered from the scene of crime. When questioned, the young man confessed to having committed the murder: "The woman I have murdered was my wife. I had deep suspicions about her character and my heart was consumed with an uncontrollable rage. I simply couldn't rein in this unnatural anger and used that knife to kill her with my own hands inside the carriage. I am prepared to take whatever punishment is considered fit for me." But even though the young man confessed to the crime unequivocally, he refused to speak when asked questions about who he was, where he lived and what his wife's name had been. The police tried every possible means to extract answers to these questions, but to no avail. Finally, after failing in their efforts, they sent the arrested man to the Magistrate. There the trial began by stating that the young man had refused to reveal his identity. The witness statements of some of the inhabitants of that lane, the coachman and some others were then examined before the Magistrate.

II

The summary of the various statements gathered by the Magistrate Sahib ran thus:

The first witness, the coachman said, "The young woman hired this carriage at the Howrah station and after getting in said that she wanted to go to Kalighat. As soon as I started driving the carriage, the young man leapt in and when I asked him who he was and where he wanted to go, he said: 'This woman is my wife and she is going away after a fight with me. When I realised she was going away, I pursued her and seeing her get into this carriage, have got in to talk to her. You don't have to take the carriage to Kalighat. We have a relative staying in Kolkata. Drive us there.' He said all this standing in front of the young lady and she didn't protest. As a result I believed all that he said, and followed his orders. When the carriage reached Gopal Bose Lane, it seemed to shudder and then I heard an indistinct sound emanating from inside it. I stopped the vehicle and on turning back saw the blood-drenched corpse of the woman in the coach. Her limbs were flailing a bit at the time but after a while, they became completely still. I noticed that the young man held a bloodied knife and that his clothes were also stained heavily with blood. He was trying to straighten the woman's body. When I saw all this I said nothing to them but simply started shouting, 'Murder, murder.' Soon people from the neighbourhood gathered over there and subsequently a policeman also came and the young man was brought to the *thhana*."

The people from the neighbourhood also gave a similar statement. They all said that when they had gathered near the carriage after hearing the shouts of murder, they had seen the blood-soaked body inside it and also noticed the young man with the knife sitting in front of it. Besides these two there was no one else in the carriage. The carriage driver was sitting atop the coach. They also described the arrival of the policeman in an adequate manner: what he saw, the questions he asked the youth, the answers he received and how the young culprit was taken to the *thhana*. A few of them testified to the fact that there was no one other than the young man in that carriage. The doctor who performed the post-mortem testified that the young woman had died as a result of the terrible stab wounds on her chest.

When the Magistrate asked the young man some questions, he said, "Please don't ask me any more questions. And even if you do, I won't give you any answers. I'm only going to tell you this that the dead woman was my wife. But I won't tell you her name. Nor will I tell you where she lived, where we were coming from or where we were planning to go. I'm only going to tell you that I'm the killer. The grievous blow that killed her was struck by me."

The Magistrate heard his words and then said, "If you don't tell us all this, how will we know the truth of your statement about being the killer?"

"When I am saying that the murder was my doing, what reason would you have for not believing me? Surely when the accused admits of his own free will, to having committed the crime, I see no reason for doubting his word. You can sentence me to death based on what I'm telling you."

Magistrate: "I have the power to believe or disbelieve what you say. Besides, I don't have to take your opinion on how to sentence you. You, on the other hand, need to give answers to the few questions that I ask you. For this will only benefit rather than harm you. If you tell me your name, your address or the details of your family, then maybe I'll be able to get them to help you. They could enlist a good solicitor to try and help you. You should agree with this suggestion."

"Please forgive me Sir, but I am not going to give you any of this information. I don't wish to take any favours from anyone. I should be punished for whatever I have done. Please don't ask me anything more about this. Just give me the punishment I deserve and I'll accept it with a smile."

Realising that it would be futile to ask the accused any further questions, the Magistrate asked him to be taken to the Sessions Court and said to him, "Such is the magnitude of your crime, that it is beyond my powers to decide a befitting punishment. Hence I'm sending your case to a higher court; that's where your sentence will be decided."

III

Around the time when a month was left for the trial to begin in the higher court, my superior officer called me and said, "You must be aware of the recent Gopal Das Lane murder case and you must also know that the accused in this case has still not revealed his identity. The reasons why this gruesome crime was committed remain shrouded in complete darkness till date. The Government Counsel who is going to fight this case has now written this letter to me. He writes that quite often in a homicide trial the sentencing of the culprit becomes difficult if the motives of the crime are not ascertained. And so I have decided to hand over the responsibility of solving this crime to you. Try your best to see if through some means you can find out the identity of the man and dig out his reasons for murdering the woman."

It is so very easy for a superior officer, to issue orders of this kind to his junior officer. But what never ceases to surprise me is why our superiors are unable to give us any suggestions about how such orders are to be followed. At any rate, once I get my orders, I have no choice but to follow them to the best of my abilities whether I succeed or fail in my mission. Where do I begin, where to go, whom to ask: these were questions to which I could find no answers, despite mulling over them for quite some time.

After spending the entire day thinking along various lines, I even spent the night with such thoughts. But having failed to come up with a solution, I got up in the morning and went off to the Harinbari prison. According to the laws of this land, the prisoner has to be in custody while the trial is in progress. When I went into the prison to meet the accused, I was in civilian clothes, for quite often I don't need to wear my uniform at work. I walked into the prison wearing my regular, everyday clothes.

The prison warden knew me well and so he let me enter without raising any objections. I went in and met the Englishman who was the prison officer there and told him that I wanted to meet the accused in the recent case of homicide. I also told him, "I want to meet him in such a way that he doesn't suspect I am a police officer."

The officer agreed with my proposal and then asked me to wait in a room. When I had set off in the morning with the intention of meeting the prisoner, I had carried a set of clean *dhoti*, a white shirt and a warm wrapper with me.

The prison officer brought the accused to the room where I was waiting for him. The officer sat in the other chair in the room, while the convict remained standing before us.

The clothes on the prisoner's body had become extremely grubby. I said to him, "Your clothes look very dirty. Why don't you take them off and wear these clean clothes?"

The young man: "Who are you? I have no wish to take the clothes you are offering, until I know who you are."

When I heard his words, I thought for a moment that I would reveal my real identity and then cajole him with kind words to disclose the truth about himself. But then I thought to myself that the man who had refused to disclose anything of his identity to the first investigating officer, and had even managed to thwart the Magistrate's efforts to extract information out of him, was unlikely to reveal anything to me. And if he refused to talk, then I would simply have to abandon my mission there and then. Any chance I might have of getting something out of him, would be completely lost. Thinking on these lines, I said to him, "Are you likely to recognize me if

I told you who I am? I am not an acquaintance and I doubt you have ever seen me before."

Young man: "If you don't know me and I have no way of recognising you then why pray have you taken the trouble of getting clean clothes for me?"

"I had no need to do this and I haven't got clothes for you out of any ulterior motive. I carried all this for you because I couldn't ignore the heartfelt request of someone very close to you. If you take this then well and good, else I'll return all this stuff to them."

The young man looked slightly alarmed upon hearing this and then muttered in a faint voice to himself: "Has my father found out about my situation?"

"I didn't say that your father has got to know the truth about you and sent all this clothing for you."

"Whether you say it or not, I know that only a father's heart can be filled with this kind of concern."

"I don't know whether the person from whom I took these clothes was your father. But if you tell me your father's name, I can verify if it was he who gave me these clothes."

"No Sir, I am not going to give you my father's name. What if he doesn't really know any of this? My telling you his name might in that case reveal all that I don't want disclosed. He lives far away so I am hoping against hope that the news would not have reached him."

"Do you really think that this news hasn't travelled to your father yet? Don't you think your relatives and acquaintances living in Kolkata haven't got wind of this affair? Do you believe that the person whose house you were visiting that day wouldn't have any inkling of what's happened? This murder has created such a furore in the city that probably everyone—from mansion-dwellers to those who live in hovels—has gotten to know about it. That being the case, don't you think that someone has surely carried this news to your family?"

"Whatever you might say, whether my father has come to know about this or not, I am neither going to tell you anything, nor accept this gift of clothing from you. After all what difference does it make to a man who is determined to die, whether he wears clean or unclean clothes?"

"Alright then! Don't take the clothes today. But bear in mind that when I visit this prison with whoever has sent these clothes, your father or an acquaintance, you'll have no choice but to accept this gift."

The young man said nothing when he heard this. Seeing him sit in complete silence, I realised that I wasn't going to extract anything out of him that day and left the prison. The officer then led the young man back to his cell.

After meeting the young man, I felt that my conjectures about him were close to the truth. I gathered that he did have relatives or acquaintances living in the city. What I had also divined was that his father was alive and lived at some distance from Kolkata.

IV

I returned home that day from the prison. My ruse having failed, I began thinking of other ways and means of succeeding in my project. After spending the day and most part of the night brooding over this, I visited the *thbana* where the first report of the murder had been filed.

At this point I must apprise my readers of something that I forgot to tell them earlier. At the time that the convict had been apprehended, his clothes were blood-stained. When he was brought to the *thbana*, those clothes had been taken away from him and he had been given something different to wear. The clothes that he was wearing at the moment were those given to him by the police.

On reaching the *thbana*, I said that I wanted to see those clothes for myself. The officer at the *thbana* heard me and said that the clothes were no longer with them. The clothes of the young man as well as those of the dead woman had been sent to the "chemical examiner" for examination.

I then went to the Medical College and met the examiner. I didn't really know him well but I saw that he was a real gentleman. When I told him what I wanted, he agreed to help and brought in all the clothes for my inspection. I began to examine them right there in front of him.

Amongst all the clothing was a black coat. It seemed a little old but not as if it had been worn too much. I realised it belonged to the killer. On its inner collar was stitched a white cloth label. Though white, it had become fairly grubby. I was aware of the fact that in coats and jackets such labels often carry the name of the seller. Hence I examined it very carefully and was able to discern the following details written on it in English letters: Ganguli Brothers, Kolkata.

Having found this out about the coat, I felt some hope flooding my mind yet again. I thought to myself that it would be really good if I could use this lead to find out some more things; for until then, I had not been able to come up with any other means of satisfying my curiosity. Anyway, after examining the clothes minutely and failing to find anything else that might prove useful for my investigation, I left that place.

Finding the shop called Ganguli Brothers didn't prove difficult at all. I located it easily after a brief search. It is co-owned by one Mahendranath Ganguli. I didn't know him extremely well but we were vaguely acquainted. I went there and told him everything. I spoke to him about the investigation, what stage of the investigation I had reached and finally asked him if he would be willing to accompany me to the Medical College and take a look at the aforementioned coat. He agreed to help and we then set off towards the Medical College.

The coat was with the chemical examiner and the law did not allow us to remove the coat from there while his examinations were going on. That's the reason why I had to take Mahendra *babu* to that place.

Mahendra *babu* saw the coat and said that he could recognise it as belonging to their shop but he couldn't say at that point who had bought it or when the sale had taken place. However, even though he couldn't identify the buyer of the coat, he confirmed that the coat could have been bought only at the price indicated on the label. He also said that as far as he was aware, nothing from their shop had ever been sold at a lower price.

I went back to the shop with him and after a great deal of discussion, it was decided that we had no other choice but to sit there and go over the details of sales records of the last few years with a fine tooth comb. If we came across the sale description of such a coat, then it might just lead us to the details of the buyer we were interested in.

Once this decision was taken, it didn't take me long to translate it into action. It was only after a relentless examining of the sales books over fifteen long days that we completed looking at the information for the last six years. Our study had yielded that only five coats that cost Rs seven had been sold in that period. The first had been bought by Sureshchandra Dutta of Simla, the second by Shashi Chandra Ghosh, the third by Ramjadu Sarkar of Boubazaar, the fourth by Trailokya Biswas of Bhavanipur and a fifth whose name was not known and the entry simply said, "Cash Paid".

Despite knowing that this lead would be nigh on impossible to follow, I decided to pursue this line of investigation since there was precious little for me to go on. The four gentlemen whose names we had managed to retrieve from the sales records were all known to Mahendra *babu*. As a result, locating them proved quite easy. We found Suresh Dutta in his Simla house. His coat was with him. The second buyer, Shashi Chandra Ghosh, had been staying in Tangra when he had bought the coat, but when we reached his address, we found out that he had left that house two years ago. Thankfully one of his neighbours knew his subsequent address in Tallygunge and we took him along and paid Mr. Ghosh a visit. When we met him in Tallygunge and asked him about the coat, we found out that it was still with him.

V

Ramjadu Sarkar of Boubazaar used to live in the house mentioned in the records some time ago. About six months ago he had left that house and moved back to his village. His house was now in a small hamlet near Bardhaman. Not having any hopes of finding him in Kolkata, we decided to visit Trailokya Biswas of Bhavanipur. There we learnt that he had died three months ago. From his brother we later learnt that his black coat was still with his widowed wife.

All our hopes were now pinned on Ramjadu Sarkar. If the coat proved to be his, then my efforts would bear fruit. Thinking along such lines,

I decided not to delay the matter any further. Post haste, I began my journey to Sarkar *babu*'s village. His house was not more than four or five miles away from Bardhaman so I was able to reach his house the very next day. I noticed that Ramjadu *babu* was stepping out of the gate of his house and it looked like he was about to go somewhere. My hopes were dashed, as soon as I saw him. Over the last few days I had fixated on the idea that the coat I had seen at the chemical examiner's in Medical College belonged to Ramjadu Sarkar and that the killer was none other than Ramjadu. The surprise on seeing him was nothing compared to the shock I felt on seeing his coat. For Ramjadu *babu* was wearing the same coat that I had come all the way to investigate!

When he saw me, he said, "Who are you Sir and whom have you come here to meet?"

I had to answer his questions. I gave him my actual identity. But I did not immediately reveal to him my reasons for being there. Instead I said to him, "I have some business with you and that's why I'm here to meet you."

"If you have some work with me then why don't we go inside the house and talk? I had plans to go out of town, but I can shelve those for a while. Once your work is finished, I can take care of mine."

I agreed with what he said and my junior officer and I went into his house. He first led us to the drawing room, asked us to take a seat and then went into the inner apartments. Afterwards, he came out to the room where we were seated and sat down with us. I could guess why he had gone in. He was planning to ask us to spend the night at his house and when he went into the inner quarters, he made arrangements for our meals and accommodation within the house.

Ramjadu *babu* sat next to us and then said after a while, "Sir, now can you alleviate my anxieties and tell me why you have come to pay me a visit? Given that even the mere mention of your department is enough to fill people with fear, imagine the effect that an actual visit by your kind can cause! I'm not sure you can understand what I'm going through right now."

Upon hearing these words, I smiled a little and then said to him, "You don't have any reasons for feeling nervous about our visit. In fact, our work here is done. I am now ready to leave this place and go back."

"I haven't the faintest idea as to what your work here might have been and how it has suddenly got completed. At any rate, if you have no reservations about telling me what your assignment here was all about, I'd be terribly pleased. Besides, you can forget about leaving this place today. Please spend the rest of the night in my house; tomorrow we can set out on our separate journeys."

I heard Ramjadu *babu*'s request and replied, "Alright then! I'll stay here tonight." Then I explained to him in great detail the reason why I had paid him a visit. I told him about the various leads and clues that I had been investigating from the very beginning of my involvement in the case, the circumstances that had led me to his doorstep and the reason why my investigation had come to an abrupt halt in that place.

He heard my account very carefully and then said, "I'm finally feeling a great sense of relief. For I was so sure that you were here to conduct an investigation against me." He also added, "Your conjecture is correct. This coat is indeed that very coat that you are interested in. I had bought this coat for seven rupees and nine annas from the shop of the Ganguli Bros. At that time, a young man called Lalit used to stay in the house that I was living in. We both bought a similar coat on that same day."

Hope flooded my heart afresh when I heard Ramjadu's words. I asked him, "Did Lalit's coat look the same? And was it bought at the same price?"

Ramjadu: "The two coats were just the same and their prices were identical."

"Did you have credit with Ganguli Bros.? Did you pay cash for the coat or did you buy it on credit?"

"As far as I can recall, I had got it on credit. Subsequently I paid off the money I owed them for the coat."

"Can you also recall if Lalit paid for the coat with cash or took it on credit?"

"I think he had paid for it with cash."

"And what is Lalit *babu*'s full name?"

"Shri Lalit Mohan Mukhopadhyay."

"Do you have any idea as to where he might be at present?"

"I'm afraid, I have no clue regarding his present whereabouts. I do know that his brother Jogendranath Mukhopadhyay is a clerk in the General Post Office in Kolkata. But I don't know where his house is or where he might be staying at the moment."

I saw some glimmerings of hope upon hearing all this from Ramjadu *babu*. I felt that my investigations related to the coat would surely conclude with the finding of Lalit *babu*. But in case going to him failed to produce any results, then I would have to start looking for other leads. And all my efforts devoted to pursuing the present set of leads would have been in vain. Anyway, I spent the night at Ramjadu *babu*'s house but I refrained from discussing the case any further with him. The very next day I left his house and travelled back to Kolkata. Ramjadu *babu* also left the house at the same time and went off towards his destination. By the time I reached Kolkata it was too late to visit the GPO and so I couldn't look for Jogendranath that day.

VI

The next day I went to the GPO at around 10 o'clock and asked for Jogendranath. When I found him and asked him about Lalit *babu*, he informed me that Lalit was working in Kolkata's main telegraph office. The two brothers resided in the same house and their present house was in the fishermen's colony.

After bidding him farewell, I went to the telegraph office and found Lalit *babu*. He then asked me to wait outside. After I had waited for him for nearly half an hour, I saw him walking towards me. When he came to where I was standing, I introduced myself and then asked him a few questions.

I: "Do you remember that at the time that you were living in Boubazaar, a gentleman called Ramjadu *babu* used to live in the house that you stayed in?"

"Oh yes Sir! I remember that Ramjadu and I were roommates."

"Do you remember going to a shop called Ganguli Bros. with Ramjadu and buying two similar-looking, warm black coats?"

"Yes, I can recall that a little faintly now."

"Isn't it true that you had paid seven rupees in cash for that coat whereas Ramjadu *babu* had bought it on credit?"

"Yes, I possibly paid for it with cash."

"Where's that coat which you had bought that day?"

"I really can't say where the coat is. The truth is that I had bought it for someone else, not for myself."

"Well, whom did you buy it for?"

"I have no idea whom it was meant for. I had bought it on my uncle's instructions that he sent to me in a letter. In order to fulfil a friend's request, he sent me eight rupees and some measurements, based on which he asked me to buy a coat and send it to his address. Accordingly, I bought the coat and sent it to him."

"From where was your uncle's letter posted and where did you send the coat?"

"My uncle wrote the letter from Kanpur and that's where I sent the coat."

"And where does your uncle stay at present?"

"He's still in Kanpur. That's where he runs his business."

"What's his name?"

"My uncle's name is Kantichandra Mukhopadhyay."

"Would you have any idea at all about the person for whom your uncle had bought that coat?"

"I told you earlier I haven't got the foggiest. But I know for sure that he didn't buy it for himself."

After gathering all this information from Lalit, I left that place. And Lalit went back to his office.

My investigation of this case in Kolkata was petering out and so I felt that it was essential that I go to Kanpur and pick up the pieces by talking to Kanti Mukhopadhyay. I decided that I needed to follow the lead to its logical conclusion without any further delay, and so I took the mail train to

Kanpur that very night. The train reached Kanpur the next day. I alighted from the train and then wondered for a while as to where I should go. I had been to Kanpur a few times before this but since I didn't really know too many people living there I stopped in my tracks for a bit and then decided to hire a carriage and go into the city.

There's a fairly substantial population of Bengalis in Kanpur and as such I didn't really have to try very hard to find Kanti *babu*. I found out his address after asking one or two Bengalis who lived there. When I reached his house, Kanti *babu* was not at home; he returned after I had waited for him for almost two hours. When he saw me he asked me who I was. I disclosed my actual identity to him and then said, "Sir, I have come here from Kolkata to ask you a few things. I would be greatly obliged if you answer my questions truthfully. After that, I'll tell you my reasons for all the questions."

When Kanti *babu* agreed to my proposal, I said to him, "Sir, do you remember that your nephew Lalitmohan used to stay in Kolkata's Boubazaar area some years ago?"

Kanti: "Of course! I remember that very well."

I: "Do you also remember that at that time you had sent him some money and measurements and asked him to buy a coat from Kolkata?"

Kanti: (after thinking for a little while) "Yes, I think I can recall that Lalit had bought a coat for me and posted it from Kolkata."

"May I take a look at that coat?"

"I'm afraid I don't have it. That coat wasn't bought for me. I had got it for Ramsundar *babu*'s son Upendranath."

"Where might Ramsundar *babu* and his son be, at present?"

"Ramsundar *babu* stays in this very city and he is a fairly successful contractor. I don't really know where his son Upendra is. I haven't seen him in quite some time."

"How far from here is Ramsundar *babu*'s house? Will I be able to meet him, if I go there now?"

"His house isn't very far from here. I can take you to his house right away. But I really wish you would tell me what it is that you are investigating and what has brought you so far from your city?"

VII

I then said to Kanti *babu*, "I can definitely tell you about the case and the leads that I am following in this place, but please don't utter a word about any of this when we meet Ramsundar *babu*." Then I recounted all the details of the case to him in chronological order. I didn't keep anything back and described the killer's arrest with a blood-stained knife right next to the dead woman, his confession as well as his insistence on being punished, and also his refusal to reveal his identity to the Magistrate or the police. I told Kanti *babu* everything. Then I also told him about the manner in which the case had fallen into my hands, my visit to the prison to meet the killer, the ruse that I had devised in order to make him reveal his identity and how after the failure of that plan, I began to follow the lead of the coat and eventually landed at his doorstep in Kanpur. After hearing all of this, Kanti *babu* sighed heavily and said, "It'll be terrible when Ramsundar *babu* hears all of this. For Upendranath is his only child. The old gentleman will be driven mad with anxiety and my fear is that he might even lose all sense of equilibrium and try to kill himself."

When I heard Kanti *babu*'s apprehensions, I felt they might not be entirely far-fetched. It would be wrong to accost the old gentleman with this kind of news, without any prior warning. After a great deal of discussion with Kanti *babu*, it was finally decided that I would not go to meet Ramsundar *babu* immediately. Kanti *babu* would go to meet him in his usual manner, and while casually chatting with him would try to find out about Upendranath's present whereabouts, along with the whereabouts of the coat that had been bought for him from Kolkata.

After all this was decided, Kanti *babu* left for his friend's abode. I stayed back in his house. Kanti *babu* had told everyone in his house that I was a distant cousin and so no one knew about my real identity.

Late in the evening, Kanti *babu* returned home. I learnt from him that around two months ago Upendranath had left Kanpur to visit his in-laws' house in Kashi. At that time, his wife had been staying with her mother in Kashi. After reaching Kashi, Upendranath had written two letters to his father but subsequently there was no further news from him. Ramsundar *babu* then wrote several letters one after another to his son and when they went unanswered, he became terribly worried and sent one of his competent employees to Kashi to find out what had happened to his son.

That employee was back in Kanpur and Kanti *babu* had managed to meet him as well. Kantibabu learned from him that he had gone to the house where Upendranath's mother-in-law was staying, but he didn't find anyone there. Upon asking around, he found out that Upendranath's mother-in-law had died very soon after he reached Kashi. Till around two days after her death, everyone had seen Upendranath and his wife, but soon after that, nobody knows where they went. When the employee returned to Kanpur and gave this news to the old gentleman, he was prostrated with grief. Crazed with sorrow, he has been weeping continually and was refusing to listen to anyone's words of comfort. It had become difficult to convince him that his son is alive.

When Kanti *babu* asked some of the domestics about the clothes that Upendranath had carried with him to Kashi, he found out that he had indeed taken the coat—the one I had been investigating for so long—with him to Kashi.

I thanked Kanti *babu* profusely for all the information that I had gathered with his help. I also felt a little happy within my heart. All my painstaking efforts had finally borne fruit and the identity of the killer had come to light. I had successfully concluded the task given to me by my superior and unravelled the mystery that so many other officers were desperate to solve. Now only one thing remained in this investigation—to find the reason for this murder. And I felt that since the killer's identity as well as his address had been established, before long, the motives for the murder would also be revealed.

However, I was deeply distressed to hear about the sufferings of the old gentleman. I also wondered how I could bring myself to visit him and pour hot ghee over the burning sorrows of his heart by telling him the truth about his son.

VIII

After a heated discussion with Kanti *babu* over this matter, I decided that I was duty-bound to tell the gentleman about the investigation. Firstly this would mean that Ramsundar *babu*, who was completely clueless about his son's whereabouts, would finally have some information about him. Secondly, given the nature of the case, Upendranath had very little hope of being acquitted, without some help. If his father were not informed about the case, who would help Upendranath by finding out relevant facts for his defence? After reflecting awhile, I eventually decided that I would pay Ramsundar *babu* a visit the next day and tell him everything.

The following day both Kanti *babu* and I went to his house early in the morning. He was in the inner quarters at that time. Kanti *babu* asked one of the domestics to go in and inform him that a *babu* had come from Kolkata with news about Upendranath.

Ramsundar *babu* rushed out to meet us as soon as he got this news. Both Kanti *babu* and I were sitting in the drawing room at that time. As soon as he saw us he cried, "Who has brought me news of Upendra? Where is my Upendra? Is he alright?"

Replying to his queries, I said, "Sir, I am the one who has brought you news about your son. He is alive and well but he is in great trouble."

"My Upendra is in trouble?! Where is he? What kind of trouble is he in?" Saying this the old man collapsed into a chair.

"I have in fact come here to tell you everything about Upendra's crisis. But unless you calm down, how am I going to give you all the information? Upendranath is not here, he's in Kolkata. He is a convict in an ongoing case. The judgement is yet to be delivered, though." I told him all these things, one by one.

"I feel a little better after hearing that my son is alive. I am not that concerned about the fact that he has been arrested in a criminal case. I'll spend as much money on lawyers as I can, and then surely he'll be free. But how do you know all this? Who are you?" Ramsundar *babu* asked me the last two these questions after he had recovered a little bit. I said, "I'm a police officer. It is on your son's request that I have come this far to give you this news."

"If you are a police officer, you'll definitely be able to tell me on whose complaint my Upendra was arrested. What's the nature of the allegation? And how did he land up in Kolkata?"

I was in a quandary after hearing the old man's questions. If I were to tell him everything truthfully, he might fear the worst and then my well-laid plans would end in a disaster. And what if he fell ill a second time, and it became impossible to revive the old gentleman? With all this running through my mind, I felt I had to lie to him. I'm not sure if such lying is a sin but it was fear of the far greater sin of causing his death that drove me to say, "I didn't come to Kanpur to deliver this news to you; nor am I all that aware of the details of your son's case. Before coming to Kanpur, I had visited the Harinbari prison in order to meet a prisoner related to one of my cases. While I was there, I met your son and when he heard I was about to go to Kanpur, he asked me to inform you about his crisis. He also said, 'Please bring my father along with you when you return from Kanpur. Without him I have no way of finding my way out of this problem.' When I had asked him about the nature of his case, he had simply said, 'I have been accused of a very serious crime. Once my father gets here, he'll get to know everything.' I can't tell you anything more than this. But you may come with me to Kolkata if you wish. I'm leaving Kanpur tomorrow morning for I've completed my work here."

I could see that Ramsundar *babu* was listening to me very carefully. He then decided that he would leave for Kolkata the very next day with me.

IX

I spent that evening as well at Kanti *babu*'s house. Kanti *babu* did not reveal anything of the case to Ramsundar *babu*. The next day Ram *babu* left Kanpur with me accompanied by one of his clerks and a servant. In due course, we reached Kolkata.

As soon we reached the city, Ramsundar *babu* said that he wanted to meet his son immediately and began pleading with me to take him to that prison. I agreed to take him there and said to him, "Alright, I'll take you to the Harinbari prison right away and I'll also make sure that you get to meet your son while you are there." Taking him with me, I set off for the Harinbari prison. On the way there I said to him, "Look Ramsundar *babu*, Upendranath is a convicted prisoner. It is therefore not very easy to get access to him. No one can meet a prisoner without the permission of the prison officer and that's the reason why most people go there early in the morning to seek his permission. That's the stipulated time for meeting the officer or getting his permission. As such, I cannot assure you that you'll be able to meet and talk to your son today when we go there. The only advantage you have is that I'm a police officer and am allowed to go into the prison at whatever time I wish and talk to whoever I want to. Since you are desperate to see your son, I'll go into the prison on your behalf and get Upendranath to a spot where you can see him, while standing at the gate. I can also convey to your son the questions that you wish to ask him and communicate his answers to you. Beyond this, if you want to meet him and talk to him personally, then you'll need to go there another day early in the morning and seek the permission of the prison officer."

Ramsundar *babu* accepted my suggestion without any protest. I asked him to wait outside the prison and went inside. The old man stood outside the railings that fenced the prison, waiting to catch a glimpse of his son. Just as I had stepped into the prison, he had told me, "Please find out from Upendra what kind of a criminal case he is involved in, why he is in prison and what sort of help he needs. Also ask him how he has come here and where his wife is." I assured him that I would ask him all these things and went in.

As I have mentioned earlier, I knew all the prison officers quite well. When I saw the Jailor *sahib* approaching me I told him all that had transpired. He agreed to what I proposed and soon brought Upendranath to me. As soon as I saw him I said, "Upendranath! Look, I'm back and this time I've brought another person along who wants to meet you and who's waiting there just outside the prison gate." I then pointed to where Ramsundar *babu* was standing.

Upendra looked at the old man but only for a few seconds. He then quickly averted his gaze and sat down heavily on the ground and began trembling all over. It looked like he was unable to utter a single word.

I felt a little worried when I saw his condition. I thought to myself that Upendranath was arrested for murder and undoubtedly his mind must be wracked with all kinds of anxieties. On top of that, not only had his identity, which for some reason he had wanted to keep a secret, been revealed, his old father had got to know of his troubles and come rushing to his aid. It was impossible for us to gauge what Upendranath was going through, in that moment. Given his situation I feared that maybe I had exacerbated his pain. Would the frail and distraught-looking young prisoner be able to keep his mental balance?

When I gestured to the Jailor, he led Upendra out of that place into a room where he again collapsed on to the floor. I sat down next to him and the Jailor *sahib* also sat in the room.

In those moments, Upendra's endurance was being tested to the very limit. If he could pass the test I would know the extent to which he was capable of repressing his emotions. I was about to find out if his determined vow of silence was the result of a fickle, emotion-driven youthful impulse or the unyielding decision of a strong and guileless mind. I was also going to find out the reason for that vow.

I addressed him, "Upendranath!"

Upendranath looked at me. His gaze was no longer like what I had seen earlier. It was not the hard gaze of a man who had taken a rigid vow and was fearless of consequences. Today his eyes seemed like those of a helpless little boy. The dry-eyed young man of that day had disappeared. Today as he sat before me, his eyes were like lotus leaves brimming with water; the tears moved inside them like iridescent crystals, but did not spill out.

"Upendranath! Now do you see that when I had come to meet you earlier, I had come on behalf of a relative and not because I meant you any harm? Perhaps you see that now. And since you do understand this, will you tell me the truth now? Do you really think you can die without telling us the truth? Maybe your wish to remain anonymous and silent would have been fulfilled if we hadn't found out anything about you and if your father had not come here to help you. But that, as you know, is not going to be possible now. Whether your wish was a good or a bad one, it will now remain unfulfilled. We have consulted a number of renowned lawyers for your case. We have even shown them copies of the witness statements. After looking at all the documents, they have all said that despite the confession, it's unlikely that you would be hanged. In these circumstances, it's quite pointless for you to conceal the truth. Especially since your old father has come this far to meet you and find out what has happened. He had even gone to Kashi when he had heard about your troubles and he found out all that had happened there. The questions that I'm asking you now are those that he would have come and asked you. But then he's your father, and you are his son. Lest you feel embarrassed about revealing everything to him, he decided to wait outside and sent me in to meet you on his behalf. You shouldn't keep anything secret now; especially since your father has found out a few things already." I stopped to gauge his reaction, after saying all this to him.

X

Upendra said, "Please tell my father that it would be best if his worthless son left this world. How can a man who doesn't know his own heart and can't distinguish right from wrong, deserve to live? Surely a sinful wretch who, on a mere suspicion, recklessly loses the brightest and most precious possession of his heart, has no right to show his face to anyone in this world." With these words, Upendra's throat began to choke with unshed tears. After being unable to speak for almost ten minutes, he finally said, "Sir! Please tell my father that my mother-in-law passed away after two days of my reaching her house in Kashi. My wife, who was heartbroken at her mother's death, wept incessantly. I consoled her and then went off to complete the last rites. Later in the evening, I came back to my mother-in-law's house. The house that she lived in was divided into two sections, inner and outer. She had lived in the outer section, while some other women stayed in the inner quarters. That night, as I was entering the house I noticed a young man whom I had never seen before, darting out of our section of the house. I thought that he must be an acquaintance of my mother-in-law and so I didn't probe the matter any further. When I went in, I found my wife mourning for her mother and crying uncontrollably. I tried to comfort her in whatever way I could.

I realised that the intense grieving over a loved one's death that one sees on the first day wanes inevitably over time. Over time, my wife did not seem as devastated as she was earlier. I decided that soon after completing the rites of the fourth day, I would return with her to Kanpur.

That day, I had to go out for some work in the evening. It was almost ten at night by the time I got back. As I was entering the house through the main gate, I nearly bumped into the same male figure I had espied last evening. It seemed as though he had emerged out of my wife's room. Upon seeing me all of a sudden, at first he baulked and then he ran off at the speed of lightning, without uttering a single word. His manner of running away filled me with unease that night. Truth be told, my heart was overrun with suspicions and doubts of all kinds. When I went into our room, I found that my wife was awake. I asked her about the young man, but she said she knew nothing about any such person. I became more and more certain that she was feigning ignorance. She kept saying, 'I know nothing about this.'

I felt suspicions surge in my heart. I thought to myself that my wife had become unfaithful while she was staying away from me in Kashi. But that day I didn't ask her any more questions.

The next day I had to go out again on work. When I returned home that night, it was past eleven. After entering the house, I rushed towards my wife's room and found that the door was ajar and in the dull glow of the lamp burning inside, it seemed, that my wife was asleep. As I was about to sit down on the other side of the bed, I saw the same youth dashing out of the house. I chased him but he ran at such speed, that I couldn't see which of the several lanes outside he went into.

I returned to our room and shook my wife awake. But when I asked her about the young man, she again replied, 'I have no idea about this!'

I didn't like her answer. I had just seen a person leaving her room so how could I believe that she knew nothing about the matter? It was not something that I had heard from someone else; I had seen the man not on one, not on two but on three consecutive days with my own eyes. So I found her short answer 'I don't know' very difficult to swallow and be content with. As a matter of fact, that day, I was filled with grave suspicions about my wife's character. And was it just restricted to suspicion? No, I spelt out my thoughts very clearly and shouted, 'You wretched woman, you slut, I had no idea till date that you are a deceitful witch in disguise.' With these words, I worked myself up to an immense rage and throwing away all sense of right and wrong, I acted like a terrible coward and kicked her with great force. The poor feeble girl, already traumatised by her mother's death, fell to the ground as a result of my kick. I rained a few more kicks on her prone body before sitting down angrily in that room. Poor thing! The virtuous young woman slowly lifted herself up from the floor and then clasping my feet she said in plaintive tones, 'My Lord! I have never been unfaithful to you. I have never even thought of anyone else. It is your image alone that resides in my heart. Whether you believe me or not, I can swear while touching your feet that I know nothing of this. Please don't cast a slur on my character; I have not sinned in any way.' She held my feet and continued to weep.

For some reason, the sound of her weeping aggravated me even further and my rage escalated into a terrifying thing. I flung her arms off forcefully and after administering a few more kicks, cried, 'Sinful creature! I don't believe a word you say, anymore. Just get out from here, I don't wish to see your face ever again in my life.' Then I shoved her out of the room with all my strength and slammed the door shut.

The poor helpless woman addressed me in a piteous voice from outside the door, 'My Lord! Since you no longer believe me and have vowed never to set eyes upon me again, then how can I shamelessly insist on showing you my face. But do remember this, I am not unfaithful. If I'm uttering the truth and have laid my heart at your feet alone, then surely God will one day show you whether my heart is full of poisonous deceit or brimming with pure love and devotion for you.'[1]

I was of course so consumed with an inhuman fury at the time, that her words did not stir me in the slightest bit. I was awake that entire night in the house but not for a moment did I wonder where the poor woman could have gone in the dead of the night.

I stepped out of the house very early in the morning next day but I made no effort to find out where she might have gone. I was still fuming and I spent the next day in that manner. I barely ate or drank since I didn't feel either hungry or thirsty the whole day.

That night at around nine, I was sitting all by myself in the house. I was sitting in the dark and had left the door ajar. All of a sudden, for some reason my eye was drawn to the main gate of the building. And I saw that same young man entering the building, in a furtive manner. I thought to myself that if he came anywhere near our apartment, I would definitely murder him and avenge my humiliation.

The young man entered the gate and then turned and went off towards a different apartment. Since he didn't come into our apartment, I got up and began following him with extremely light footsteps. I saw that he walked beyond our apartment and entered another apartment which was housed in the inner part of the building. I followed him and then began watching his activities from a distance.

Upon reaching the other apartment, he knocked very gently on its door. Soon the door opened from within and I could see that a lamp was burning inside. In the faint glow of the lamp I could see that the person who had opened the door was a twenty-year-old widow. As soon as she opened the door, the youth darted into the room. Once he entered the room, the door was firmly shut once again.

That was the moment when I realised the grave mistake that I had committed. God himself had made me see the truth with my own eyes and I realised how I had fallen into an abyss of false assumptions and how terribly I had wronged my devoted and defenceless wife. I could barely stand still; my entire body trembled after making this discovery. Feeling dizzy, I slumped down to the floor and I lost count of the hours I spent like that. But as soon as the door opened again, I recovered my senses and leapt up in order to enter that apartment. I found the young man still sitting inside the room. When he saw me he again tried to flee but since I was standing right next to the door, he failed to make good his escape.

Upon seeing me in the room all of a sudden, the young widow couldn't decide what to do and hastily fell at my feet and pleaded, 'Sir, you are like my father; please save me from facing disgrace. Else I'll never be able to show my sinful face to anyone in the world. If you raise an alarm or talk about my sinful act to anyone, I'll have no choice but to hang myself or think of some other way to end my life in order to escape the public shame and disgrace that'll follow.'

I considered the widow's words and thought, "Do I really need to make a hue and cry about this? Why should I unnecessarily partake of the sin of killing a woman?" I then said to her, "In that case, tell this young man that if he answers my question truthfully, I'll keep silent about what I've seen. Else I'll gather a crowd over here with my shouting and ensure that the two of you are thoroughly humiliated in front of all the residents of this house."

When they heard this, both of them said, 'Since we have called you our father and are completely dependent on your mercy, we promise that we'll answer your questions truthfully.'

I asked the young man, 'Why had you entered my apartment yesterday?'

He replied, 'When I was leaving this apartment yesterday I had suddenly espied you. I couldn't think of any way to escape and so quickly entered your apartment. At that time I had no idea that you lived there. Finally, when I saw you enter that same apartment, I realised my mistake, but didn't know what to do. So I just barged out of the door, right in front of you. Believe me, I had no evil intentions.'

I left that place after hearing his account. I didn't tell anyone about their shameful behaviour and instead began searching everywhere for my wife.

But alas! I couldn't find my virtuous wife anywhere. I realised the gravity of what I had done, when I had distrusted that good woman and thrown her out of the house.

I can't describe in words how frantically I looked for her that entire night and the following day. Eventually, having failed to find any traces of her anywhere, I went to visit an acquaintance of my mother-in-law. There I found out that my wife had spent a night with her and then gone away after borrowing some money from her and telling her that she was going back to her husband in Kolkata.

I knew that she had an aunt living in Kolkata. As soon as I got this information, I set off for the city immediately. The train reached Howrah station on time and after I got off the train and was about to leave the station, my attention was suddenly drawn to a woman who looked a lot like my wife. She hired a carriage and got into it. I ran towards the carriage and found that she was none other than the goddess of my own heart. Without uttering a word, I got into the carriage with her and then instructed the carriage driver to start driving the carriage.

Inside the carriage I began to plead with my wife in every possible way. I repeatedly acknowledged the fact that caught in the grip of horrific delusions, I had behaved in the most barbaric manner with her; I fervently begged her forgiveness and implored her to return home with me. But that virtuous woman pronounced in a voice full of hurt pride, 'My Lord! Since you decided to accuse me of unfaithfulness and to abandon me, please don't bother about me any more. I'm not worthy of you and I truly don't deserve to show you my face.'

After hearing her words, when I continued my pleas and then even tried to grab her hand, which was concealed under her saree, she quickly said, 'Please don't ever touch this sinful and unfaithful woman. But I'm glad I have met you. Countless times have I prayed to various gods, begging them to ensure that I die before my husband. It now seems that they were paying attention to my prayers.' With these words, she brought her hand out of the folds of her saree and I could then see that the hand held a fierce-looking knife. I tried my best to wrest the knife out of her hand but I failed, and, in a flash, she plunged it into her heart. I drew it out soon after, but it was clear that there was no hope and after a while she breathed her last. She gave up her life, because of what I had done and right in front of my eyes. So my life needs to end as well!"

After saying all this, Upendranath passed out. The Jailor *sahib* and I tried to revive him but when all our efforts failed, the Jailor *sahib* sought the help of a few other prisoners and they all carried him to the prison hospital. After about half an hour I was informed that Upendra had regained consciousness. I left the prison and went to meet the old gentleman waiting outside.

I told him the entire story, from beginning to end, and after hearing everything he was devastated. Eventually however, with the help of all his resources, a good lawyer and the witness statements of the doctor who had examined the corpse, Upendranath was acquitted in the trial at the Sessions Court.

Priyanath Mukhopadhyay

Note

1 I have translated the word "kalkut" as poisonous deceit. While that is one way of translating it, in Hindu *Purana* mythology, *kalkut* also refers to the deadly poison that was produced by the churning of the ocean by the *deva* and *asura* (roughly translated as gods and demons). The cultural reference embedded in the word is, unfortunately, lost in translation.

7

'THE AERIAL CORPSE'

'(A shocking and sensational incident!)' Darogar Daftar, Jyeshth (mid-May–mid-June), 1894

I

This happened some years ago, during the monsoon. The sun god, knowing full well that he would not be able to weave his web of rays for much longer, had mournfully decided to retreat quite early in the day. The goddess of night seized the opportunity and marched in hastily, in her dark robes, to claim her seat of honour. The god of thunder and clouds arrived with a slight pitter-patter of rain and before long started making loud, rumbling noises. The ominous sound of the thunder was enough to strike terror in the human heart and it felt as if the Great Deluge was on its way. It was at such a time, while I sat in my office at the police station and gazed pensively at the terrifying skies, that I saw a man come rushing in. The clothes on his body were soaking wet. His first question upon entering the police station was whether I was present. On finding out that I was inside, he came to my office and after delivering a letter into my hands, stood at some distance and waited for me to read it.

I opened and read the letter and realised it was from a particularly wealthy resident of Kolkata who also happened to be an acquaintance of mine. I will keep the letter writer's identity a secret. The reason for this is that the case that I am going to describe has several shameful mysteries embedded in it. Hence, I have no wish to reveal his name and humiliate him in public. Besides I know him very well. When I asked the letter-bearer for details, he claimed ignorance though quite possibly he simply didn't want to disclose anything at that point.

In the letter it was written, "I am in a lot of trouble. I'll be deeply grateful if you could come post haste with the bearer of the letter, once you have read it. I will explain everything after you arrive. In short, please understand that I am facing a terrible crisis."

Upon reading the letter I concluded that the letter-writer must indeed be in a terrible situation, for why else would a man of his social stature appeal to me in this desperate manner? It is true that he knew me well but he had never ever written to me for any kind of help. With such thoughts racing through my head, I decided to go to his house. I hailed a carriage, and taking the letter-bearer along, set off towards the house.

Upon reaching the *babu*'s house, I found the living room milling with police officials. From the constable to the chief official, a variety of officers—English, Bengali and non-Bengali—were there. On seeing that, I gathered that an extremely dreadful incident must have occurred. For why else would so many officers collect in a single house? Wondering about what might have happened, I alighted from my carriage and entered the house.

Almost every one of those officials present in the house knew me. As soon as one of the higher officials saw me, he asked, "How did you manage to get here so quickly? It's only been a few minutes since I despatched a letter seeking the help of my subordinates for this case. So how did you come here in such short time?"

I had to lie to him. Why exactly I lied to him at that point for no obvious reason is very hard for me to explain. Perhaps if amongst my readers there's a police officer, he will understand my reasons for lying. I cannot bring myself to discuss them here even if my other readers were able to follow them. At any rate, I replied, "I had gone elsewhere for some work and on my way back, I saw all of you here. So I came here to see what had happened."

"Well it's good that you are here. No need for you to go back now. Just try and see if you can solve this matter. From what I can gather, I don't see anything coming to light easily. The problem is not going to get resolved anytime soon. For one, it's the house of a wealthy gentleman and on top of that, right from the beginning of the investigation, there's been a posse of lawyers following us around as we go about our business. Moreover, the very individuals from whom one can hope to get any relevant information about the case cannot be summoned and asked specific questions. For they are all *antahpur*-bound women.[1] What then does one do in such a situation? I have done everything that I could possibly do; now let's see you give it a shot. After all, you have been involved in investigating several cases and have acquired quite a reputation for solving particularly difficult ones. Try to see if you can do something about this one." Saying this, the officer pointed to a large chest made of tin and said, "Go and first examine the contents of that. We'll then tell you what we've been able to find out about it."

At that very moment a servant from within the household came and said to me, "My *babu* is waiting to talk to you in a different room. He has sent his regards and has said that you should first go and meet him before beginning your investigation of this case."

On hearing this, I said to him, "Please tell your *babu* that I'll go in to meet him as soon as I have finished examining this chest." The servant bowed deeply and departed.

II

I then went near the aforementioned chest to examine it. I saw it was a fairly large chest, about four feet in its length and three feet high. Its lock had been broken. When I opened it and looked inside, there lay the body of a woman, with its arms and legs twisted out of shape. The corpse had rotted so badly that even the slightest attempt to move it had led to skin and flesh peeling off. The head was bent at an unnatural angle, the face was contorted and the eyes were beginning to fall off. Indeed, the stench was so unbearable that it was nigh on impossible to stand there for more than a moment. It was equally impossible to ascertain the identity of the person by simply looking at that corpse. Parts of it were covered with a black-bordered saree. And barring a few metallic bangles on the left wrist, there were no other ornaments anywhere on the body. After looking inside the chest, when I returned to my superior he asked, "So what do you make of it?"

"I saw the body Sir but given its state there is no way it can be properly identified. And without it being identified, how do we start our investigation? Where was it found?"

The officer said, "The chest with the body inside was found in the *antahpur* of this very house."

"What do the people of the house have to say about this?"

"They say they are completely clueless about how it got here."

"Is any woman missing from the *antahpur*?"

"Well, they claim they are all here. No one's missing."

"Has anyone new come to the house lately?"

"No, no one has talked of any such thing."

After talking to the officer for a while and gathering all this information, I set off to meet the *babu*. On reaching the drawing room upstairs, I found him sitting in a corner looking extremely anxious and distraught. A few lawyers and some of his neighbours were also sitting around him. Everyone seemed downcast and silently preoccupied with their thoughts. When he saw me, the *babu* leapt to his feet and, after greeting me respectfully, urged me to sit right next to him. As soon as I took my seat, he began, "I am in such a dreadful mess."

I replied, "Yes indeed I can see that. But please don't worry so much. Now that I am here I won't let you or your family face any trouble."

"If you can save me from this disaster, I'll be grateful to you for the rest of my life. Please tell me now what I should do to get out of this mess?"

"I will tell you everything and I'll also do everything possible to try and help extricate you from this mess. But first tell me all that you know. I haven't really been able to get much information. Unless I hear everything, how can I give you any advice?"

"I really don't know much about this. What little I know, I'll tell you. For some days now there's been a foul stench in the house. We had no idea as to where the stink was coming from. The last three days we searched high and low both inside and outside the house to identify the source. We found absolutely nothing. Today it became so bad that we were finding it difficult to stay inside the house. The search was intensified and at one point during the search, it felt as though one of the rooms upstairs was stinking more than the others. We all then concluded that something in that room must have turned putrid and started smelling in this manner. While searching inside the room, a chest was found which seemed to give off the worst smell. We looked for its key but since no one came forward to claim ownership of the chest, we had to take it to the outer quarters and a blacksmith was fetched to break it open. That's when we all saw the body that lay inside it, in that state. Not knowing what to do in that situation, I sent someone to report the matter to the police. Before long, these police officers arrived. They are now insisting that we are involved in this murder. But the truth is, I know nothing about the chest or the corpse lying inside it. I have also asked each one of the women in the house, but none of them seems to know anything. What is even more surprising is that none of us is aware of how that chest, which no one recognises, came into this house. Who are the people who brought it in? We simply don't know! Now tell me what should I do to get out of this strange mess?"

I said, "If you don't mind, I'm going to begin by asking you a few questions."

The *babu* said, "Even though you are a police official, I don't really see you as one. You know that quite well. So why would I mind your questions?"

"It's true that we know each other well, but then I have never had occasion to ask you searching questions about your family before this. However, I do need to ask you a few questions of a private nature now. We don't need to go anywhere private. You may give me the information that I need from you here in front of everyone."

"Then please go ahead and ask me whatever you want."

"At the moment, which of your family members is present in the house?"

"I have a rather small family. There's only me, my wife, my sister, my two daughters and a son. They are all in the house."

"Doesn't your sister live in her husband's house?"

"No. She's old and a widow; her age is close to sixty. From what I have heard, she lost her husband at a very young age, when I was but a toddler. Since then she has been living here."

"You mentioned two daughters. Are they married?"

"The older one was married. But then she was widowed soon after, and ever since, she has been staying with us. She doesn't live with her husband's family. As for my younger daughter, she's not married. She is 10 years old."

"When did your older daughter get married and by when did she lose her husband? And how old is she now?"

"She was married when she was nine years old. She lost her husband when she turned thirteen and now she would be around twenty-five years old."

"How old is your son?"

"Younger than my other daughter. Around five or six."

"Are all the women that you have talked about present in the house?"

"Yes, they are all in the house."

"Besides those you have just mentioned, who else stays in the house?"

"There's a Brahmin couple that cooks for us. There are four maids who look after the children and do other household chores. Two male servants who are meant to run errands for me and four guards who sit in the courtyard outside."

"Of these people, who all are allowed to go inside the female quarters?"

"Barring the guards, none of them is restricted from visiting the inner quarters."

"Do all the domestics stay in the house at night or do they go off to their own houses in the evening?"

"No, none of them goes anywhere at night. They all stay in this house."

"Did any female acquaintance of the family, or perhaps of one of the domestics, visit the house recently?"

"As far as I know, no one has visited the house in the last one month."

After asking the *babu* all these questions, I expressed my wish to see the place where the chest had been found. He readily acquiesced and led me to the room.

III

I was taken into a room in the inner quarters. In the northern section of the house on the first floor, there were only three rooms, in one of which the *babu*'s sister lived. In the room adjoining hers, which was not inhabited, large almirahs, boxes and chests were kept for storing odds and ends. This was where the chest with the body had been found. The room next to this was where his elder daughter lived. Flush with it was a terrace that had a five-foot wall going around it so that no one could look into the rooms. Right below these rooms, at the back of the house, was a huge garden. In front of the house, there was a courtyard, along the side of which there were more rooms where the *babu* and the rest of the family lived. The inner quarters were in that area.

Having surveyed the inside of the house, we came out. I reassured the *babu*, "Please don't fret any longer. I'll try my best to see that you are not inconvenienced in any way. At the same time, I'll also try and get to the bottom of this mystery."

On hearing my words he looked somewhat pacified and then he spent the next few minutes thanking me profusely. After promising him that I would help in every possible way, I came down and then took a seat where all the rest of the officials were sitting.

I wanted to find out what methods would be adopted by the different police officers gathered there to solve the case, and so I sat with them for a while. What I could see was that everyone there was groping in the dark in much the same way as I. Despite a great deal of confabulation, none of them had arrived at any firm conclusions regarding what might have happened or how to go about solving the case.

I sat there for some time listening to the discussions and then went out of the house and wandered into the garden at the back. I searched the garden thoroughly and even looked closely at the climbing vines but found nothing suspicious anywhere.

At some distance from the garden there were a few other houses. Walking towards the houses I realised that the neighbourhood was quite familiar to me since I had only lately investigated a case of theft-through-underground-tunnelling over there.[2] After walking around for a bit, when I was convinced that exploring the area any further would be of no use to my investigation, I retraced my steps.

When murder investigations begin, it becomes imperative to first ascertain whose body it is. Without knowing the identity of the body and how it had got to the *babu*'s house, it was impossible for us, at that stage, to investigate a murder of that kind.

All the domestics, right from the Brahmin couple to the guards, were subjected to a thorough interrogation but they were all either unable to or unwilling to provide any answers. So at the end of it, we were still completely clueless about the body. People from the neighbourhood were also shown the body and asked about it but everyone seemed to be in the dark.

Who had dared to commit this horrific crime? For some time this question was sidetracked as we all became engrossed with trying to find out whose body it was.

"Can you identify this body?—Anyone who can give us any information about it will receive a reward of Rs 50." An announcement of this kind was made all over. A variety of officers were sent off in different directions, all of whom began to investigate whether any woman had gone missing in the recent past. But their efforts bore no fruit. None of them could get any useful information that would have helped in the case. The corpse meanwhile had rotted so badly that it was futile to assume that anyone now would be able to recognise it. We became concerned about the performance of its last rites.

Before this, I had investigated many cases and with god's grace had also succeeded in solving their mysteries; but never had I confronted a problem of this kind. All those previous investigations had always yielded some clue in the beginning which had finally led to a complete unravelling of their hidden mysteries. This time the case refused to throw up a single clue with which we could move ahead. And yet this was not for the want of trying, on our part. Everyone racked their brains and started making every possible effort to come up with something but nothing seemed to lead to results that night.

IV

Next morning, as I sat pondering over the case and thinking, "What should we do now?", it suddenly occurred to me that if the saree we had found on the body was an old one, then it would surely have gone to the cleaners' house. In which case it would bear a mark that could perhaps open up some avenues for our investigation. For if such a mark is found and we can then find the cleaner, he would be able to enlighten us about the owner of the saree, on the basis of that particular mark. And if we could find the owner of the saree then we could identify the body and thereafter maybe even the murderer.

With these thoughts in my mind, I asked for the saree to be brought to me but once it was brought in and I had examined it thoroughly, all my hopes were dashed. The belief on the basis of which I had presumed I could take the case forward was utterly crushed. For I noticed that the saree was fairly new and made with Farashdanga cloth.[3] It bore no marks that could have helped our efforts in any way. Thus, a possibility that had opened up momentarily proved to be a false door. And I went back to reflecting on the case.

The following day the investigation seemed to take a slightly different turn. I felt that most of the investigating officers had decided to turn on the *babu*. They all seemed to feel that he had either committed the murder himself or knew about it but was deliberately concealing things from the investigating officers. Since I knew him and what his nature was like, I said to them, "It is absolutely impossible that he could have done something like this." But they refused to listen and dismissed my belief as being a delusion. Soon a serious investigation was launched against him. A number of officers started asking him all sorts of questions.

Since I didn't like what was going on, I walked away from there and went to the place where the maids of the house had gathered. I decided to ask them a few questions, thinking their answers might throw up some leads. With this in mind, I took aside a maid named Kamini and asked her several questions about the household. I tried to find out about the character of the various people in the *babu*'s family but she described each of them as being good and above board. She also said that in the last two weeks nobody had come to visit either the family or anyone else in the household. However, she added, a month ago, the granddaughter of the maid called Bama had come from her village to pay her a visit and after staying with her for two days had gone off somewhere in search of work. When I had finished interrogating Kamini, I asked her to wait nearby and then summoned Bama.

As with Kamini, I initially got no real answers from her and so finally turning to her I shouted, "Enough lies Bama! Kamini has told me everything. Isn't it your granddaughter that you have killed and stuffed inside that chest?"

Stunned by my accusation Bama first hurled a few abuses in the direction of Kamini and then cried out, "My granddaughter came here for just two days and that was a month ago! Based on this that wretched Kamini has insinuated that I killed her and put her in the chest? And what about her sister who came for a visit, just a week ago? Has that slipped her mind?" With these words, she started squabbling fiercely with Kamini. I stood watching their fight and also listening carefully to what they were saying to each other. What I noticed was that despite all the abuses hurled at her, Kamini refused to admit that her sister had come to the house. As a result I grew extremely suspicious of her. And when I told my fellow officers about this they were all equally surprised and suspicious. They then left the *babu* alone and accosted the maid. Bama left the place in the midst of all this and then, returning soon after with her granddaughter, declared, "Here Sir! This is my granddaughter. Now let's see if Kamini can bring her sister and present her here."

Kamini however stuck to her guns and continued to deny that her sister had paid her a visit. When we asked the other domestics they also claimed not to have seen her sister. However one of the guards, Ram Singh, said, "About a week ago a girl had come to the gate wanting to meet Kamini. I called Kamini and she came and took the girl inside. I did not see her leave the house afterwards."

V

This one piece of information turned the tide of the investigation completely. Everyone turned their attention from the *babu* to Kamini who was then subjected to all kinds of questions. But despite everything, Kamini refused to change her earlier statement saying that both Bama and Ram Singh were lying. Did Kamini in fact have a sister? If she did, had her sister come to Kolkata? And where was she now? These, we decided, were some of the questions for which answers had to be found. When it was found that Kamini hailed from a small village in Medinipur district, an officer was sent there to further investigate the matter. We meanwhile continued with our work related to the investigation in Kolkata.

The officer who had been sent to Kamini's village returned after a week. He then gave us an account of what he had unearthed.

"In Medinipur," he said, "it was only after a lot of intense searching, that I finally found Kamini's house. The house is nothing but two rooms with thatched roofs that have been locked from outside. When I asked around, I learned that about six months ago Kamini had gone to her village and after staying there for a month had gone back to Kolkata. She did indeed have a sister called Sundari but nobody had clapped eyes on her in the last ten years. Sundari had been married to Ramhari, a native of a village that was about twenty miles away and after the wedding, she had never returned to her native village. When I heard all this, I decided to visit that village and walked for hours before I finally found Ramhari's house. Ramhari's wife was not inside. I learnt from the neighbours that she, along with some other women from the village, had gone to Kolkata to bathe in the holy waters of Ganga but while all the other women had returned home, Ramhari's wife had not come back with them. A number of those women who had gone on that trip to Kolkata were right there in the neighbourhood and so I asked them what had happened. From what they said, it seems, they had all travelled together in a steamer to Kolkata. But subsequently, on reaching Kolkata while they were their way to Kalighat, Sundari got lost in the crowd. They searched high and low for her in the city, but could not find her anywhere. And so finally they gave up and returned to the village without Sundari. When he heard what had happened, Ramhari began searching for his wife in Kolkata and it so happened that he returned to his village even as I was gathering all this information. In fact I have brought him along with me. Here he is, Sir." Saying this, the official produced Ramhari before all of us.

Ramhari knew Kamini and on seeing her, he said, "This is my wife's sister. She visits our home once or twice every year. At times we also receive letters from her." Kamini had just heard the account of her sister getting lost in Kolkata and how despite several attempts she had remained untraceable. Yet her face betrayed no sign of grief or concern and not a single tear trickled down from her eyes. I did not feel too happy about Kamini's reaction and every little thing about her added up to make me even more suspicious. Somebody expressed my thoughts quite clearly when he said, "It has to be Kamini's sister's body. It can't be anybody else's."

All the officers over there became suspicious but there was little we could do. The body had already been cremated. Ramhari might have been able to identify his wife by looking at the body but that was no longer possible. So what was to be done now? The clothes and the bangles were shown to Ramhari but he wasn't very sure that they belonged to his wife.

Why was Kamini lying: this now became the focus of the investigation. Despite being the maid in a rich *babu*'s house, Kamini was no longer treated with kid gloves and the investigating officers began to hound her with all kinds of questions. Subsequently, she was handed over to a constable with instructions to take her to the police station. Kamini then realised that there was no escape possible for her. Tormented by all kinds of terrible accusations, she left the house in a flood of tears along with the constable. All of us assumed he would put her in custody. But before long, the man returned and everyone stared with wonder at that amazing epitome of valiant and enterprising masculinity when they heard what he had to say. For it turned out that as he was taking Kamini to the police station, she gave him the slip somewhere along the way and that despite all his efforts, he had failed to find her.

VI

Why did Kamini flee? Did this prove that she had indeed been responsible for this heinous crime? Was the body that of her sister Sundari? We had seen that the body bore the traditional marks of a married woman. There would never have been iron bangles on the wrist of a widow or an unmarried woman. And according to Ramhari his wife had gone missing in Kolkata. Did all this add up to mean that Sundari was the victim and Kamini the culprit? Everyone became even more suspicious of Kamini and finding her became our top priority. Searches were conducted in a number of places, but all our efforts proved futile. The next day, again several men were sent to find her but none of them could bring any news of her.

The following day, as we were sitting at the gate of the *babu*'s house, we saw two women approaching the house. Seeing one of the women someone shouted, "There comes Kamini," while someone else said, "No, no that woman resembles Kamini but it's not her." Yet another voice exclaimed, "It *is* Kamini I'm quite sure." As the gathered crowd speculated in this manner, the two women came quite close to where we were sitting and we realised that one of them was none other than Kamini, the woman whom we had all been desperately searching. The other woman had her head partially covered with a veil and as soon as he saw her, Ramhari shouted, "This is my wife Sundari!"

We were all taken aback on seeing Kamini and then even more so upon hearing Ramhari's words. For a few minutes there was utter silence as we were struck dumb and could only stare at each other. After a few minutes, I collected myself and said to Kamini, "Why did you lie to us from the very beginning? You kept denying your sister's visit even after it was proved. And then when everyone suspected you or thought that you had killed your sister, you ran away. And now you have surfaced along with your missing sister! What does all this mean?"

On hearing this Kamini said, "Whatever be my motive, you had all decided that I was Sundari's killer. But now that I have brought her here and presented her to all of you, do you have any reasons to suspect me of murder? Whatever secret designs I might have had for keeping her here in the city are no concern of yours. Even if you ask me about them I am not obliged to tell you anything, am I?"

Surprised to hear Kamini's answers and embarrassed by our inability to counter her statement we said, "Go then, go into the house." And Kamini walked into the house with her sister.

Ramhari spent the night in that place and the next day he went back to his village along with his wife. Now we shifted our focus to finding some other clues that would help us solve the case at hand. However, even though I had to turn my attention back to solving the murder, the mystery behind Kamini having misled us with her false stories continued to niggle away at the corner of my mind. I did succeed ultimately in solving that mystery. Unfortunately I can't assuage the curiosity of my readers, for were I to describe the Kamini-Sundari case in detail, it would surely sully my narrative. Suffice to say, Kamini had every intention of ruining her sister's most priceless possession—her virtue—and ruining her life.[4] In fact, there is no doubt that had she not been forced to bring her sister to us because of the fracas following the discovery of the body, she would have succeeded in her evil designs.

VII

One of the houses in the aforementioned *babu*'s neighbourhood was that of one Ramgopal Biswas. Ramgopal would often be away from Kolkata for his work as contractor in the area around Mymensingh. Ramgopal's old mother and his young wife stayed in the house in his absence. Ramgopal would only come twice or thrice a year to the house and spend five to ten days before leaving again. At the time we are talking of, he had been in town for a week and word had got around that this time he had returned with a great deal of gold jewels for his wife and much more wealth than usual.

Within two or three days of his return, a thief started digging an underground tunnel into his house. In the night, when Ramgopal was about to sleep, he heard the noise of someone digging. He immediately understood that there was someone sitting in the garden at the back of the house, trying to dig a tunnel to get inside. However, despite having heard the sounds and guessing the cause, he didn't stir out of bed. Almost from his childhood, Ramgopal had been travelling widely for various reasons. He had seen and heard all sorts of things and had encountered many kinds of people. Maybe it was because of this, or perhaps because of his inherent nature, he was quite brave and confident. As he lay quietly in bed, he planned out how he would pounce on the thief once he emerged out of the tunnel into the room and teach him a lesson that he wouldn't forget in a hurry.

When the digging ended and the two feet of the thief emerged out of the tunnel ready to enter the room where Ramgopal had been resting, the latter leapt out of his bed, grabbed the intruder's feet with as much force as he could muster and started shouting at the top of his lungs. With his feet stuck inside the room and the rest of his body dangling outside it, the thief had little hope of being able to escape. Ramgopal's shouts woke up his wife as well as his neighbours and the thief was caught quite easily. His hands and feet were then tied and he was sent off to the police station in the custody of a guard.

There the thief answered the questions in such a manner that at first the officers believed everything that he said. I was then summoned to investigate the truth of the matter, and that's how I came to be involved in the case and happened to be in that neighbourhood once again.

The thief had said, "Ramgopal quite often doesn't stay at home, leaving his wife all by herself. Almost five years ago, I had gone to that neighbourhood for some work and that's when I first saw her. And from that very day, either due to her fault or mine, we started having an illicit affair. Ever since then, I have gone to that house almost every night. Not realising that Ramgopal *babu* was back from his travels, I had gone as usual to the house, that night. As soon as I entered the house, I saw Ramgopal *babu* right in front of me and he was immediately able to gauge the reason for my clandestine visit. Without saying anything much to his wife, he beat me up badly and then went out to dig a tunnel behind the house and later raised an alarm shouting 'There's a thief who has dug a tunnel in my house etc', so that some of his neighbours collected over there. Then he had me sent to the *thhana* with my hands and legs tied. Have you ever heard of any thief worth his salt, digging tunnels on a clear, full moon night like this?"

Subsequently, after my investigations, I discovered that what Ramgopal *babu* had said was all true and not one word was fabricated. Everything that the thief had said was false. Not the slightest bit in his account was true. When the case was finally brought to trial, the thief was presented before the Magistrate and the chief witness called upon was Ramgopal Biswas. Ramgopal *babu* having suddenly fallen ill, the trial could not however be continued. It got postponed for a fortnight.

VIII

Finally, the day that had been fixed for the thief's trial arrived. Ramgopal had come to the Magistrate's court and many of his neighbours had also come to gape at the thief. The Magistrate began the trial right on time, and Ramgopal and some of his neighbours gave their witness accounts. Finally, I saw a man named Mahendranath Das get up to give his account of what he had seen that night. I had not seen him during my investigation and I wasn't sure what he was going to talk about. As such I was quite keen to find out what he was about to say and started listening to him quite intently.

Mahendranath's statement was somewhat like this:

Lawyer: What is your name?
Mahendra: My name is Mahendranath Das.
Lawyer: Where do you stay and what do you do?

Mahendra: I stay quite close to Ramgopal's house. And I work as a clerk at the Bodom Brothers.

Lawyer: Can you recall the events of the night that a man had been caught in your neighbourhood?

Mahendra: Oh yes Sir! I remember them very well.

Lawyer: Well, please describe to us in detail what happened that night.

Mahendra: One night, about a fortnight ago, I had an argument with my wife over some minor issue. My wife is extremely prickly by nature and quick to take offence. On hearing my words, she lost her temper and decided to kill herself in a fit of rage and then stormed out of the house. Since I was feeling quite upset myself, I didn't try to prevent her, nor did I try to find out where she had gone. I simply assumed that having left the house she would go to a neighbour's place and seek shelter for the rest of the night. After she had been gone for some time, my anger began to subside and I thought to myself that since she had left the house having threatened to end her life, I must try and find out where she had gone. A woman's rage can be ferocious and she rarely values her own life. They are quite capable of ending their precious lives without much hesitation on the slightest of pretexts and for fairly minor reasons. Given all this, I felt it was my immediate duty to find my wife, and so I started looking for her. I could not find her anywhere in the house. In another room my mother and sister had been sleeping and when I went to look, I found the door to that room locked. I stood outside their room for a while, hoping against hope that if she were inside, I would be able to hear them talking to each other. But my hopes were in vain for I heard no such sounds emanating from their rooms. In fact, the occupants of the room seemed to be fast asleep. I became frantic with worry and found myself shaking with anxiety. Not knowing what to do, I just stood there stock still. For a few moments I toyed with the idea of waking up my sister and mother and telling them everything, but then I was too overcome with embarrassment and couldn't bring myself to do that.

I began searching for her yet again in the house. I looked for her in the rooms I hadn't searched earlier. I searched in the kitchen and I even entered the bathroom and looked around carefully. But I couldn't find her anywhere. Gradually I think I started losing my mind and could no longer decide what would be the best place to look for her. I went back to my room and searched on the bed, under it and even inside a large trunk, but not finding her anywhere, I went out again.

I sought her frantically in places that I had already looked in and then finally collapsed in an anxious heap. It was almost as if I was compelled by some force to sit there.

Sitting over there I thought of all kinds of terrifying possibilities and that's when I noticed the back gate of our house. In the moonlight, I saw that it was open and immediately I was filled with hope. For a split second I thought that my wife must have opened it and was sitting outside. I ran out, panting for breath, but could see no one around. I looked everywhere and searched all around the house but couldn't see my wife. The hope that had lifted my spirits just a few moments ago, was now completely gone. In a state of despair, I fell to the ground and then, like a madman, began imagining all sorts of horrible things that might have happened.

IX

"I can't say, for exactly how long I kept sitting over there. At that time, in the bright moonlight, everything around me could be seen very clearly and that's when I felt I could see someone sitting very still under a mango tree, in a garden nearby. Mustering all my courage, I slowly went up to the tree and what I saw there took my breath away. The person whom I had been searching for so long like a lunatic, my dear wife, was sitting calmly over there. Gone were the traces of the fury that had made her storm out of the house. Indeed, more than anything else, she looked anxious and frightened. She made a sign and bid me to be quiet and then started whispering certain things in my ear; afterwards she got up from there and went back into our house. I was quite taken aback to hear what my wife had to tell me. I gazed for a while towards the front part of the garden but failed to see anything. But when I closely examined the back of the garden, I was shocked and I realised that my wife had been telling me the truth. I saw this thief digging a tunnel in that portion of Ramgopal's garden. Before long, he finished digging and then as soon as he started going into the house, feet first, he was nabbed by Ramgopal. Then he was bound with a rope with the help of several neighbours. Subsequently I returned to my house and shut the door. But I can vouch for the fact that it was this very man who was digging the tunnel that night in the garden."

After hearing Mahendranath's account, the Magistrate believed him and returned a verdict of guilty to the thief but did not immediately decide the extent of his punishment. His case was deferred for another week for this thief had been imprisoned earlier as well, and it was to collect information about those earlier charges that the date of this case was postponed.

From what Mahendranath had said, it was clear that his wife had told him about the thief digging a tunnel in the garden that was Ramgopal's house. But had she told him anything else? For instance, I couldn't make head or tail of what exactly he was looking for, when he gazed towards the front of the garden. I therefore became extremely curious to find out what it was that his wife had told him. What was it that had made her forget her anger that night?

I knew where Mahendranath's house was located and so a little before the evening, I set off to meet him. He was at home and since he knew me, we sat down and chatted for almost two hours. Finally, I said to him, "I am curious to know some details about a few of the things that you said before the Magistrate today. What all did you hear from your wife that night and also what did she try to show you? I don't know why, but I am really quite keen to find this out."

At first Mahendranath was a bit reluctant to accede to my request, but then after a while, he acquiesced and he repeated to me in great detail all that he had told the Magistrate and also added everything that his wife had said to him and showed him while standing under the mango tree that night. After hearing his words, my curiosity was satisfied. I also felt quite pleased and more than a little hopeful. Mahendranath of course could not have had a clue as to why I was feeling happy or what it was that had made me hopeful. I don't think my readers can understand either.

I came back home late in the evening and went to bed at my usual time. But I could not sleep a wink that night. In my mind, I kept going over all that Mahendra had told me that evening, and tried to decide what my course of action should be, in order to fulfil my mission. That is how I spent that night.

X

The next day in the morning, I visited the prison in Harinbari to meet that thief. I said to him, "You do understand that the Magistrate *sahib* has found you guilty of the crime of digging a tunnel for burglary, don't you?"

He replied, "Oh yes I do understand only too well that now there's no escape possible for me."

"Well since you have more or less accepted that you are going to be punished, would you have any objections to my attempting to save you?"

"I have no objections to your proposal but I refuse to give you any answers to questions related to the case."

"I am going to ask you one or two things, but you needn't worry. I'm not about to ask you anything that might put you in a sticky situation."

"Alright then, what is it that you want to ask me?"

"You don't deny that that day when you were caught by Ramgopal, you had indeed gone to their house, do you? For it's been established that you had gone there, although whether you had gone there to steal or for some other purpose remains a contested issue.

"Yes Sir. It is true that I had gone there. But my motive wasn't theft. I have already told the court what my purpose was."

"Can you recall the time that you were waiting there? At that time there were two men going past. They were acquaintances of yours. As soon as they saw you, they stopped and after exchanging a few words with you they left."

"Why do you want to know? Why are you interested in what those men had to say? Are you thinking of calling them to give witness against me in court?"

"The case has already been decided against you so there is no need for further witnesses. No, I want them for some other reason. If the purpose for which I am seeking them is fulfilled, I daresay you might also stand to gain from this."

"I will have to fulfil my destiny. But if knowing their names will help you in some way, I am willing to give those names to you. Why don't you write them down somewhere? Their names were Shaatkodi Das and Makhomlal Dutta."

"Can you also tell me where these two men stay?"

"A few houses away from where I had been standing that night is the house of a landlady called Prasanna. They are both her tenants."

Having found out these things from the thief, I returned home. Then after taking a bath and eating lunch, I set off towards the house of the *babu* in whose *antahpur* the corpse had been discovered. The *babu* was at home. I took him aside and told him a few things as a friend. He was completely mortified upon hearing what I had to tell him and sought my advice on how he could protect himself from the shameful repercussions of what I'd just revealed. I promised to do everything possible to save him from this calumny and then expressed a desire to revisit the inner quarters of his house. He agreed to my proposal and we both repaired to the room where the body had been found. We searched the room again with greater care than earlier. But we found nothing. All that we saw was a rather sturdy and thick pair of ropes lying there. A piece of wood—about a foot long—was tied to one of the ropes.

I went to the terrace that I have mentioned earlier to my readers and found a wooden bench on it. I dragged the bench towards one of the walls, climbed on it and realised that I could look over the wall and get an excellent view of a large part of the garden below. I took a good look all around the garden, from my perch. On examining carefully, I noticed that in a number of places on the outer part of the wall, sand and cement had come off and longish marks had been made. All the marks that I saw, began from almost the top of the boundary wall and ended close to the bottom. Having seen all this, the two of us went back inside.

The *babu* sat down rather mournfully in his drawing room and after a while, I took his leave.

XI

The landlady Prasanna used to own another house besides the one that she lived in. It was in that other house that Makhomlal Dutta and Saatkodi Das lived as tenants. Makhomlal stayed in a room close to the exit of the house. He had no relatives in the city and lived by himself. He worked in the Railways office. In that same house, there were three other rooms where Saatkodi Das lived with his wife. Saatkodi was also in the railway office. Both men would leave home for work around ten in the morning and wouldn't return before six in the evening. Only one person used to be all by herself, the entire day in the house, and that was Saatkodi's wife Biraaj.

I went to this house after seven in the evening. At that time, they were both in the house and I met both of them and when I asked them certain things they both denied knowing anything. When I entered their house, I found that Saatkodi's wife Biraaj was not inside. I asked them about her and they both claimed that she had gone to her parents' house. I didn't believe this and so I started searching inside the house. My search revealed various objects that made me even more suspicious. I found a box full of old and used ornaments. I was told they belonged to Biraaj. I found it a little hard to believe that a woman from these parts had gone off to her parents' place without carrying any of her jewels with her. In another box I found a washed saree with a black border. I had the saree that had been discovered with the corpse in the chest brought over from the police station for comparison with this one. After examining them closely, I concluded that the two were part of a set of two similar sarees that had been sold as a pair. What was also clear was that the two sarees had even come back from the cleaner's place at the same time. They had then been snipped apart with a pair of scissors. While cutting it, some of the edges of the sarees had become jagged while other parts had been cut in a very even manner. Based on the way in which the two pieces had been cut, it became quite clear to me that they were part of the same original set of sarees.

When I didn't get proper answers to my questions from either of them, I took both men to Mahendranath's house. I told Mahendranath to repeat before them all the things that he had heard from his wife that night. Mahendranath knew me well and I had also clearly explained to him the nature of the investigation that I was involved in. He started from the beginning and went over each of the things that he had already told me earlier. The things that he recounted at first are those that the readers have already heard. Finally he added, "When my wife had stormed out of our house in a huff, she had seen two men going past, on that road. One of the two had a large tin chest on his head, while the other was following him. The two of them had then entered the *babu*'s garden with that chest and moved slowly towards the back of the mansion. After keeping it on the ground, they sat there for a while. What then became visible was that a pair of thick ropes was hanging from a wooden plank on the boundary wall of the inner quarters of the *babu*'s house. They tied the tin chest to the wooden plank and stood aside. After a while it seemed that the chest was being gradually pulled up by someone with the help of the ropes. As she stood and watched, the chest went up the boundary wall and then it seemed as if someone pulled it inside. After a while the two men went away from that place. They walked back to where they had come from. On the way, they encountered a thief who it seemed was an acquaintance of theirs, for they chatted with him for a bit, and then walked away."

Saatkodi and Makhomlal heard everything that Mahendranath had to say. Then I added my bit to their account, based on what the thief had related to me. I said, "In fact, it is because the thief gave me your names and other details that I was able to come here to arrest you."

The two men also found out that an official was being dispatched to Saatkodi's parents-in-law's house. As soon as the official would reach that house, it wouldn't take him long to find out that Saatkodi's wife Biraaj had never been there. After seeing and hearing all this, they looked crestfallen and then finally confessed their sins and related in front of everyone what had happened that night.

XII

Makhamlal Dutta began by saying, "I'll tell you everything. I don't plan to conceal anything. All that you've said and that we just heard from Mahendranath *babu* is true. Not one bit is false. The day all this happened, I was returning home from work at my usual time. On reaching home, I noticed Saatkodi sitting on the porch, looking dazed. His eyes looked bloodshot. When I went and stood near him, he didn't even notice that I was there. Finally, when I called him by his name, he got up and stood in a state of stupor. Then without answering any of my questions, he grabbed my hand and led me to his bedroom. At first I didn't understand why he had grabbed me and taken me there. But soon I was paralysed with shock and then I fainted and collapsed on the floor. When I came to, I saw Saatkodi's wife Biraaj sprawled on the floor. Her body lay in one place while the head was somewhere else. And it wasn't as if the body was only divided into two halves; it looked like it had been stabbed several times in several places. After staring for a while I shouted, 'What happened here!'

Saatkodi answered, 'What do you think? I have killed my wife. After what that shameless sinful hussy has done, I gave her exactly what she deserved, with my own hands.'

'You may have given her her just desserts. But what happens to you now?'

'What can I possibly say to that? Do what you have to do. Else I'll just wait for fate to take its course. Can a man value his life so much that he sits passively despite having witnessed his wife's depravity?'

Seeing Saatkodi's state, and hearing him speak in that manner, made my heart swell with genuine pity for him. I started thinking about ways to save him. I considered informing the police but I was sure that doing so would definitely lead to Saatkodi being hanged. If by some means the body could be moved to some other place and suspicion be cast on someone else, then maybe Saatkodi would have a chance—however small—of being saved. I uttered a few reassuring words to Saatkodi and then went out. I bought a strong and large tin chest and then skilfully shoved the dead body into it, after removing all the ornaments.

I first thought of throwing it into the river Ganga at night. But then I felt terrified about taking this course of action. For if we were to be intercepted on our way to the river by a policeman, neither of us would have been able to escape. Besides, we also felt that neither of us had the required strength to carry that heavy chest that far. Given these circumstances, we then started wondering what we should do. All of a sudden, I was struck with an idea and immediately stepped out of the house. What I saw outside confirmed the plausibility of my brainwave and I went back into the house.

The thing is that quite often I used to take the narrow path that went past the *babu*'s house. It was not a public thoroughfare. One night, as I was going on that path for some work, I had caught a glimpse of a man entering the garden. Seeing him enter that place in the middle of the night, I became quite suspicious and thought to myself that I had to see where he was going so late at night. So I stood and waited silently over there. I saw the man cross the garden and go towards the adjoining two-storeyed building. I then noticed that a wooden plank was hanging with the help of two ropes along the wall. The man stood on the plank and then as soon as he jerked the rope, the plank started getting pulled up slowly along the wall, to the very top. I was completely amazed to see all this and stood there watching for a long time. But I didn't see the man climb down. After that, every night I would notice the ropes dangling in that manner.

So on the night that we are talking about, I went there and found the ropes hanging in a similar manner in the garden. I thought, if I could somehow manage to send the tin chest with the corpse up their wall, then we would be out of trouble. Later when the corpse would be discovered, everyone would harass the *babu* and his family. Thinking such things, we went to that spot with the tin chest and, after tying it firmly to the plank attached to the ropes, shook the rope a little bit. We then saw someone gradually pull it up from above. We returned from there, cleaned the blood in the room as thoroughly as we could and then consigned the blood-stained clothes to the fire god Agni. This is all that I can tell you. Now you may do what you think is right."

XIII

Everyone believed Makhamlal's words and he then went on to become a witness in the case. The person arrested was Saatkodi.

When the Magistrate questioned him, Saatkodi confessed to the killing and only added these few words, "Sir, I had returned home a little early that day, around two in the afternoon. I found the main gate of the house locked from inside but it gave way when I pushed it a little forcefully. I entered the house and found the door of our bedroom slightly ajar. And what I then saw left me reeling with shock. I saw my wife in our bed with a stranger. When I saw this, I just couldn't control the maniacal rage that engulfed me. I knew there was a scythe somewhere in the house. When I rushed off to find it, the man made his escape. Not knowing what else to do, I struck my wife with the scythe and killed her. I can now barely recall the number of times I hit her in that frenzied state. The rest of the story you know from Makhamlal's account."

The Magistrate heard all that he had to say, and subsequently the case was sent to a higher court where a jury pronounced him guilty and punished him. However, Saatkodi did not get the death penalty; he only got two years of imprisonment.

A lot of people flocked to the High court in order to find out how and why the mysterious chest had travelled into the inner quarters of the *babu*'s house. In court Bhava, a maid servant from that household gave the following statement. "I feel deeply ashamed to confess that I have been involved in an illicit liaison with a man. My employer's instructions prevented me from stepping out of the house at any point in the daytime or at night. As such, I could find no way to satisfy my desires, and then I hit upon this idea—as you have all heard—of pulling my lover up with a rope every night and then after a while, helping him climb down in the same manner. As long as the wooden plank tied to the rope dangled from the roof, I would sit and wait near the rope on the terrace. When the rope moved, I knew my lover had arrived and it was time to pull him up. Luckily, one of the rooms on the roof had a heavy lock on the door, to which I fixed a hook so that the rope could be attached to that and the pulling became easy enough. One night, when I had slowly pulled up the rope thinking he had arrived, I found a tin chest attached to it. Assuming that for some reason he had sent a gift for me in it, I pulled it in and kept it in one of the rooms upstairs. I decided that I would open it in his presence. But he did not come and I never saw him again. In this court I don't see him anywhere among the witnesses or the people present. I only know his name is 'Ram' but he never ever told me where he lived. And as for the contents of that chest, how that was revealed after a few days, is known to everyone here."

Of the people gathered in court, some believed Bhava's testimony while others had their own views about her account.

From that day onward, no one saw the *babu*'s widowed daughter ever again in the city. Later on, many people got to know that she had become a resident of Kashi.[5] Meanwhile, speculation was rife that it was in order to save the *babu*'s daughter from public disgrace that Bhava had taken on the blame for all those shameful acts that had actually been committed by the highborn girl. Apparently it was for this very reason that she did not reveal the identity of the secret lover.

It is true that while investigating the murder we had followed every possible lead to find the culprit, but if the events surrounding the case of theft had not fortuitously come to our attention, then we would have remained as clueless as ever. Especially if the aforementioned thief had not given us the names and addresses of Saatkodi and Makhomlal, we would perhaps never have been able to arrest the actual murderer. Since it was with his help that we could unearth the truth about this murder, the Magistrate *sahib* requested the government to reduce his punishment. The government acceded to his request and the prisoner's sentence was reduced by three months.

Priyanath Mukhopadhyay

Notes

1 The inner quarters of upper caste/class households where the women of the family resided were out of bounds for outsiders. About *antahpurs* (women's quarters) in wealthy households in late 19th-century Bengal, Chitra Deb writes,

> Everywhere, as far as women were concerned, there was overwhelming emphasis on *aabroo* (seclusion though the word also means honour), *purdah* (the veil), closed windows and doors. Women in their own houses, were prohibited from stepping on to the courtyards, going to terraces and there was of course never any question of their crossing the threshold on foot.
>
> (Chitra Deb, *Antahpurer Atmakatha*, Kolkata: Ananda Publishers, 1984)

2 *Sheendhh kaata* refers to a particular kind of burglary which involves digging a tunnel in order to break into the house.

3 Chandannagar, a town in Bengal, was also known as Farashdanga since it had been a French colony. *Farash* is the Bengali/Bangla word for French.

4 In all probability refers to Kamini planning to trick/force her sister (Sundari) into a life of prostitution in the city.

5 Within the caste patriarchal system, a widow's sexual life was relentlessly policed by extremely rigid and austere codes of enforced celibacy, bodily mortification and food restrictions. Their marginalization and exclusion from normal familial existence and sexual life often also resulted in being sent off to social oblivion

(and not infrequently, indigence) in places of pilgrimage like Varanasi/Kashi, Vrindavan and Nabadwip. Despite the possibilities of social change opened up by the Widow Remarriage Act (1861), the formalization of usufructuary rights of widows over their husbands' property, and also the radical marriage regulation of 1872, it was celibate widowhood that was apotheosized in the late nineteenth century context. In this case, even though the *babu*'s daughter lived with her family, once her secret liaison becomes known to her father, she is exiled to Kashi.

8

'A SEVERED HEAD'

'(The search for unclaimed property)' Darogar Daftar, Kartik (mid-October–mid-November), 1894

I

Today is the first of Kartik (approx. mid-October to mid-November in the *Saka* calendar) and the first day of Durga Puja celebrations. My Hindu readers must all be so happy on the occasion of *saptami*.[1] From poor hut-dwellers to regal residents of mansions, everyone is terribly eager to catch a glimpse of the great goddess. Everyone's heart is dancing with joy. The excitement of seeing the goddess on her annual visit has made even long-suffering widows and recently bereaved mothers forget their grief. All those who had been travelling for work are back in their own homes. They are all busy meeting and spending time with their friends and family after being away for a year. They are all beside themselves with the joy which only that heavenly treasure of being reunited with loved ones can bring. In short, everyone's in the throes of euphoria today and even Mother Nature seems to be participating in all the merrymaking.

Readers might well be asking themselves why I am describing *saptami* celebrations before narrating the incident of murder that I have set out to present to them. What could be the connection between Puja celebrations and the incident? In my reply, I would like to say to my readers that the author of these accounts works in an office where no one gets any holidays during this or any other Puja. As such, there is no scope for meeting friends or relatives who have returned from their places of work.

For many years, I had failed to fulfil my wish of getting some time off during Durga Puja. In the year that I am now talking of, I had somehow managed, with great difficulty, to get a fortnight's worth of holidays. My holidays began two days before *saptami*, that is from the day of *panchami*. On *shashthi*, I left Kolkata and reached my beloved birthplace. That day I couldn't really meet my relatives or friends, barring one or two. The next day, as soon as I stepped out of the house with the intention of visiting some friends, I spotted a peon carrying a telegram. I soon gathered that the telegram-bearing man was searching for me. I signed the receipt and accepted the telegram. And then when I opened the telegram, I was consumed with rage and sorrow.

Dear readers, let me ask you this. How would you feel if today, on the day of *saptami*, someone were to uproot the vine of your hope and expectation that you had been carefully nurturing for an entire year?

I don't think I have the ability to describe adequately what I went through on that *saptami*, upon receiving the telegram. Maybe today if you could try and imagine my state, you might be able to understand the anger that I felt that day.

The aforementioned telegram carried the following words: "A corpse has been discovered in very strange circumstances. We are cancelling your leave so that you can begin investigating the case. Come to Kolkata as soon as you receive this telegram."

The telegram had been sent by the highest official in my department. There was no way I could have resigned from my job, for that would surely have meant starvation and death for my family and me. So even on such a joyous day, I became heavy-hearted. Wiping the tears that rose to fill my eyes, I set off for Kolkata that very day.

I reached Kolkata and met my superior officer. He looked extremely happy to see me and said, "A terrible murder has happened. We have no clear idea as to where the heinous crime was plotted or where it was committed. But whether we like it or not, we are lumbered with this corpse and have no choice but to start investigating the murder. The corpse was found this very morning and we have yet to figure out how we should proceed in our investigations to solve this case successfully. It's good that you have arrived promptly after receiving the telegram; I must say I would have been extremely offended if you hadn't. Once this case is solved, I'll make special arrangements to ensure that instead of a fortnight, you get an entire month off from work. But right now go to the place where the body was found and begin your investigation."

II

After hearing what the official had to say, I didn't waste any further words. I set off for the office where I could see the body and try to understand what had happened. When I reached that place, the chief police officer of the *thhana* had gone out to take rounds of the neighbourhood. As such I had no choice but to take a look at the box myself. A guard was standing very close to it. When I asked him about it he said, "Last night, I was assigned the job of guarding a warehouse that stores goods, located very close to the river Ganga. When I went there and started walking around in the warehouse, my attention was drawn to this box. As I walked towards it, I realised that it didn't seem to belong to anyone. At first I thought that its owner might have gone somewhere nearby on some errand and that he would return soon. But even after waiting till four in the afternoon, there was no one who came to claim the box. Just then one of my bosses walked in and I told him about the box that seemed to have no owner. After listening to me he said, 'Well, if the box is unclaimed by anyone, go and deposit it in a nearby *thhana*.' So I obeyed his order and with the help of a coolie brought the box here. Please keep this and allow me to leave. There's no one guarding that warehouse in my place." After hearing the guard's account, I felt that there was no reason to keep him waiting. I could let him go after completing the formalities of getting the box deposited in the *thhana*. However, no sooner did I bring out the ledger in order to fill in all the details of the deposit than I saw the chief officer walk in.

III

I asked the officer with whom I had earlier talked, "Has the box been deposited by our superior officer?"

Officer: "No, where was the time for that! Let me tell you the exact sequence of events. If you listen patiently you'll understand everything. The chief official came and asked me, 'What's this box?' I replied to the best of my ability and added, 'I'll get this box deposited and let the guard go, why don't I?' The chief officer then said, 'It won't be enough to simply have it deposited. First, you'll need to open it and check the contents. Then in the presence of the guard who brought this, draw up a list of the contents and have them deposited individually. I don't want anyone claiming later that they can't find all the stuff that they had put in the box.' I felt this was good advice and began to try opening up the box. But when you look at the box properly, you'll realise how difficult it is to prise it open. I tried to break it and when even that didn't work, I summoned an ironsmith and pressed him into service. The ironsmith finally managed to prise it open after struggling for some time. I asked the guard whom I had instructed to stand near the box, with a pen and paper ready to note down the contents, to lift the lid and look inside. As soon as he lifted it, he began screaming and then scuttled off to stand at the furthest corner of the room.

I was completely taken aback to see his reaction but then when I went and lifted the lid myself, I was filled with panic. The papers in my hand slipped and fell to the ground. Shocked and befuddled, I began to shout and call my boss. He came rushing to the spot and asked, 'What's happened, what's happened?' Such was my state that I couldn't even bring myself to answer his question. All I could do was point a finger at the box. He then opened it and we all could see very clearly that there was a woman's body that had been tied up and stuffed into it. After that there was no question of depositing the box. The guard could also not be allowed to go anywhere. In due course, the news travelled to the highest officer and when he came, there were many others who came with him to see the corpse and to help with the investigation. Subsequently I was ordered to take the body for post-mortem to Medical College. I followed the orders and took it there. While I was there, the Coroner *sahib* came with some members of the jury and inspected the corpse and then the doctor arrived and it was he who pulled the body out of that box. That's when I saw that the neck of the corpse was bound tightly and several times with a very thick rope."

I: "But from what I can see, this corpse is headless. Where's the rope that was used to tie its neck?"

The officer: "First listen to all that I have to tell you and then you'll have a better understanding of the matter. When the doctor found the body trussed up in the manner that it was, he asked a Dom to untie the ropes. The Dom immediately cut off the rope around the neck.[2] We examined the rope and found that it was not any common or garden variety rope, but one made from branches of the *sika* tree. The doctor preserved that *sika* rope very carefully and then proceeded to cut open the corpse. After finishing his examination, he said to me, 'This woman was strangled to death with the rope that we found around her neck.' Then he said to the Dom, 'The chief police officer has requested us to preserve the head since the body has yet to be identified. Once the last rites are performed, there'll be no way left to have it identified and it'll become impossible to investigate the murder.' Upon hearing these words, the Dom promptly took out a knife and chopped off the head and put it inside a glass container. The doctor then poured in some preserving fluid into that container and sealed it. Later he took it with him in his car. The rope and the box were given to me. So here's the *sika* rope and here's the box! So this is how things are placed at the moment. Right now I can't tell you anything more than this."

After hearing this account, I studied the headless corpse once again. I also examined the rope and the box very carefully and then decided to leave. But just then a thought flashed through my mind. I remembered that there had been a few cases earlier where we had succeeded in having the corpse identified through its clothes. So then why not try the same method with this one? I quickly asked the officer, "What kind of clothes did you see on this corpse, when you first found it? Where are those clothes now?"

"It's usual for bodies to be found with some clothes on them but this one didn't have a shred of clothing covering it. It was completely naked when we discovered it."

"What about jewellery of some sort?"

"Forget about jewellery. It didn't even have a single glass or iron bangle on the wrist."

"You saw the corpse with its head earlier on. Could you discern whether the woman was married or a widow?"

"No sir, there was no way to find out anything of the sort. I didn't see any traces of *sindoor* on her head."[3]

"What was the state of her hair?"

"Her hair was very thick and long. It was in a completely dishevelled state when we found the body."

"Since you saw the corpse when it was whole, and since you are an experienced officer, let me ask you a question. From her appearance were you able to ascertain where she might have come from? Did she come from the western parts of the country? Was she a Bengali? Hindu or Muslim?"

"I got the feeling that the woman was Bengali, not someone from the western regions. She also seemed like a Hindu woman."

It was late in the evening when I was having this conversation with the official in that morgue. Everywhere around us, the worshipping of the Durga idols had begun as part of *saptami* celebrations. All Hindus had collected in front of the idol and were closely watching the evening *arati* with folded hands, their hearts overflowing with a sense of utter fulfilment and joy. And here I was, a luckless wretch, who had had to forgo all the festivities, toss all pious thoughts into the very morass of sinfulness and, instead of gazing at the radiant face of the goddess, was standing in a morgue looking at the corpse of a dissolute woman! What utterly debased creatures we are!

IV

Later at night after leaving the mortuary, I went to the doctor's house. After talking to him for a while, I asked to see the severed head of the corpse. When he took me to the place where it was kept, I saw that it was exactly how the officer had described it. The head, that looked more alive than dead, was preserved inside a huge glass container. Her unfettered tresses were floating freely inside the preserving fluid. Looking at the head I felt that it belonged to a young and beautiful Bengali young woman. But there was no easy way of knowing whether she was a married woman or a widow. I looked at it for some time and then after asking the doctor a few questions about her death, I left his house.

In due course, I met all the wise and experienced police officers who were involved in investigating this case. What I found was that after being involved in the case, they had investigated the point where it had started and found out how the box had reached the warehouse. While they were asking questions about the box, a coolie had come and informed them that on that particular night, at around two o clock, he was walking down that road to do some work on a ship. That was when he had noticed that a man was struggling to pull a huge box out of a horse-drawn carriage. But he just couldn't get it out. The carriage didn't have a footman, only a driver. The horses seemed to be new to their task, which was why the carriage driver was unable to leave the reins and help the passenger with his box. The man with the box had then spotted the coolie and hailed him. Helped by the coolie, he then dragged the box out of the carriage and managed to put it on the ground. Subsequently, after paying the coach driver and waiting till he drove off in the opposite direction, he had sought the coolie's help in dragging the box to the warehouse. After the box was kept inside the warehouse, the man had then paid the coolie 4 *anna*s. Then the coolie had left for his work and the man walked off towards the banks of river Ganga, saying that he was going to hire a boat.

The officers had succeeded in gathering all this information from the coolie and they had also found out that the man with the box had been a Bengali youth. The coolie had said he might be able to recognise the young man if he were to see him again.

After the coolie had given his statement, the officers had then started searching for the carriage. They had scoured all the stables of the city and finally succeeded in locating the carriage they were looking for. In fact, the carriage was from the outskirts of the city and the officers had found it in a stable in Kashipur. Upon being interrogated, the carriage driver had confirmed all that the coolie had said. He further added that it was while the carriage was resting in the Kashipur stable that a man had come and hired the carriage. But he didn't take him to a house. Instead he took him to a road where another man had been waiting with a large box and the two of them then placed the box, with some difficulty, into the carriage. Once the box was put inside, the man who had hired the carriage, had left. The man who was waiting on the road then travelled to Kolkata in the carriage. He had finally taken the box out with the help of the coolie.

The officers then put all their efforts into investigating how the box had reached that point on Kashipur road and who the people were who had brought it there. But all such efforts led to nothing and everyone went back home after searching fruitlessly for those men.

Meanwhile, following the instructions of the Chief Police Officer, all inhabitants of that town and its nearby places were shown the corpse; and yet no one was able to identify it. The entire night of *saptami* was spent showing the body, as well as the severed head, to a great variety of people brought in from a great variety of places.

V

On the morning of *ashtami* also, several people were shown the corpse and, of the many who saw it, one piped up, "This looks like the face of Gopal Biswas's daughter! He belongs to Kashipur." I couldn't bide even for a moment after hearing this and set off for Kashipur immediately. Gopal Biswas was at home when I reached his house. I told him everything and then brought him along to show him the head. Gopal *babu* stared at it for a very long time and then finally said, "Sir! I think this is my daughter." When I prodded him for more details, I found out that following a skirmish with his son-in-law, he had brought his daughter home and had not allowed her to go back for four years. But a few days ago, his son-in-law had come to their house and had pleaded with him to let him take his wife back to her marital home. Unable to turn down his son-in-law's requests, Gopal *babu* had sent his daughter back with him on *shashthi*. After his son-in-law had left that day with his wife, Gopal *babu* had not received any news of their having safely reached their house. Even as he recounted all this, the poor old man broke down and then began sobbing loudly while looking at the severed head.

After the old man had composed himself a little, I found out his son-in-law's name and the details of where he stayed. His son-in-law's house was not very far; it was in a small hamlet about three to four miles from Sheoraphuli station. On *ashtami*, as soon as I heard the old gentleman's tale, I decided to visit Sheoraphuli and having made this decision, I took Gopal *babu* along with me to the Howrah station. We then climbed into the first train that we could catch going to Sheoraphuli. We reached Sheoraphuli in due course and then set off for that small hamlet where Gopal *babu*'s son-in-law resided. We reached his house a little before darkness fell. And what did we find when we reached our destination? For after that, it became impossible to reassure old Gopal *babu*. The more I tried to comfort him, the more loudly he wailed.

What we learnt when we went there was that his son-in-law had not returned to his house after he had left to fetch his wife. Not only had he not come back to the house with his wife, he had not even dropped a letter to anyone in his family to inform them about his whereabouts, whether he was returning with his wife or when exactly they might return.

Even as I tried to console the old man, I was becoming fairly certain that his son-in-law had duped him and, as revenge for the four-year conflict between them, had committed this heinous and savage act, before fleeing for his life.

Seeing the two of us standing there, several gentlemen who lived in that area came and stood around us and after hearing what we had to say, they seemed to share our worst suspicions. The conclusions they finally reached were the same as ours.

Gopal *babu* had also mentioned that when he had sent his daughter away with his son-in-law, he had given her jewellery worth nearly Rs. five hundred. But we had not found any jewels on the body. I thought to myself that if the body was that of Gopal *babu*'s daughter, then surely the jewellery had been stolen by his son-in-law. Even though from all accounts, the son-in-law had not returned home, I felt that I could not leave the place without searching the house myself. In case he had secretly returned to the house at some point and hidden the ornaments somewhere, I would be able to find them during the search. So I decided that I would do a thorough search of his house.

I entered the house in the presence of a few gentlemen standing there. His (the son-in-law's) mother and a widowed sister were in the house at that time. When I told them what I intended to do, they left the house and waited elsewhere. We then searched the house quite thoroughly but couldn't find any traces of the jewellery. But one part of the mud floor of the house looked like it had been dug up fairly recently. Needless to say, we became extremely suspicious when we saw that spot. And then when we dug up that area, we unearthed a brass pot that was full to the very brim with gold coins and gold and silver jewellery, as well as some cash. It looked like the jewellery was the same as what Gopal *babu* had described. These looked like the bangles, armlets, bracelets and anklets that he said his daughter had been wearing when she'd bid them farewell.

Everyone who had gathered there appeared more shocked when the hidden pot and its contents were discovered. Even the few remaining doubters were now convinced of the son-in-law's guilt. The unanimous opinion was that none other than that man had killed his wife.

It was in this manner that I spent *ashtami*.

VI

A list was drawn of all the ornaments that had been dug up from that house and I left that very night with all the seized goods. The immense sorrow that I had felt earlier at having missed my officially sanctioned leave, and at not being able to meet my friends and family and celebrate Puja with them, was slightly alleviated by the finding of the jewellery. I felt that while it was true that I'd been dragged away from my well-earned leave for this investigation, with god's help I had managed to save my reputation by cracking the case quite easily. With such thoughts in my head, I reached the Sheoraphuli station where I then spent the rest of the night, since there was no train leaving for Kolkata before the next morning. I got into the very first train that was leaving for Kolkata the next day and with great excitement in my heart, I reached Howrah station. Gopal *babu* also returned with me.

A few moments after we alighted from the train, Gopal *babu* moved very close to me and when I stopped walking, he whispered into my ear, "Sir, look over there! That's my son-in-law standing over there."

I thought to myself that when a case begins to get resolved, all the pieces fall into place so very neatly. The corpse had been identified, the stolen goods had been recovered and now all that remained was nabbing the culprit. And such was god's grace that lo and behold, there he was, right in front of our eyes! I leapt forward towards the man whom Gopal *babu* had pointed towards and held him firmly. Startled out of his wits, the man shouted, "Why Sir! What are you doing? Why are you holding me like this? What have I done?"

I: "I am not just restraining you, I'm about to place you under arrest and take you away from here."

"Who are you? How can you talk of arresting me?"

"I'm a police officer. Why don't you try and figure out for yourself why I would be placing you under arrest?"

"What are you talking about! I have no clue about why a police officer would want to arrest me!"

"Do you think this pretence of innocence can help you go free? Don't labour under any such illusions! A murderer can never escape my clutches."

"A murderer! What are you talking about? Whom have I murdered? No Sir! You are making a terrible mistake. You are arresting the wrong man!"

"Let me be the judge of that. I'm in no mood to waste time standing here and talking to you. I'm going to take you to Kolkata now."

"Sir, since you are a govt. official I won't argue any further with you. I have no choice but to go wherever you take me. But sir! I have a request. I am travelling with a lady and if I have to leave with you, then you'll need to make arrangements for her travel. For I have no one with me who can accompany her for the remaining journey. Can you please organise something for her? Otherwise I'll be sick with worry thinking about how she'll manage on her own."

"Who is this lady that you are talking about?"

"Why Sir, my wife!"

Gopal *babu* who had been standing at some distance from us and listening to our conversation could no longer contain himself when he heard the last few words. Rushing forward, he grabbed his son-in-law and exclaimed, "What did you just say, son? Did you just say your wife is with you? Who are you talking about? Where is she?"

Son-in-law: "But Father don't you know who I'm talking about? Have you forgotten who my wife is? What's going on?! Have you lost your mind? How many wives do you think I have? Your daughter is my only wife. There she is, sitting over there."

We were completely astounded upon hearing his words. Gopal *babu* ran towards that young woman and after staring at her for some time, began shouting, "My daughter! This is my daughter! She has not been killed! She's alive and well!"

As soon as I heard these words, I released the old man's son-in-law. So overcome was I with embarrassment that I could barely walk any further. I climbed back into the train and sat down to collect my thoughts. Gopal *babu*'s son-in-law kept asking me, "Sir! What does all this mean? Why did this fracas happen?" but I felt too ashamed to give him any answers. I just kept sitting inside the train in complete silence. He then ran to his father-in-law and asked for explanations. Gopal *babu* then told him everything that had happened so far and how it had all started when he had seen the severed head and mistakenly assumed it to be that of his daughter. He also related the sequence of events that had led us to his village and thence to search his house and finally dig up a pot containing valuables. Finally he said, "Things got out of hand because you left my house some time ago with your wife, and yet neither did you reach your village on time nor did we get any news of where you might have gone."

His son-in-law then said, "That wasn't my fault, Sir! What could I have done? That day when we left your house, we had set off towards Howrah station but then on the way I ran into my cousin who lives in Kolkata. He said that he was planning to celebrate Durga Puja in his house this year, and refused to let us go back without visiting his house. Even though we were not very keen to go with him, he insisted on taking us there. We ended up spending four days at his house and that's why the delay. He was reluctant to let us return even today but we finally set off after much begging and pleading with him and then we found ourselves in the midst of these strange events at the station! You said you had discovered the pot that was hidden under the floor of my house. But what did you do with it? Where did you take it?"

Gopal *babu*: "Nothing was left there. This police officer carried everything with him."

He pointed at me while saying that and then instructed his son-in-law to retrieve all his valuables from me. Without any demur I immediately matched every single valuable with the list that I had drawn, handed everything to him and also took a receipt from him on that same list. Looking happy, the three of them then hired a carriage and set off for Kashipur. I wended my way to the *thhana* feeling both miserable and deeply embarrassed.

VII

Thankfully no other officer at that *thhana* was aware of the lead that I had been pursuing. So I didn't reveal any of this to them and instead wallowed privately in the immense chagrin that I felt in my heart. I cursed my own brains a thousand times. A little later I heard from my fellow officers that at the time I was in Sheoraphhuli, another officer had been investigating the case and had found out a few things. And then while some of us were sitting and discussing the case, that officer came into the *thhana*. When I asked him what he had been investigating, I found out that he had also believed a man and set off on a wild goose chase. He had been told by a man called Ganesh that the head was that of his wife. A month ago, Ganesh's wife had conspired with some men in their neighbourhood and then eloped with someone. Ganesh was well aware of the identity of the man his wife had eloped with. But despite all his efforts he had failed to trace their whereabouts. That's the reason why Ganesh had deliberately identified that head as being that of his wife. He wanted the police to go after the people who were involved in his wife's elopement. He hoped those people, fearing arrest, might then lead the police to his wife. And thus he would accomplish what he had set out to do, without loss of face.

Ganesh's plan worked. When the officers heard his tale they became terribly excited. All the men whom Ganesh had suspected of being involved in his wife's disappearance were arrested. They were accused of murdering her. When those people realised that things were getting out of hand, and that it would be foolhardy to keep Ganesh's wife hidden any longer, they quickly brought her out of the secret hideaway. When this happened, Ganesh was severely reprimanded for giving false information. However, Ganesh turned a deaf ear to all the abuses and with a smirk on his face said, "I became a little confused when I saw the severed head and felt it was my wife's. That's the reason I gave the information that I did. I didn't deliberately mislead them."

The officer who had been pursuing that lead was also stumped like me by the turn of events and returned to the *thhana* with feelings of embarrassment and dismay. Most of the other officers also got to know about the debacle. But thankfully no one came to know about my embarrassment. I never disclosed anything of those events to anyone. But despite all my efforts to conceal what had happened, gradually a few of my colleagues got to know everything from Gopal *babu* and his son-in-law. And then they talked about it to others. Thus the news of what had happened travelled to several ears and eventually it reached the ears of my superior officer as well.

At any rate, this was the manner in which we were stumbling between genuine and false leads in this investigation. But now we reached a point when we could not see any other paths on which we could move forward. At our wits' end, we all sat together and had no other option but to reflect on the case and discuss it with each other. We carried on talking about it till late in the afternoon.

VIII

On the day of *navami*, everyone left the *thhana* at one in the afternoon. I went back home and then later in the evening I went to the *thhana* where the young woman's corpse had been discovered. I had examined the box and the *sika* rope on *saptami* but I wanted to examine them carefully all over again. So I went back there and then studied them very closely. They didn't look like the ordinary *sika* that's used in homes; the ropes had been pulled together with great force. Nobody would have such *sika* ropes in their houses for domestic use; it looked like the kind of rope that a milkman, or some other worker, who carried heavy stuff by hanging them from a long stick placed on his shoulder, would use.

The box looked new at a cursory glance. But when examined thoroughly, it became clear that while it was a very strong trunk made of extra-durable tin, it wasn't very new. It looked like someone had put fresh paint on top of its original colour. Once I realised that it was a newly painted old trunk,

I began to scrutinise its entire body even more carefully. For if the old trunk could reveal any marks then those could help us in our investigation.

As I was scanning it, I thought I espied something written on its side. It was not entirely visible, let alone legible. After a great deal of effort I thought I could discern the names of a person and a village. But the letters were so faint, that I could barely read them. Finally I got a lens and tried reading the letters once again. But even with the lens all I could make out was the word "nimta", which made no sense whatsoever to me. So I sat down in a state of despair and wondered what to do next.

Suddenly it struck me that around a few miles from Kashipur there is a tiny hamlet called Nimta. What if this trunk had come from there? I decided to go there and investigate. I hired a carriage and set off for Nimta and after the carriage had taken me till the point beyond which there was no proper road, I walked the rest of the way to the village. Nimta seemed like a very small village with very few houses. Of those, only four or five were Brahmin households and the remaining ten to twenty were of people of other castes.

In the village I asked a few passersby and children I met on the road some questions but received no satisfactory answers. Thinking that I had failed in my mission, I was about to turn back from there when something very ordinary caught my eye. These were nothing special but just a few old earthen and well-worn pots that bore signs of many years of cooking; they were lying on the side of the road.

Dear readers, I'm not sure whether this scene evokes any particular feeling in you but I definitely thought of something and that's why I mention this here. For a few moments I thought that nothing would come of this. And yet at the same time I couldn't quite relinquish the thought that had arisen in my mind.

But what was it that had suddenly occurred to me? If my readers haven't got an inkling, then bear with me while I explain what I mean.

What suddenly occurred to me was that the discarded utensils didn't seem to have been abandoned a long time back. Rather, they looked like someone had got rid of them just a few days ago. It is only amongst Hindus that the custom of discarding old pots is prevalent. But in my entire life, I had neither heard of nor seen a Hindu household discarding their old, unbroken pots during the auspicious period of Durga Puja, unless they have some truly intransigent reason for doing this. If my conjectures are correct and it is in some house here that the murder was committed, then that would also explain the mystery of the pots that were thrown away. Deaths that happen due to aberrant causes, like snake bites, falling off a tree or suicides through hanging or poisoning oneself or murder, are not considered natural deaths. In the case of a natural death, Brahmins have to observe purificatory rituals for a period of eleven days, but if the death is unnatural, then the period is that of three days. After the three days are over, the cooking utensils used on those days are thrown away and new ones are acquired.

If this had happened in this case and my conjecture was right, then undoubtedly the pots had been discarded for one of the aforementioned reasons. At any rate, I decided that I would not leave that place without investigating the entire matter. And so I started making enquiries about those utensils. What I found after asking four or five people in the village was that the cooking pots had been discarded by a Brahmin. His name was Gorachand Chakrabarty. Upon further enquiries I found that Gorachand had three brothers. Gorachand was the eldest of the brothers. The second, Ramchand died about five years ago. The third and fourth brothers, Kevalchand and Rupchand, lived in the same house as Gorachand and were not married. Gorachand's wife and two infant sons were also in that house. Ramchand's widow was living with them as well. It was a joint family. None of them was employed in an office; their livelihood depended on cultivating their own land.

IX

After secretly gathering all this information, I then landed up at Gorachand Chakrabarty's house. Gorachand was at home that day and stepped out as soon as I called him. When he saw me, he asked, "Who are you, Sir? Where are you from? And what brings you here?" Truth be told, even though he uttered just these few lines, his manner aroused my suspicions. He looked very nervous while speaking to me. Also, his speech seemed to be slurring a little.

I: "I am a police official and I'm here to investigate a crime. Perhaps you know what I am referring to, and why I've come to see you."

Gorachand: "Why, sir, how would I possibly know what you're investigating. I can't think of anything that we have done that would necessitate a police investigation."

"It won't be long before all that you've done will come to light. So why get impatient? Meanwhile, just answer this one question for me. Why did you throw away all your old cooking utensils at this time?"

"Who told you we have got rid of our cooking pots? We haven't done anything of the kind."

"Don't lie to me. I won't let you off lightly if you lie. I can step into your house this very moment and check the utensils in your kitchen to see whether they are new or not. You know very well that I can search your house to allay my suspicions, don't you?"

Gorachand looked somewhat crushed when he heard this and said in a subdued voice, "Sir, what is going on? Is it a crime to throw away old cooking pots and use new ones in their stead?"

I: "I know that there's no harm in getting rid of one's old cooking pots. But don't assume that you can pull the wool over my eyes by saying this. I'm not an Englishman who resides abroad and is unfamiliar with all the customs here; like you I'm a Brahmin who lives in this very country. So don't think that you can pull a fast one on me by saying such things.

Unless you give me a satisfactory explanation for throwing away your utensils during this auspicious period, you are going to be in a lot of trouble."

Gorachand was not able to give me any satisfactory answers, but he did eventually admit to discarding cooking utensils a few days ago.

While we were talking, the two brothers of Gorachand also arrived on the scene. It appeared to me that they also looked quite concerned when they saw me and heard who I was.

It was customary for a junior officer to accompany me whenever I travelled to such places. There was an officer with me that day as well. I whispered to him, "Go quickly to the nearest *thhana* and come back with some more officers to this place, as soon as you can. It's getting dark and we don't know what might come up." He left the place after hearing my words. I called a few of the village *chaukidars* to come and help me. Keeping my purpose in mind, I sat down over there and began chatting with various people of that neighbourhood. Needless to say, many of the neighbours had gathered in that spot of their own accord.

While one *chaukidar* stayed with me, to the other I said in hushed tones, "Go and try to find out where Gorachand's widowed sister-in-law is at present. Return to me as soon as you investigate this matter." He then departed with my instructions.

He came back after nearly two hours and said to me in private, "I have found out that Gorachand's sister-in-law used to live in the same house as them. But no one has seen her in the last four or five days. Apparently she was not a woman of good character. Many things were said about her by many people and she was generally regarded with suspicion. She seems to have had affairs with her elder and younger brothers-in-law. I had asked a female informer to go inside the house and gather information. She came back and said that the widow was not at home. Some people are saying that unable to bear the constant humiliation inflicted by those around her, she has fled to some other place. Others say that having failed to control her sinful instincts, she has run away and sunk her family into the depths of disgrace. There are so many such rumours flying about that it has become almost impossible to separate the truth from lies."

The shadow of suspicion that had arisen in my mind deepened when I heard the *chaukidar*'s words. I felt certain that it was Gorachand and his brothers who had killed the widow. But then I also immediately remembered Gopal *babu* and the debacle that I had caused with his daughter and son-in-law. Meanwhile, the officer whom I had sent to the *thhana* also returned with more policemen.

I felt a little emboldened when I saw them and thought that I could now move ahead with some confidence. So, putting all my faith in my luck and in whatever the Mother Goddess' Grand Design might be, I braced myself and plunged right back into the investigation.

X

Subsequently, the eight of us—my fellow officers, the two *chaukidars* and I—surrounded Gorachand's house. We did this to prevent anyone inside the house from escaping with anything. When Gorachand and his brothers saw all of us guarding the house in this manner, they came out to meet me. I asked them in a clear voice, "Tell me Sir, aren't you four brothers in all?"

Gorachand: Yes Sir, we are indeed four brothers but one of my younger brothers died quite some time ago.

I: So then where's his widow? Wasn't she staying with all of you after her husband's death?

Upon hearing this question, the brothers looked crestfallen. None of them was able to give me a straight answer to the question. Gorachand seemed dumbfounded. After a while Rupchand said, "Indeed she used to live with us, but she left the house a few days ago to go and stay at her father's place."

We were not convinced by this and decided to search the house.

Dear readers, I have to ask you one thing at this point. Why, do you think, did I decide to search their house? Was it really possible for me to get anything worthwhile by way of evidence from that house? To begin with, we could find out if the widow was inside. According to them, she was not. Which meant she was either at her father's house, or her severed head was floating inside a glass jar. Secondly, the motive behind this murder was not theft and there were no stolen goods to be recovered from anywhere. And then lastly, there was the mystery of the discarded cooking utensils. The family had already admitted that they had thrown away their old utensils and bought new ones. So then why was the search needed? If you are able to answer this question then I'll know that all these years of writing *Darogar Daftar* have not been in vain. And if you are unable to answer my question, then you'll need to ask me. What I'll then say is that you should try and cast your mind back to the time when the body was discovered. Try to recall the state that it was in. Think of that *sika* rope that was around the neck. You all must know that no one buys just one strand of *sika* rope. Everyone usually has at least two. In that case readers, imagine what a piece of luck it would be, if we were able to unearth the other *sika* rope during our search! Where would that finally lead us? It was for this very reason that I wished to search the house and not only did I then translate my wish into actions, I also succeeded in my real mission. We managed to find *sika* rope in the house.

Whatever doubts had started crowding my mind disappeared completely once I saw that rope. I decided to place all three brothers under house arrest. They could not go anywhere without my permission. I wrote and sent off a letter to Kolkata along with my junior officer. He left the village and then took the carriage in which we had travelled from Kolkata to return to the city. The rest of us waited for him in the village.

It was around three at night that the officer came back. And I noticed that my superior officer was also there with him. What's more, all the other officers who had got involved in the case were also accompanying him. And they were also carrying all the things that I had requested for in my letter. Has my reader been able to guess what that stuff was? It was the glass jar with the head in it, the *sika* rope and the tin trunk. The head was shown to many residents of the village, both old and young. All those who used to know that young widow confirmed that it was Gorachand's sister-in-law. My doubts might have persisted if it were just one or two who could identify her. But if every single person claimed it was that young woman, where was the room for any doubt? The maids who worked in that house also said that they had seen the rope and the tin trunk there. But no one said that they had seen the murder being committed and Gorachand's family didn't own up to it either.

We did what we usually do in such circumstances. We arrested the three brothers and took them along with us to Kolkata.

Finally, we also found out where the young woman's natal home was. The wretched girl's parents were both alive and were able to identify the head as being that of their daughter.

When the driver of the aforementioned carriage was brought in again, he looked at Rupchand and said that it was he who had hailed the carriage that day while Kevalchand had then travelled with it to Kolkata in the carriage.

The coolie who had met us earlier also identified Kevalchand as the man whom he had helped carry the trunk to the warehouse.

All the three brothers were charged in this case. Subsequently all three were presented to the District Magistrate. After taking the statements of all the witnesses in the case over a few days, the Magistrate sent the brothers for a trial at the Sessions Court.

The trial began in due course and the brothers hired a lawyer to defend them. They refused to admit that they had anything to do with the crime. Since there was no actual evidence to prove that they had committed the murder, Gorachand was soon acquitted. Kevalchand was imprisoned for two years as punishment for hiding the body while Rupchand was sent to jail for only a year for assisting him.

These men were punished in this manner for killing and dismembering a fallen woman; and here I was, denied the holy sight of the great goddess, for no fault of mine. I thought that perhaps the goddess was offended with me for always being involved—consciously or unconsciously—in various underhand activities as part of my job. She had therefore denied my eyes the privilege of savouring the divine sight of her glorious visage.

Priyanath Mukhopadhyay

Notes

1 The seventh day of the Durga Puja festivities. *Panchami, shashthi*, *ashtami* and *navami* are respectively the fifth, sixth, eighth and ninth days.
2 Dom refers to a so-called 'unclean' caste group found in large numbers in districts in the western fringe of Bengal. Traditionally, Doms were basket-makers, cultivators, labourers, musicians and midwives. Some were also scavengers. Refer to footnote 23 of the Introduction.
3 *Sindoor* refers to the vermilion mark on the forehead of Hindu women and is meant to be an identifiable mark of her being married.

9

'GIRIJASUNDARI'

'(A woman killed on the capital's thoroughfare)' Darogar Daftar, Baisakh (mid-April–mid-May), 1895

I

It was on a day in the month of *Poush* (approx. mid-December to mid-January in the *Saka* calendar), just as I was preparing to take a bath at around 10 o'clock, that someone arrived with the information that a woman called Girijasundari had been killed in the Mathhaghasha Lane. No one knew who had committed the murder or why. I was instructed to reach the scene of crime forthwith and begin the investigation.

When we receive an order to the effect of, "Leave immediately and begin investigations into a murder case", we are not allowed to tarry. Therefore as soon as I got this information, I sent off a man to hire a carriage for me and then hurriedly prepared to complete my ablutions while he was gone. As soon as the carriage arrived, I left for Mathaghasha Lane. When I saw a crowd gathered in front of one of the several two-storied tenements that have been built in a row on the Mathaghasha Lane, I decided that must be the house where the murder had happened. Since this incident occurred quite some time ago, I can no longer remember the number of the house. Nor can I find the diary where I had recorded these details at the time. At any rate, when I alighted from my carriage, I realized my guess had been right. I was informed that it was in one of the apartments in the ground floor that the murder had taken place.

When I walked up to the apartment, I found that the room where the murder had been committed was on the main road. The room was a little cut off from the rest of the apartment and was extremely small. In its width it would have been about five feet, and in length not more than six feet or so. All that was there in it by way of household items was a wooden pallet with a mattress and a pillow on it. Next to the pallet was a box made of mango wood and on it were a few copper vessels. In the little space between the pallet and the door lay a corpse. The corpse was covered with a coarse white cloth and the room was awash with blood. But there seemed to be even greater traces of blood on the street right outside the door. It is not easy for ordinary people to imagine the large quantities of blood that can come out of a human body. But we have seen such things many times, and so we know that it is not unnatural for such quantities of blood to flow out of the murdered body of a healthy young woman. I observed all this while standing outside the room and after some time, I slowly entered the room.

When I did go in, I could not find a single spot in the room that was free of bloodstains where I could stand and observe the corpse without being distracted. As a result, I had to stand on that blood-soaked floor and begin my investigations. The coarse cloth that covered the corpse had to be removed for me to examine it properly. Once it was lifted, I saw a horrifying sight. I saw a sight that is extremely rare, for despite working on millions of cases, one doesn't usually come across the kind of thing that I saw.

While starting the investigation, I had decided that I would first examine the corpse meticulously and then proceed in my work depending on how I would find the corpse. But once the cloth was lifted I realized I would not be able to go according to that plan. For I could see only from the feet up to the neck; beyond that I was unable to see anything.

And it wasn't just me; everyone who had gathered there to help me was in a similar situation. No one could see anything beyond the corpse's neck. How could we? For not only had the head been severed from the body, it was nowhere to be seen. Everyone searched for it carefully in that room and around it but no traces of it could be found anywhere.

Looking at the body it seemed that the woman could not have been more than thirty or thirty-five years of age, but she could very well have been somewhat younger. Her colour was dark, her body well-proportioned and round, but not very tall. There were two pairs of diamond-cut gold bangles on her wrists and she was wearing a clean white saree. I turned the body and examined it thoroughly and found that there were wounds on the chest and the back, as well as on the sides, and almost all of them were pretty severe. What was quite clearly evident from the wounds was that a machete or some such sharp weapon had been used with such force that a single blow alone would have been enough to fell a well-built woman and send her to the House of Death.

When we searched the inside of the house thoroughly, not only could we not find the head, we couldn't locate the weapon either. Everything else in the room appeared to have been untouched; nothing seemed to have been either stolen, moved or even disturbed in any way.

After examining the inside of the room, I stepped out. The officer who had received the FIR of this incident was standing outside. When I asked him who had filed the FIR and at what time, he said that that morning, around nine, when he was sitting in the *thhana*, the landlady of this house, Bama Bewa, had rushed in and informed him that one of her tenants living in an outer room of her apartment block, Girijasundari, had been killed by someone. Girija, or Girijasundari, used to work as a maid in the house of one Rammay *babu*. Since she had not gone to his house for work that day, her employer Rammay *babu* himself had arrived in the early hours of the morning and gone to her room to check her whereabouts. Being the first to see her in that state, he had raised the alarm and called the landlady. On hearing his voice, many others from different houses also soon gathered in that place. Finally, Bama had gone to the *thhana* to inform the police about what had happened.

After hearing this description, I summoned Rammay *babu*. He was present in the neighbourhood, at that time. When he arrived, I asked him some specific questions and then listened to his answers very carefully and even wrote down all that he said. Here's a summary of what he told me: "I live in this Mathaghasha Lane. This is not where I was born but this is where I had to come and stay for work. I rarely get any days off at my workplace. Hence even though my salary is meager, I have to keep my family with me; besides, my son's studies would be affected if he didn't stay with me. That's why my wife and child stay with me in Kolkata. I have no one else in this city besides my wife and my ten-year-old son. My wife is often unwell and therefore not able to do all the domestic work by herself. As a result, even though I could ill afford it, I was forced to employ this maid. For almost the last two years she has been working for us but she doesn't spend the night in our house. By nine o'clock in the evening, once our meals are over, she leaves for her own apartment and then returns for work in the early hours of the following day. I had come to make inquiries in the morning today since she had failed to show up for work. About a month ago, she had not turned up for work, saying she was unwell, and I had then come to this place and found out her house and confirmed that she had indeed been sick. Today, when I came to her house, I found the door of her house shut. I assumed she was inside. But as soon as I started knocking on the door, it flew open. I started calling her from outside. Not getting any reply when I made to step in, I was met by this shocking scene. I even lost consciousness for a few minutes. When I came to, I was at a complete loss as to what I should do next. For a while I thought I should probably just run away from there. But immediately after that, I thought what if everyone begins to suspect me of the crime if I flee? So I started calling the landlady and many others then came with her to see what had happened. Soon a crowd gathered. Eventually, after much confabulation, it was decided that the *thhana* needed to be informed and the landlady then went off to the *thhana*. Gradually all of you came here. This is all that I know. I don't have any other information."

II

After listening to everything that Rammay *babu* had to say, I summoned the landlady Bama in order to ask her a few questions. Whatever she said to me tallied with all that Rammay *babu* had just told me. I wondered if they were both lying or they were both telling the truth. But Rammay *babu*'s manner of answering my questions had definitely not suggested that he was hiding anything from me.

I also wanted to ask Bama a few questions about Girija. But before doing that, I thought of a few other things. These were very simple thoughts indeed! They were as follows:

1 Was this suicide or murder? Given that I couldn't find the head of the corpse, that there's no weapon to be seen anywhere and there's blood on the street outside the room, only a lunatic would think of this as a suicide. Hence this was murder.
2 If it was murder, then what was the motive? It didn't seem to have been motivated by theft. Girija was a penniless widow; she earned a living by working as a maid. There was nothing valuable in the room and nothing seemed to have been disturbed in any way. Besides, the gold bangles had been untouched. If theft was the motive, wouldn't the bangles have been taken?
3 Also, where did the bangles come from? Everyone in that house, including Rammay *babu*, claimed that Girija had been a widow. Nobody had ever seen gold bangles on her wrists. Nor did she have the money for buying such bangles. So how did these bangles reach her wrists? A lot of thieves steal valuables after killing someone; till now I had seen this. As opposed to this, it was completely unthinkable that someone would bring ornaments from their own homes in order to put them on the victim.
4 Did the poor woman die as a consequence of some dispute? If that were true, why could we not find a single person with whom Girija had a terrible spat? Surely if she had had acrimonious relations with someone, some resident of this apartment block would have got wind of the matter. Besides, even if it was a dispute that had led to the murder, why would the killer make away with her head?
5 Was it possible that the head had been dragged away by jackals and stray dogs after the murder? But if what Rammay *babu* had said was true, then how could that be possible? For given the manner in which he had found the door of the room when he came here in the early hours of the morning, it would be very difficult to imagine a stray animal to have gone in or come out.

As I mulled over these things, I just couldn't fathom what the motive for the murder might have been. Why did this murder happen? If this cannot be established by the investigating officer, then it is impossible for him to establish the identity of the perpetrator. Therefore, how do you think, dear readers, would I have been able to succeed in this investigation? But then, what could I do? We are a colonized race; we take orders from others.

So despite being sure that the case was going to be a hard one to crack, I could not relinquish the investigation. Whether I succeeded or failed I had to remain a part of the investigation.

I got up from where I was sitting and then, taking Bama with me, I entered her house. After sitting down in her house, I gradually started asking Bama several questions. Besides the information about Girija that I had gathered from Rammay *babu*, I now found out that she had been staying at Bama's house for the last two years. Before coming to this house, she had stayed in many other houses in the neighbourhood and worked as a maid. Her hometown was in a tiny hamlet in Medinipur. Her brother, sister-in-law and many other relatives were still living in that place. They belonged to the caste of Kaivartyas.[1] Since the time that she had come to Kolkata she had been earning a livelihood by working as a maid. It wasn't as if her character was entirely free of blemishes. She had eloped with a man to Kolkata after facing social disgrace back home. And then when he left her after a while, she eventually turned to the only option of earning a livelihood that is available to wretched women like her in the city. She began working as a maid and, like many other housemaids, her character became increasingly smothered under a veritable heap of disreputable activities. That is the reason why despite staying till late in the evening in her employer's household, she refused to spend the night there. And yet whatever salary she earned every month was spent on the rent for the room.

I got to know all this from Bama. Neither she nor any of the others could give me any details of the men who would come to visit Girija in her room; however, they all confirmed that some man or the other would be in her room from time to time.

I stepped out of the house after gathering all this information from Bama. I saw that the corpse had been brought out of the room and kept on the street outside; it would soon be sent to the "deadhouse" for forensic examination. Since there were no family members or acquaintances of the dead woman present, and no one was willing to carry the bier, we had to seek the help of Doms. They stood there waiting to carry the body away from there.

After removing the corpse, the room was searched more thoroughly. But no traces could be found anywhere in the room of either the deadly weapon that had been used to perform the foul deed or of the dead woman's head. We sat there feeling extremely disappointed and, after a while, started recording the statements of the various tenants who lived in Bama's house.

III

That day was spent in this manner and we were left completely clueless as to who might have committed this murder. The next day was also spent without finding out anything.

On the third day my mind was engulfed with curiosity. I wondered whether the dead woman, who had spent most of her life working as a housemaid, would have left something behind. With these thoughts, I entered her room all over again and decided to examine the insides of the mango wood box that stood there. But I wasn't sure how I was going to open the box. For when we had searched the room earlier for the murder weapon, we had not found any keys anywhere. We had even checked the waist of the corpse; the thread she wore as a girdle bore a gold amulet and nothing else. Unable to find a key, I toyed for a few moments with the idea of breaking the box open to see what lay inside. But then I stopped to wonder if it might be wise to make one last attempt to find another key that would open it before breaking the lock. Even as I was musing in this manner, it struck me all of a sudden that quite often, instead of keeping the keys to a safe on their person, Bengali women prefer to hide it somewhere in their rooms. If that was what this woman had done, then I must scour all the possible hiding places in the room, like the space next to the fence, under the bamboo tatty, inside the container for storing rice and below the mattress. If my search yielded the keys, then well and good; else I would go back to considering the option of forcing it open. With this in mind, I started going over every visible and not-so-visible, secret place that I could find in the room. And yet despite spending three hours searching that tiny room, I couldn't find the keys. All I found were some papers that were kept hidden near the boundary wall of the house. Accompanying me in the search that day was a junior officer. I gave the papers to him and said, "Read each one of these papers carefully and see if there's anything in them that might help us find something of relevance to our case." The official took those papers from me and went outside. Soon after that, I did manage to find a set of keys and prised the box open. But all I found inside it were some pieces of clothing and a vessel with a few coins in it.

After completing the search inside the room, I stepped out. When I asked my junior officer about those papers, I was told there was nothing of any importance to us in them. There were just a few receipts and papers related to a house in them. Even though I learnt that there was nothing useful in those papers, I asked for them and began scanning them myself. I saw that three of the documents were indeed receipts. The remaining piece of paper was a letter written to the deceased by someone in her village. The letter was quite long but amidst everything else, this had also been written:

> I am now fairly certain that Prasanna has left me to be with you. She had informed many people here that she would be going to visit you. Also talked of how the two of you shared a special connection. That's why when she left my house she could only

have gone to you, especially given that I have looked for her at her parents' house and haven't found her there. I see you in the same light as I did, earlier. I have never despised you simply because you ran away from the village. It's true that you have suffered the disgrace that was your lot but I didn't see that as a reason to hate you. While Prasanna is not your sister, she's definitely like a sister to you. And if you have thought of her as your sister, please do not ruin our lives. If she has indeed sought refuge at your place, please don't use this as an opportunity to sow seeds of her ruin. Don't wreak havoc in our lives by helping her sully her virtuous character. If you do this, it won't help you in any way; in fact if anything, it'll only increase the chances of harm befalling you. More often than not, men don't care about their lives when it comes to defending their honour. Don't assume that I won't go down that road if I have to. Reply to my letter as soon as you have read it and if Prasanna is with you (and I'm sure that she is), then treat her with care and send me information about her. If you don't reply to this letter then I'll come to your house and take a decision about what needs to be done. Don't blame me if that happens. And don't take too much time to reply to this letter.

Your brother-in-law
Shri Nabakrishna Das

IV

I read the letter four or five times and went over it very carefully. And yet I was neither able to glean all that was being said, nor could I find the date on which it was written. This much I had gathered: that the letter writer was Girija's brother in-law. He had married a second time after her (Girija's) sister's death. What I could also gather was that his second wife had left her husband and run away, and that he suspected that she had come to Kolkata to Girija's house.

If Nabakrishna Das' conjecture was correct, and his wife had indeed come here against her husband's wishes, and if the husband had begun having suspicions about his wife's character, then was it not quite likely that the murder had been committed by him? Nabakrishna had written clearly at one point in his letter that people often didn't care for their lives when it came to preserving their honour. If something like this could surface in his mind, would it be impossible for him to commit the murder? Perhaps he had made good his threat and come here, committed the barbaric act and then dragged his wife back home. But then no one had said anything about seeing another woman staying in this room. It could very well be that Girija had kept her locked in the room in order to keep her presence a secret; in which case there would be little chance of anyone becoming aware of her presence. I decided to investigate this matter and left the place, taking that letter with me. It was quite late in the evening by the time I returned to my office, so no further work happened that day. The following day when I showed the letter to my superior officer, he too concurred with my thoughts and agreed with what I proposed.

That day in the afternoon, at around four, I took a steamer on the River Bhagirathi and left Kolkata. Later in the evening, the steamer reached Uluberia. After getting off there, I saw a canal right in front of me, leading towards Medinipur. In that canal was a small steamer and it was beckoning passengers enthusiastically with its melodious whistle and large amounts of smoke that it emitted at intervals. Next to the canal stood a row of shops that were selling a variety of snacks and betel leaves; the shops were mostly run by women. There were hardly any men in them. This kind of business meant that the shop owners had other intentions and it wasn't just food that was being sold. The running of the shops was merely a front.

Keeping a watchful eye on all this, I approached the steamer. But I couldn't get into the steamer and I had to keep waiting there on that extremely narrow place. A lot of people were standing there along with me. When it was time to get into the next steamer, many who had been waiting with me jostled and pushed in their bid to get in as soon as possible, and some even started singing praises of the 'Siren' *sahib*. But 'Siren' *sahib* remained impervious to such flattery and refused to favour them with any special attention. From time to time some men who worked on the steamer came and showered the passengers with honeyed words and even pushed some of them in order to clear the way for the station master to enter. Where there was a cluster of women, the jostling had a stronger impact and an old woman lost her balance in this melee and fell into the canal. She didn't drown and her companions soon managed to save her life and drag her back on to the banks.

When it was time, 'Siren' *sahib* made noises to indicate that it was time to leave. The steamer was fairly small and the people who had climbed in didn't dare step into the area that was occupied by the staff working on the steamer. As a result, most of the steamer was filled up even before less than half of the waiting population got in. What then could be done with the rest? The steamer would face losses if they were left on the banks. So even though it seemed as though there was no way of letting them all enter, the officers ushered them in and then made them sit in such a way that they resembled a solid human block. There was not even an inch of space between them to allow the slightest bit of movement, let alone getting up or turning sideways. Even though I had to climb into this steamer, thankfully I was spared this ordeal. I had luckily bought a second-class ticket and therefore could travel in relative comfort.

The steamer started moving along the waters of the canal. It crossed a few bridges, went over rivers like Roopnarayan and Damodar and kept moving at a steady pace. Anyone who has visited Medinipur would have been surprised at the state of these bridges. But since this waterway also has a wondrous bridge that few people know about, I need to describe it a little bit here. Once one has crossed Panchkura and gone on for a while, one comes across this bridge that's not less than two hundred feet long. It's quite different from the kind of bridges that one encounters ordinarily. That is to say it's not the kind of bridge which has water flowing under it and people walking on it; in fact, it's just the opposite of that. This bridge has a huge field under it and quite often cattle can be seen grazing on this field. One can also see lots of people walking on these fields. The waters of the canal have been diverted in such a manner that they flow on top of the bridge. And steamers, boats and other vessels go over these waters that flow over the bridge. I have travelled to very many places in India but I have yet to see a bridge like this anywhere else.

We travelled on the waters of the canal the entire night and the next morning we reached the town of Medinipur. The village that I had to visit was quite far from Medinipur. The only way to travel in that direction was to take a bullock cart and even then one is not able to go the entire distance. For the last seven miles that lead up to the village, there's no vehicle available. Those seven miles have to be covered on foot or in a cart.

I hired a cart driven by an Oriya man and started my journey. We went past a charming place located on top of a small hill which, according to legend, used to be the cow shed of King Virat.[2] Many Hindus still come here to see this place. The remnants of the old building are visible till today. We crossed it and moved ahead. After crossing a few miles, our carriage reached a huge Sal forest, full of wild animals. We kept moving and I sat in the cart gazing at the beauty of the thick forests on either side of the road.

V

After travelling in this manner for two whole days and then walking for an entire day, I finally reached my destination. Nabakrishna Das was at home and as soon as I reached his house, he came out to meet me. Till I met Nabakrishna Das, I had concealed my real identity from everyone in that place. When I met Nabakrishna I revealed my true identity to him and said, "I have come here to meet you for a very special reason."

He replied, "You have come here specially to meet me? Please tell me what you want."

I said, "When did you come here from Kolkata?"

Nabakrishna: "It's been almost two years now that I have come home. I haven't gone back there after that."

"Do you know Girijasundari?"

"Of course I know her. I used to be married to her younger sister."

"Where's your wife now?"

"She died a while ago."

"Did you get married again after that?"

"Yes, I did get married again."

"Is your second wife's name Prasanna?"

"Yes Sir, it is! But how do you know her name?"

"I'll tell you later how I know her name. First tell me where she is."

"I can't quite tell you where she is right now. She fought with me and went away somewhere. I have no idea where she has gone. I have searched for her in many places but haven't found her. Do you have any idea where she might be?"

"Do you know Girija's house?"

"Yes, indeed I do. She lives in the Mathaghasha Lane in Kolkata."

"Do you think your wife Prasanna gone there?"

"No, I have no reason to think such a thing."

"Do you remember writing a letter to Girija claiming that your wife has gone to pay her a visit?"

"Yes of course I remember that. I had at first suspected that that's where my wife had gone. But later I got to know that she wasn't there."

"How did you realize that Prasanna hadn't gone to meet Girija?"

"I found this out from Girija herself."

I felt a little encouraged by this response from Nabakrishna. I thought to myself that it's hard to keep secrets and lies concealed for too long. The truth had come out of Nabakrishna's mouth as he spoke. If he hadn't even visited Kolkata, how did he meet Girija? Earlier he had claimed he hadn't visited Kolkata in the last two years and yet he had just talked of hearing from Girija that his wife hadn't gone to see her. All I needed to do now was to confirm that he had visited Kolkata recently, and then I could surely start suspecting him of the murder that had been committed. I began to feel that finally, after a long time, the investigation was moving in the right direction.

With such thoughts in my mind I said to Nabakrishna, "You said your wife had not visited Girija in Kolkata. You also said you got this information from Girija herself. If you haven't been to Kolkata in two years, then how could you have met Girija?"

"Why Sir! Is it not possible to meet people without going to Kolkata? Couldn't Girija have come here?"

"Of course she could have come here. But she hasn't been to this village lately so how could you have got news of your wife from her?"

"Who told you that she hasn't come to the village lately? I met her three days ago and, what's more, she's in her own house, at present. When I heard that she had come to the village, I went to meet her and then I got to know from her that Prasanna hadn't visited her in Kolkata."

When I heard these words, I felt as if the world around me had plunged into darkness. The Girija who had definitely left this earth and whose mortal remains I had seen with my own eyes, was not dead! How could I believe that she had left Kolkata and returned to her village? Could it be that Nabakrishna was trying to throw me off the scent and dupe me into believing that he didn't have anything to do with the crime? Did he think that I would simply accept what he was saying, leave him in peace and go away from there? At any rate, now that a new and bizarre thing had surfaced, it needed proper investigation. I would have to see Girija for myself and only then would I believe Nabakrishna's words.

With such thoughts in my mind I said to him, "Since you claim that Girija's in her own house and that it has been three days since she came here and you have even met her, then I would like you to take me to her. For I really need to meet Girija quite urgently." He agreed and the two of us then set off from there. Girija's house was just two miles from there so we reached it after walking for almost two hours.

Girija's brother was working in the field outside their house at that time. He came and stood near us when Nabakrishna called him. Nabakrishna then introduced me to him and also told him the reason why I had come to their house. After hearing what Nabakrishna had to say, Girija's brother replied, "It's been a few days since Didi came to visit us from Kolkata. She never really talked to anyone about why she had decided to come all of a sudden after such a long time. All that she said was that she was planning to go off on a long pilgrimage and that before leaving, she wanted to meet all of us. In fact she left the house the day after you (Nabakrishna) met her. She didn't tell us where she was going. She had first told the women of this household that she would go back to Kolkata and then start her pilgrimage from there. But later she had also said that she wouldn't return to Kolkata without completing her pilgrimage. She told them that her first stop would be Vaidyanath and after staying there for a few days, she would leave for Kashi. She promised to write a letter once she reached Kashi."

VI

After hearing all this from Girija's brother, I had to sit down on that very spot. Meanwhile, the news that a *daroga* had come to that small village had spread with meteor-like speed all over the place. The *chaukidars* of the village tightened their cummerbunds, settled the turbans on their heads and, with a clout in their hands, began arriving where I sat. They all came and greeted me respectfully and then went and sat at a distance. Boys and girls of the village collected there and stood around, staring at me with curious eyes. Before long, the *zamindar*, the *panchayat* members and other important men of the village had also arrived.[3] All those people who had thronged there confirmed that Girija had indeed come to the village. Some had seen her with their own eyes while others had heard about it.

After all that I heard from the crowd, I was left with no doubt whatsoever. It was quite clear to me that Girija had not been murdered; what's more, she had also paid her village a visit. And the next inevitable question was whose body it was that we had found in Girija's room, if not hers. Several questions began to crowd my mind simultaneously. Did we find the corpse in the room of the same Girija who had come to her village and then left on what she claimed was a pilgrimage? Or had the dreadful murder happened in the room of some other Girija? Was our investigation of this Girija a huge mistake and instead should we have been investigating a different Girija altogether? How were we going to find the facts of this case? If I could find this Girija, I would have taken her back to Kolkata, shown her to the people there and then decided whether we were on the track of the right person or not. But with this one also gone missing, there was no way of doing that. And yet the brother-in-law's name is Nabakrishna Das. And it was to this very Girija that Nabakrishna had written a letter inquiring about his wife's whereabouts. And he had asked her the same question when she had come here. If the room where the murder had happened did not belong to this Girija, then how could the letter have been found there? But then it was also possible that there were two Girijas living on Mathaghasha Lane and the postman had delivered the letter meant for a different Girija by mistake to the Girija in whose room the murder had then happened. Seeing that the letter was not hers, she had simply kept it in her trunk. If this had happened then it was not strange that we had found the letter in her room. Given all of this, finding the identity of that corpse was by no means going to be an easy task. As far as I could see, there was only one way of solving the matter. There could be no better solution but to get the description of that Girija from the people who knew her well and then match it carefully with a description given by Nabakrishana and others of the Girija that they are talking of. Alternatively, I could take Nabakrishna or some other person who knew her place along with me to Kolkata, so that they could identify the room as being hers. If they could identify the room where the body was found as hers, then we could at least be sure of one thing. Our suspicion that it was Girija who had been killed in that room would be proved wrong. Girija had not been killed. It was some other woman who had been killed in her room while Girija had fled in fear.

My next thought was—if the murder had happened in the room of the same Girija whose house we were now sitting in, and she herself had not been murdered, then who was the woman who had been killed? How could we be sure that woman wasn't Prasanna? How could I be sure, given what I had read in the aforementioned letter, that Prasanna had not in fact gone to Girija's room and the two had not met? Was it not possible that Prasanna had also lost her virtue in the city and that Nabakrishna had gone to

Kolkata, witnessed everything with his own eyes and committed the gruesome deed in a fit of anger?

If my second conjecture was correct, then it was not at all improbable that having witnessed all this, Girija had run away from her own room. But if that were true, how would she dare to come back to her village and then meet Nabakrishna? And would Nabakrishna then ask Girija about Prasanna's whereabouts in front of everyone?

Many such possible and impossible thoughts and suspicions thus began to whirl around in my mind at that time. The great hopes with which I had started this investigation began to slowly ebb away. I was back to wondering what road to take and whom to investigate.

I spent that day in the village in an agitated state of mind. When I got up from where I had been sitting, I was led to the abode of an aged Brahmin who lived nearby. The people who had gathered there took me to his house. Preparations were made for my meals and for my stay. From somewhere milk, fish and curd made an appearance and I have no idea who had acquired these or who paid for them. I tried to pay for them but everyone refused to take any money. It seemed the *chaukidaars* had made all the arrangements. I had the food and spent the night in that house. Then the following day, without having the foggiest about what my next step in the investigation would be, I left the village.

VII

Nabakrishna had told me earlier that Girija lived in the Mathaghasha Lane. He had also said that he hadn't been to Kolkata in the last two years. Hence I didn't want to travel to Kolkata without taking him along. Girija's brother whom I met for the first time in that village had also travelled to Kolkata three months ago and had stayed with her for five or six days. This I had learnt, while I was in the village and so I also asked him to accompany me to the city. In addition, I took down, to the best of my abilities, the details of Girija's physical appearance as described by the villagers.

We arrived in Kolkata, taking the same route that I had taken while going to the village. Then, leaving Nabakrishna in the *thhana* where I worked, I took Girija's brother with me and went to the Mathaghasha Lane. On approaching the lane I said, "Now take us to the house where your Didi used to stay." Hearing this, he started walking ahead of us and then after a while, when he reached the apartment where the murder had happened and from where I had retrieved the letter, he stopped and said, "This is where Didi used to stay and this is where I spent my days when I visited Kolkata." Indeed, many people in that house recognized him when they saw him and said, "He had come and stayed here with Girija for a few days and had introduced himself to everyone as her brother."

One part of the investigation came to an end at this point. Everyone's conclusions were proved wrong. It had been decided that Girija had been killed but now the opposite was proved. Everyone was convinced that Girija was alive. She had gone off somewhere, having informed everyone that she was leaving for a pilgrimage.

Before beginning the second phase of the investigation, we all decided that the corpse could belong to none other than Prasanna. Therefore we all focused our attention on Nabakrishna. We started badgering him and insisting that it was he who had killed Prasanna. Even though there was not one shred of evidence against him, we asserted, "The corpse that was found in Girija's room is Prasanna's. And no one but you could have killed her."

Meanwhile, since no one was paying any attention to Girija's brother, he furtively scarpered off once we turned our attention to Nabakrishna. Later we couldn't find him anywhere in Kolkata. Subsequently, we heard that he had left the city that very day and set off for his village.

The news that Nabakrishna had murdered his wife soon spread like wildfire. The newspapers didn't take long to spread this news everywhere. Everyone got to know that the body that had been earlier identified as being that of Girija was actually not hers; it was someone else's—it was in fact the body of Nabakrishna's wife Prasanna.

However, despite all our suspicions, we weren't able to fulfil the primary requirements of the investigation. For we could not find a single person who could say that they had seen Nabakrishna on the day of the murder or even around that time in Kolkata. And then there was Nabakrishna himself who kept denying the entire thing. He insisted that he had not visited Kolkata and had definitely not murdered his wife. However, despite his vociferous protests, no one was willing to believe him; everyone scoffed at his claims with a dismissive laugh. Thereafter, it was decided that we would go back to his village and meticulously investigate the truth about him. Where exactly was he when this murder had happened? If we could confirm in the course of our investigation that Nabakrishna had been in his village, then it would be proved that he had not killed his wife. Someone other than he had committed the murder. It was also decided that I would be the one to go back to his village and that two other officials would accompany me.

The following day I left Kolkata once again. In due course, we reached Nabakrishna's house. Nabakrishna had told us that he was in his village on the night that the murder had taken place in Kolkata. He had been in the Ghosh household till around midnight that day along with some of his neighbours. It was only after midnight that he had returned home to sleep. His old mother had opened the door for him when he returned.

The news of Nabakrishna's arrest for the murder had preceded our return to his village. Nobody could say who had been the first to carry this news there and yet everyone had heard what had happened. On reaching the village, we first took Nabakrishna to his house. I left him standing with one of the officials at a little distance from the house, and went in to meet his mother. The old woman came out and stood before us as soon as we summoned her. When we asked her whether Nabakrishna had been there at home that night, she failed to give us a proper answer. Instead she started wailing loudly and cried, "Please let my Naba go. We'll leave this place and go somewhere else and beg for a living, if we have to." From time to time she also directed a barrage of vicious abuses at her missing daughter-in-law Prasanna. But there were no proper answers to any of our questions. In fact, she worked herself into such a state at the prospect of her son's imprisonment, that she became more and more incoherent as we spoke to her.

Eventually, we all went to Kaliprasanna Ghosh's house. None of the male residents of that house, it seemed, were in. Whoever we wanted to meet, we were told, had gone out somewhere. It was clear to us that the people of the village were deeply shaken by the new developments and were now refusing to co-operate with us. Everyone we tried to talk to in the village gave us evasive answers. They even denied spending most evenings in the Ghosh household. As such, in those circumstances, it became impossible for us to ascertain what the truth was; we had no way of finding out whether Nabakrishna was guilty or not.

VIII

That day we decided we would spend the night in the village. In the village there was no house other than that of the Ghoshs that could have arranged for our stay. As a result, we decided we had to stay there. None of the men of that house came out as we waited outside the house. After a while, a servant came and said to us, "None of the *babu*s are at home so it's not really possible for you to stay here. Please look for some alternative accommodation." We chose not to pay any attention to the servant's words and continued sitting there. One of us said to him, "Whether your *babu*s are here or not, we are not going to stir from this place. We'll spend the night right here. If you can give us some food, that'll be fine. Else we'll manage without it. We are not going anywhere at this hour."

The servant went in after hearing us out and didn't come out. We entered the drawing room of the house and saw two large mats in a corner of the room. We rolled them out and sat on them. No one came out to greet us. Nor did any of the neighbours peep out. Only a few children from the village stood at some distance, watching us.

After an hour had elapsed in this manner, and everyone realized we were not going to budge from there, the same servant returned to us with some tobacco. My colleagues had a smoking habit so they took the tobacco from him and used it to relax after a long and tiring day. Before long, the servant got us some clean water with which we could wash our hands and feet. We washed ourselves and settled down again on those mats. Eventually arrangements were made for us to eat something. Since in that tiny village there was nothing much available by way of sweets other than the humble *batasha*, the man who had been serving us placed a plate full of *batasha* and a large jug full of potable water near where we were seated and then went back inside. By then it was quite late in the evening. We drank the water and relaxed on the mat. Some of us even lay down. Around that time, a gentleman came out of the house and sat down near us. He seemed to be an important and senior member of that household. After introducing himself to us, he told us that he had had to leave the house for some work earlier in the day and had just returned. He sat with us for a while and soon realized that we were neither behaving rudely with him nor planning to arrest him for the murder. Gradually, after observing all this, many others in that household also summoned up the courage to come and sit with us. The mat, on which we had been sitting with some difficulty, was soon replaced with a comfortable mattress. A wonderful meal was prepared and given to us. A Brahmin appeared from somewhere and cooked for all of us. We ate to our heart's content and then fell asleep over there.

Next morning we could see that no one was afraid of us any longer. When we painstakingly explained to the people in the village why we had gone there and what we wanted to know, we found that they no longer hesitated to tell us whatever they knew about the matter. Some of them told us that Nabakrishna had indeed been in the village that night. Some said that he had been with them till very late on that night in question. There were others who told us that they had seen Nabakrishna in the morning that day. In this manner, one by one, many people gave us whatever information they could about his whereabouts that day. However, we weren't able to decide whether they were telling the truth or had conspired to tell lies in order to protect Nabakrishna.

The people of the village were very pleased with the way in which we treated them. The same people who had refused to talk to us the previous day now pleaded with us to stay on for some more time. They made special arrangements for us to stay another day and we didn't raise any objections.

Around noon we saw a postman arriving at the Ghoshs' house. After delivering a letter to Kaliprasanna Ghosh, he took a seat in the house. Dear readers of Kolkata, you might wonder at this point as to why the postman sat in the house, since they normally go away after delivering letters. In my reply to this question from my Kolkata readers, I would say that most village postmen don't have to spend any money of their own on their meals. For every village has a few houses which the postman can visit for his meals. As such, the postmen make sure that they complete distributing letters in the rest of the village by the afternoon, and then reach such houses in time for their meals. That's the reason why the postman had come and settled down over there.

Kaliprasanna read the letter and then left that place with the letter in his hand. Some others also followed him out at his behest. We couldn't see where they had gone. After about half an hour a man came and said to me, "Kali *babu* wants to say something to you. Please come with me. I'll take you to him." Hearing this without saying another word, I started following that man. When I reached the place to which he took me, which was a room behind the drawing room where we had been sitting earlier, I found Kali *babu* standing there with some five or six other people. As soon as he saw me, he handed the letter to me and said, "Please read it and tell us what you make of it." The letter was written in Bangla. I read it several times and as I read it, I became more and more dismayed. For a few minutes I was rendered speechless and had to sit down to steady myself. As soon as I reveal to my readers what was there in that letter, it'll be clear to them how devastating it was at that point in time for us. This is what was written in that letter:

> I have heard that Nabakrishna has been arrested for having supposedly killed his wife Prasanna in Kolkata. I am not sure if what I've heard is right. But if it indeed is true then that's a terrible thing. If someone is arrested and punished for killing a woman who is very much alive, then there can be no greater injustice than that. I am well known to you and am a relative of Nabakrishna's. I am not going to disclose my name in this letter. For who knows the police might start dragging me into this whole sorry mess. That's why I'm writing to you. If you think it right, please show this letter to the police, else do whatever you feel needs to be done. Prasanna is at her uncle's brother-in-law Rajkumar's house in Shamshay village. She had first come to my house after her quarrel with Nabakrishna and stayed with me for a few days. But then she went off to Rajkumar's house. Even today in the morning I was told by someone that she was still in that house. She has not been murdered and Nabakrishna hasn't killed her.

IX

After reading this letter I was fairly convinced that Prasanna had not been killed; we had been chasing shadows in this investigation up till now. I showed the letter to my colleagues and they also seemed startled upon reading it. That very day we sent Nabakrishna along with one of the officials to the village of Shamshay. That village was a mere fifteen miles away. I waited in this village along with the remaining officials. After three days, that officer returned along with Nabakrishna. And we also saw that the Prasanna, whose murder we had been investigating till now, was also accompanying them. We were all embarrassed by this turn of events and immediately freed Naba. An elated Nabakrishna immediately went back home with his wife.

Quite a few days had elapsed after the murder. We had had to abandon each of the avenues that we had begun exploring as part of the investigation. Now our only hope was Girija herself. Could she tell us something? But where were we going to find her?

Had she written any letters to her brother? Or had he got news of her whereabouts some other way? I decided to find this out before leaving the village once and for all. That very day we set off for Girija's village. We found her brother at home. At first when we questioned him, he looked nervous and denied knowing anything. But then he conceded that he had heard from her lately.

"Where is she now?"

"She is in the Ganesh Mahalla of Kashi in the house of one Chinibash Das. She'll be there for the next eight to ten days before leaving for Vindhyachal, where she wants to pay homage to Vindhyabashini."

"From where did you get all this information?"

"I have a letter written by her from Kashi."

"Where's the letter?"

"I tore it up." This, however, was a lie, and after much persuasion he did produce that letter for us. The address that he had given us was the correct one.

Taking that letter from him, we first came back to Kolkata. I then explained the entire matter to my superior officer and it was decided that I would travel to Kashi. This time there would not be anyone accompanying me; I would have to travel alone. I was familiar with Ganesh Mahalla and so I was able to locate Chinibash Das' house without any difficulty whatsoever. Girija was also in the house at the time and I was able to locate her quite easily. At first, I didn't reveal my true identity to either Chinibash or to Girija. I said to Girija: "Even though you don't know me, I know you. My house is a few miles away from your village. When your brother heard that I was coming here, he asked me to come and meet you. That's why I'm here." However, when Girija started talking to me, her manner made it quite clear to me that she hadn't believed a word that I had said. In fact, she said, "Why, I've got a letter from my brother this very morning and nowhere in it does he mention anything about you."

When I heard her say this, I realized that she must have got to know everything from her brother's letter. As such there was no point lying to her. It would be far better to continue with my investigation by telling her the truth. Especially since I was in one of the places considered holy by all Hindus and visited by Hindu pilgrims, it would be far better to tell the truth rather than to commit the sin of lying in this place. As such, I decided to reveal my true identity to her. It was not easy to behave in a way that was completely different from the style of working that came naturally to us as members of the department that we worked for. It is not easy to abandon the road that one has been habitually traveling on for so long. Even though I vowed to myself that I would not lie any more, right after I disclosed my identity to Girija, the following words tumbled out of my lips, "You have run away after murdering a woman in your room. There is a warrant out for your arrest. We were going from place to place searching for you and finally after learning that you were here, I have come and found you. Now, if you have anything to say you could tell me. Else if I take you back with me to Kolkata, you will definitely hang for the murder."

When I finished speaking, Girija looked pale and ashen-faced. Trembling all over, she soon collapsed on to the floor. Finally, after a long time she said, "I haven't killed anybody and I don't know anything about the murder."

I decided that it was futile to ask her any further questions and therefore took her along with me and left that place. Girija began protesting loudly as I took her from there and also got various people to plead with me on her behalf. Finally, she resorted to a woman's ultimate weapon—tears—and managed to get the entire neighbourhood to gather over there as a result of her loud wailing. However, I refused to pay heed to any of this. Taking her along, I left that place.

I took her with me to a place known as Bangalitola. I used to stay in a house there, whenever I visited Kashi. I took Girija with me to that house for I thought to myself that if I could keep her there with me for questioning, I could use tactics of intimidation or persuasion and get her to reveal the facts that lay behind what had happened. For after all, she was merely an ordinary woman and I was firmly convinced that without anyone to support or advise her, she would be too frightened to hold back the truth from me. This was my plan when I took her to Bangalitola. At first, I tried scaring her into telling me everything but she remained unmoved. Then when I saw that she couldn't be terrorized into saying anything, I tried to sweet-talk her into revealing what had happened that night. I tried every possible means of extracting the truth out of her. I said to her, "If you tell me in a detailed manner all that had happened that day, then I'll try my best to save you from getting involved in the case. I'll make sure that you are spared the death sentence by the judge." After saying all this I asked her several questions, but each time she would give a different answer. I simply couldn't get the truth out of her. Finally, after a day had passed in this manner, I vowed to her that she would be alive after everything came to light. After hearing this, she was satisfied enough to gradually reveal everything to me. Instead of describing all that she said that day in the right order, I have written down the bare facts alone.

X

I was thunderstruck when I heard what Girija told me. She came out with the kind of bizarre account that neither I nor any other officer could have even dreamt of. Girija said, "Sir, while I am not to blame for what you have arrested me, I can't claim to be entirely blameless either. But not even in my wildest dreams could I have imagined that things would go this far. You know all the details of my past life. I'm a widow but I strayed from the path of virtue as a result of various temptations, and was compelled to elope with a man from my village. It was he who had taken me to Kolkata and then after some time, he left me and disappeared. All this happened quite a few years ago. Left with no other choices, I had to start earning my livelihood by working as a housemaid. I started working as a maid in the house of one Bidhu *babu*, but I couldn't forfeit my nature. So I didn't let go of the room that I had rented either. Bidhu *babu* had a widowed daughter whose name was the same as mine. She used to love me with all her heart and used to address me as *Mitin*.[4] Even though she was my employer and I was but a servant, she never treated me as such; indeed, she used to love me like a sister. From time to time she would also tell me the secrets of her heart. In fact, she soon began confiding in me without any reservations; she told me the kind of things about herself that nobody else but she would have known.

My *Mitin* had been a child widow. I don't think she had ever known what it was to be loved by a husband. Her life was destroyed very soon after she stepped into adolescence, in a manner that was reminiscent of mine. And since the wealthy household of which she was a part was forever bustling with people, she just couldn't think of a way to fulfil her desires. That's the reason why she became so very close to me. At the time that I'm talking about, my *Mitin* was no longer very young. But instead of fading away, her youthful desires grew stronger with each passing day. It was upon her instructions that I began spending the nights at her place. I didn't, however, give up my rented room. I didn't have to pay the rent for it; my *Mitin* took take care of everything. Besides taking money for the rent, I also took money from her for various other reasons.

It was around this time that she started going out almost every day to bathe in the Holy Ganges. She wouldn't go unless I accompanied her. Once she stepped out of her house, instead of going to the banks of the River Bhagirathi, she would stop for a while at my rented house. After spending an hour or so over there, she would then go to the sin-cleansing river in order to wash away the sins she had accumulated over the last hour. I am not going to spell out what she would do in my house; you are free to draw your own conclusions.

Many days passed in this manner. Finally, one day, when Bidhu *babu* became suspicious, he fired me from my job and also placed a man as a guard outside my house. From that day on, my meetings with *Mitin* came to an end. I couldn't find her on the banks of the Ganga when I went there in the mornings, and the guards of her mansion wouldn't let me in when I went there asking to meet her. Nobody told me clearly why they were behaving in that manner with me; but in my mind I knew only too well why this had happened.

Eventually I left the room that I had rented, and sought employment in the house that I'm working in at present. Some time later, I met a maid who was working in Bidhu *babu*'s house and after talking for a while, I showed her my new place of work. From her I got news of my *Mitin* and I also requested her to inform her about me.

About two months after this, that housemaid got in touch with me again and gave me this message: 'Girija will be visiting Kalighat next Monday. If possible, be there at that time and you'll be able to meet her.'

The next Monday I asked my employer to grant me leave for a day and went to Kalighat. I met my *Mitin* after a long time over there but we didn't really get the opportunity to speak too much that day. The only thing she said was, 'Rent a place near the road and then meet me again next Monday over here. You can then tell me where you have rented a place.' I followed her instructions, rented the room I am living in at present, and went back to the *ghat* to inform her about it. She left me with the words, 'I'll meet you tomorrow on the banks of the river.'[5]

The next day, early in the morning I reached the banks of the river Ganga. I saw that she had also come over there. I didn't immediately reveal myself and hid myself at some distance. When I saw that she had completed her bath and was getting ready to return home, I started walking ahead of her without turning back to disclose my identity. I had already noticed that there was just one maid accompanying her. Girija started following my footsteps and soon I led her to the lane where I had rented a room. Then I opened the door of my room and went in. *Mitin* took note of where I was staying, but left without saying anything to me.

The next day she knocked on my door at the crack of dawn and I opened it for her. After that, we fell back into our earlier routine and many days were spent in this manner. Finally, that fateful day arrived. Like always, when Hari *babu* and she had entered my room, I had gone and stood outside on the road. When Hari *babu* had left the room and Girija came out, all of a sudden, Bidhu *babu*'s son Ram *babu* sprang out of nowhere and attacked her in the most gruesome manner, with a knife. My poor Girija fell down and soon breathed her last on the road. The place where she died was awash with blood. Then he picked up her lifeless body and dropped it inside my room. He then searched for me everywhere in the room and outside, to punish me in a similar manner. I stood in the shadows next to a gaslight in death-like silence. After a while, having searched for me in vain, he chopped off Girija's head, wrapped it in a *gamchha* and left.[6] I think he completed all this in just two minutes. I was in shock after witnessing everything. Walking very slowly, I stepped into my room, collected whatever money I could and then after shutting the door, I left that room. This is all I know. There's nothing more that I can tell you."

I believed all that Girija told me. I brought her with me to Kolkata. Then I located Bidhu *babu*'s house in the course of the investigation and even managed to meet Ram *babu*. Ram *babu*'s sister, Girija, was not to be found anywhere in that house, but when we made inquiries we were told that she had gone away on a pilgrimage. Ram *babu* was subsequently arrested for the murder. But the case soon got dismissed, thanks to the clever arguments of the Defence Counsel. Besides the maid, Girija, there were no other eye witnesses to the crime. As such, it could not be proved beyond doubt by the prosecution that the corpse was indeed that of Bidhu *babu*'s daughter, Girija. As a result, Ram *babu* was acquitted despite having committed this murder. But the amount of money he ended up spending for his defence was adequate punishment for him. After his release, he was never able to regain his former prosperity. Even though he was not reduced to abject penury, he definitely could no longer be considered a rich man.

Priyanath Mukhopadhyay

Notes

1 The Kaivartyas, a scheduled caste, belonging to the regions of Assam, Bengal and Odisha, were traditionally engaged in the occupation of fishing.
2 In the epic *Mahabharata*, Virat was the king of Matsya and a cow baron, in whose court the Pandavas spent a year in concealment during their exile.
3 *Panchayat* refers to the village council or a governing body usually formed of influential old men of the village.
4 *Mitin* is a term of endearment for a dearly loved friend and is often used by a man for a female friend. It is clear from the account that the maid Girija gives to the *daroga* that both she and her employer's daughter (also Girija) think of the other as *Mitin*. There is also a tantalizingly vague hint at same-sex love between the two Girijas in her account which remains unexplored and attenuated.
5 *Ghat* refers to the banks of a river.
6 *Gamchha* refers to a piece of cloth used as a towel.

10

'PROMODA'

'(Havoc wreaked by a wife's illicit liaison)'
Darogar Daftar, Jyeshth
(mid-May–mid-June), 1895

I

Nabakumar Basu used to live in the Bosepara area of the village of Santoshpur. His house was on the western border of the village. On the eastern side of the house was a large bamboo grove that ended somewhere close to where the Muslim neighbourhood began. Anyone wanting to visit Bosepara had to use a narrow path that cut through the grove. The back gate of Nabakumar's house was on that path. There was no prohibition on anyone using that lane at any time of the day.

There was a small, old pond as well near the back gate. It remained dry on most days, except during the monsoon and at present, it had become choked with weeds and other rubbish. A corpse was lying in that pond next to the path. And *daroga* Bansiram was sitting on a stool near that lane and noting down the details of the corpse.

Bansiram asked the people who had gathered around him, "Can anyone tell me whose body this is?" Someone from the crowd then said, "Nabakumar is known to all of us. He and his forefathers have all lived in this very village. So we can all recognize this body as being that of Nabakumar Bose."

The village had six *chaukidars* all of whom were also present at that spot. They too confirmed that the body was indeed that of Nabakumar. The *daroga* then wrote down, "After being identified by many people of Santoshpur, it has now been verified that the body found here is that of one Nabakumar Bose."

After this *daroga* Bansiram got up from the stool and went and stood near the body. After examining the limbs of the corpse very carefully, he then turned to the member of the *panchayat* standing over there and said to him, "You have also been looking at the body quite carefully. Now tell me, do you have any ideas as to what might have happened?"

Panchayat member: "It's quite obvious that he has been killed by someone."

Bansiram: "That we can all see. But based on the wounds that you see on the body, tell me what you think was the kind of weapon that has been used."

"I can definitely guess that a very sharp weapon was used. Perhaps a sword; for it looks like the weapon first wounded the right shoulder and then was dragged in a crooked manner across the chest towards the left side."

"There is no doubt that it was a sharp-edged weapon. But I don't think that a sword was used. Certain parts of the right shoulder haven't been split open by the blow; some parts of the flesh are still intact. That wouldn't have been the case, if it had been a sword. I think it was probably not a sword but a smaller but fairly heavy weapon used. It was quite likely to have been a *dao*."[1]

Member of the *panchayat*: "That's possible. But from where did the blow come and what, I wonder, was Nabakumar doing while it happened?"

"You have asked the very question that I was going to raise. What do you think?"

"I don't think Nabakumar was asleep when the blow fell. I think he was sitting down when it happened. Don't you think the wound looks like that of a person who was struck while he was sitting? As you can see, the collar bone hasn't been shattered as much as the neck."

"But what if just the opposite happened? That is, if Nabakumar was struck from behind with a sharp *dao*, wouldn't it have caused a similar wound? Especially since there seems to have been no reason for Nabakumar to be sitting on the path. And there's no doubt that the murder took place on the lane. Else, why would the soil over there be soaked in blood?"

"I think what you are suggesting is also quite possible. In which case the murderer could not have been a young boy or a man of a small frame."

"That's for sure. Nabakumar wasn't of a short stature. His killer would have been at least as tall as him, if not a bit taller, and definitely a strong man. For the wound suggests that his life was ended with just one blow."

"But if the murder was committed on the road, how did the corpse travel to the pond?"

"That's easy enough to answer. The murder would have come to light much faster if the body had lain on the path; that's why the killer moved it a little and threw it into the pond."

"If that is the case, then the murder couldn't have been committed by one person alone. It would have been impossible for a single person to have lifted the body and thrown it into the pond. Under the circumstances, we have to assume there were two or more people involved."

Bansiram said, "This wouldn't have been an impossible task for one person. For don't you see the marks left on the blood-spattered lane? They suggest that a heavy load like a human corpse had been dragged and pulled over that place. If it had been two or three people, there wouldn't have been any need to drag the body in that manner. It was because he was alone that this kind of dragging happened and left marks."

"Sir, if you don't mind, may I ask you a question? The question is perhaps a bit impertinent and might offend you."

"You don't know my nature, which is why you are saying this. You think I'll be offended by one question of yours? You can go ahead and shower me with a volley of abuses and you'll see that I won't be the least bit perturbed. So tell me whatever you want to say, without any hesitation."

"Ever since I have started working as a member of the *panchayat*, whenever I have got the opportunity, I have closely watched the ways in which investigations have been carried out by officers like you in this area. Till now, none of them has asked my opinion and so I haven't talked to them about anything. Since you have asked me to make a few suggestions, I feel emboldened to ask you this question. Till date, we have just not been able to understand why, when you people begin an investigation, do you waste so much time in searching for answers to all sorts of irrelevant questions instead of focusing on finding the murderer? Take this case for example. Nabakumar has been killed, but ever since you began the investigation have you wondered even once about the identity of the killer? Your attention has not been drawn to that question at all. Rather you seem to be maundering on about unimportant issues like what the weapon might have been, whether Nabakumar was sitting or standing at the time, if the blow was struck from the back or the front, etc. Instead of conjecturing and arguing about such things, if you simply focused on catching the killer, surely you'd get the answers to all such questions from him. In my opinion, rather than wasting one's time on these questions, it would be far more fruitful to investigate who has committed this murder."

The *daroga* heard him out, laughed a little and then said, "You are all simple, rustic folk and so you have asked me this question in your natural, forthright manner. If I focused my investigation on tracking down the killer, then would such useless matters be necessary?! Well if police officers were omniscient and capable of looking into the past and the future, we wouldn't have needed to investigate anything! As soon as a crime is committed, we would have marched to the scene and then taken the criminal to court. But unfortunately we haven't been blessed with such divine powers and that's the reason one has to ask the kind of questions that you dismiss as being useless. Otherwise we'll never be able to decide how to get to the road leading up to the truth. It's from all the irrelevant-seeming issues that we are able to sift the relevant facts. As an example, why don't we take this present investigation. If it were certain that the murder was committed with the help of a sword, then would you be able to tell me who all in this village or in villages nearby possess swords? And then how long, do you think, would it have taken us to discover which one of those swords was used to commit the murder?

If, for instance, it's decided that the killer had attacked Nabakumar frontally, then don't you think even you could have told me that the motive of the murder was not a secret, given that the killer attacked him openly like a hero in a battlefield? And you would also have been able to tell me immediately who would be likely to have vengeful motives for doing such a thing to him. Besides, you would also have told me that Nabakumar, on seeing his attacker before him, may not have been able to resist his blows, but had shouted loudly to awaken his neighbours. But now that we can conjecture that the blow came from behind, then this has to be the work of a secret enemy of his. If it's decided that it was a secret enemy who killed him, then don't you think we'll be able to nab this secret enemy only if our investigation is conducted in secret?

Furthermore, if it is concluded that the murder was committed by more than one person, then the investigation will have to be carried out in ways that would be very different from an investigation into murder by a single person. I don't think I have been able to explain all this in a very satisfactory manner; perhaps I don't have the ability to convince you. But those who have spent nearly their entire lives doing this will immediately understand what I'm trying to say.

It is based on such minute details that we have to decide who the protagonists of a case are, and therefore there's nothing for it but to be extremely meticulous in finding out those very things that irritate you about an investigation. That's why before being able to nab the culprit, we first need to focus on many things that might seem totally irrelevant to you. It's only when we are able to get some leads from these observations that the case moves towards a solution and miscreants are unable to evade punishment. In the absence of any leads, the investigation hits a rough patch."

The member of the *panchayat* fell silent after hearing Bansiram's speech. Without uttering another word he then accompanied the *daroga* and watched him intently as he went about examining the crime scene, the position of the corpse, etc.

II

Besides the aforementioned wound on Nabakumar's body, there was another one that was clearly visible at the back of his head. It seemed that as soon as Nabakumar had fallen on the ground face down, after being hit the first time, a second blow had been struck to the back of his head. The first blow had been enough to kill Nabakumar so there had been no need to strike him a second time. Except for these two wounds there was no other mark visible anywhere else on the rest of his body.

With the help of a few people, Bansiram dragged the corpse out of the pond and placed it on the path nearby. He then began to look closely at the spot from where the body was removed. For he thought that he might be able find the murder weapon or some other thing that would help his case, in that place. But despite a great deal of searching, he was unable to find anything there. The only things that could be extricated from the pond were an old pair of sandals and a *gamchha*. There were no bloodstains on the sandals but it seemed as if someone had used the *gamchha* to wipe their hands and possibly also the blood-smeared weapon.

Pausing the investigation for a while, Bansiram entered Nabakumar's house.

The house had been inhabited by Nabakumar and his young wife Promoda. Even though Nabakumar was not very old, he used to look quite ancient. He had been no more than fifty at the time that he died, but having suffered from several painful diseases over the last twenty years, he had aged before his time. Promoda on the other hand was just twenty-five years old. At the time of her marriage she had been a mere slip of a girl. However, her father being a man of little means, had fixed her marriage with Nabakumar despite the enormous difference in their age. Nabakumar had no other family living with him and a *boishnobi* had become the mistress of his household, for all intents and purposes; as such no one else in the village wanted him as a groom for their daughters.[2] Besides, as long as the *boishnobi* was alive, Nabakumar had made no attempts to get married. It was after she had died that the wedding had taken place with the help of some Kayastha men in the village.

When Bansiram *daroga* entered Nabakumar's house, several people from the village entered along with him. Inside the house, Bansiram found Promoda sitting in the inner courtyard with many other women of the neighbourhood and wailing loudly at the demise of her husband. Upon seeing Bansiram and the others, Promoda and the other women immediately went inside the house. As Bansiram stood in the courtyard and asked her a few preliminary questions, he received her answers through an elderly woman who was sitting there with Promoda. Bansiram got to know that when Nabakumar had left the house the previous evening, he was dressed in a *dhoti*, his feet shod in old sandals and there was a *gamchha* placed on his shoulder. There was nothing unusual about his leaving the house at that time. Every evening around that time he would go to Ramsundar Ghosh's house and sit in his drawing room. He would then return at nine or ten, eat and go to sleep.

Bansiram then asked her, "Did he come back and have his meal last night?"

The old woman (conveying Promoda's answer): No, he didn't come back home last night. So how could he have eaten?

Bansiram: When you saw that it was getting very late and there was no sign of Nabakumar anywhere, did you try to look for him?

The old woman/Promoda: I am a woman! How could I have searched for him in the dead of night?

"The place where Nabakumar died is not very far from your house. And when he was getting killed, he must have tried to defend himself or raise some sort of an alarm. Surely there was some noise that you heard? How is it possible that you were completely unaware of what was happening?"

"No, I heard nothing. I had fallen asleep quite early."

"So when did you realize what had happened? At what time of the night did you find out that he was dead?"

"It was early in the morning that I heard voices outside and that's when I went out and saw that my life had been destroyed."

"You said that every night Nabakumar would return home and eat his dinner. Last night he didn't come back or eat anything. So where's his dinner? May I see it?"

"Last night I wasn't feeling well so I didn't cook anything for him."

"Those are not the principles of a Hindu's wife. Even if Hindu women are dying, they don't fail to prepare food for their husbands. And even when its nigh on impossible for them to cook, they manage to arrange for something that their husbands can eat. What was your illness last night?

"I had a terrible headache. That's why I couldn't cook for my husband."

"You said just now that you had fallen asleep early. But it's not possible to sleep early if one has a terrible headache, is it?"

Instead of answering this question, Promoda began to wail loudly and once it became clear that it would be futile to press her any further for answers, everyone gradually dispersed from that place.

Soon after leaving Nabakumar's house, Bansiram set off to meet Ramsundar Ghosh. At Ramsundar's house he was told that Nabakumar had indeed been there till late in the evening. It was around nine that he had set off, all by himself, to return home. This had been his routine for quite some time.

Bansiram then became preoccupied with the routine work of the investigation, like sending the body for postmortem and sitting down with various people in the village to take down their statements. But even after three days of doing this, he was unable to ascertain the identity of the person who had first seen the corpse. Everyone claimed that before them, many others had already seen it. It became impossible for Bansiram to figure out who was lying.

But then it's not just Bansiram who has to go through such experiences. Any police officer tasked with investigating a crime, finds himself facing such situations. Most people in this country have very little faith in the workings of the police and as such are extremely reluctant to open up to them. What if the truth leads to their getting dragged into unnecessary police-related complications? Hence, what better adage to live by than "the dumb has no enemies"?

After three days of trying in vain to find out what had happened, when Bansiram was sitting and wondering what to do, another police officer arrived at that place to help him out. He was an officer who was of the same rank as Bansiram, called *daroga* Shyamacharan. Shyamacharan and Bansiram had become close friends over years of working together as police officers and they had solved quite a few difficult cases. As a result, the two of them were greatly valued by their superiors. Bansiram was extremely relieved upon seeing Shyamacharan; he felt elated at having someone by his side, with whom he could discuss the case. The two of them sat together in a secluded spot and talked at length about the case. Finally at the end of their discussions, Bansiram handed over all the papers that contained his observations on the case over the past three days to Shyamacharan, and said, "I have done my best; I doubt I can make any further headway in this case. Please do whatever you can to solve it. I'll leave." Bansiram then summoned his footman and told him to get his horse ready for departure from that place.

The news that one *daroga* had failed to solve the case and had been replaced by another spread like wildfire through the entire village. Soon most of the villagers left whatever they were doing at the time and gathered to see what the new *daroga* would do. Small children stood around him and stared intently. All those who had been watching Bansiram's activities till then, forgot about him and turned their attention to the new *daroga*.

The *daroga* began his investigation in the manner that was customary at the time. He asked an excited and noisy audience to gather around him and began proceedings. The first thing he did was to assault a poor and timid-looking village *chaukidar* who was sitting there. He summoned the poor fellow and then, citing some flimsy reason, rained a few blows and kicks on him. The *chaukidar* quaked with fear as he shook off the dust from his emaciated frame, before moving away to sit down at a distance. The rest of the *chaukidars* also looked terrified and they all sat down in a frightened huddle. It was not clear to anyone, least of all to the *chaukidar* himself, why he had been suddenly accosted and humiliated in that manner. But then in our country, this kind of behaviour is hardly unusual in those who have wealth or the power to intimidate others. Who keeps count of the number of poor people who are bullied and insulted by the rich and the powerful on a regular basis?

However, even though no one could understand why the *chaukidar* had been beaten up in that manner, I am fairly certain I know the reasons for his doing what he did. Shyamacharan had realized that the *chaukidars* were taking the side of the villagers and were being secretive even about the things that they knew quite well. Hence their answer to every question was, "I don't know anything about this." That's the reason why Shyamacharan decided that a few blows were necessary to make them cough up the truth.

Meanwhile, after the footman had brought Bansiram's horse to him, he had bid everyone farewell, and got up on his horse. He then struck the animal with a whip and it began to run as fast as it could along with its rider, and before long both rider and horse disappeared completely. Those who had gathered to watch him leave, stood there and looked on till they could no longer see any traces of either the horse or its rider.

III

In the south of Santoshpur, there flowed a tiny river. In the past, the river had a great deal of water which flowed with strong currents. A lot of boats carrying cargo for trade used to sail on it. But, over time, the river had changed. It no longer flowed with strong currents and parts of it had dried up completely so that people could actually cross it quite easily on foot. The river barely had the depth that it used to have at one time. It looked fairly full during the rainy season, but with the onset of summer, most of the water dried up and very little of it remained.

For the people of Santoshpur, and even for its cows and other animals, the river was the only source of water. They had no other choice but to go to the river for their daily requirement of water. They all took their bath in that river. And there was no other source of drinking water anywhere for miles. Most mornings, the village folk would wend their way to the dying river for their ablutions. And in the evenings, young women would gather on its banks and, after washing their hands and feet, would fill their brass vessels and return home. This was pretty much the routine for most villagers.

A few days after the discovery of Nabakumar's corpse, some women of the village were taking their usual bath in the river. Dear readers (both male and female)! You know the nature of the women of our country only too well; no sooner do a few of them get together at one place, than they find it impossible to keep the doors leading to their thoughts firmly shut. So how can I say that they were washing themselves and filling their vessels, without uttering a word to each other?

One of them said, "Did you see that? What can be more important in the whole wide world than one's husband?"

Second woman: "There wouldn't have been anything to worry about, would there, if everyone realized this truth? If that were to happen, this world would turn into a heavenly place and we would all enjoy even greater delights here than those available in paradise."

Third woman: "Well, this may not be paradise yet, and perhaps not everyone serves their husbands as though their lives depend on it, but this is something that one has neither seen nor heard before. The woman's husband has died in this terrible manner and yet one sees nary a tear in her eye! How shamelessly she goes around talking and laughing with everyone as if nothing at all has happened. Why when so many people die every day, does

Yama (the God of Death) not see this girl for what she is and take her away?"

Fourth woman: "You are all completely wrong. What I have heard is that women of questionable morals, who are forever eyeing other men, have neither compassion nor any sense of right and wrong. They forget that their husbands are their gods and behave very badly with them. Don't you people know Promoda? Have you ever seen her serving her husband? So why are you all so shocked by the fact that she has neither shown any grief at his death nor shed a single tear? And what about that wretched Hari! His father begged him for so long to get married but he stuck to his guns and refused to listen to him. God alone knows what kind of spell the witch has cast on him."

Fifth woman: "Have you heard the latest? It seems the wretch ran away from our village the very day that Nabakumar got killed. The witch is frantic with worry about him! Shame on her! She refused to shed a tear for that precious husband of hers even when she saw the state that he was in. But haven't you seen how agitated she was for the other man? I have never heard such a thing till now, let alone see anything like this!"

First woman: "What did you say? That wretch has run away from our village? Do you think it's possible that it was he who killed Promoda's husband? And if that's the case, without doubt, Promoda knows what actually happened."

Conversing in this manner, the women who had gathered on the banks of the river washed themselves and then, balancing their water-filled vessels on their hips, began to walk back in a row towards the village. So engrossed were they in their conversation that none of them paid any attention to their surroundings.

Near that same spot from where they had drawn water, there was a thicket of overgrown weeds. As soon as the women left that place, a figure emerged from behind the thicket and began to follow them at some distance. The women discussed the case as they walked homewards. Based on his clothes and mannerisms, the man who followed them also looked like a rustic fellow from a nearby village. His feet were bare, and all he was wearing was a soiled *dhoti* without a *chadar* covering his torso; on his shoulder was a *gamchha* and in his hand a small brass vessel.

All of them entered the village as darkness began to fall. And once they parted ways in the dark, none of them could see who took which path.

That very night a *chaukidar* brought a letter for *daroga* Shayamacharan, who meanwhile had also been appointed as investigating officer for the case. Shyamacharan opened the letter, read it and then placed it very carefully in his pocket. Then he asked his footman to prepare his horse. Everyone who heard him thought he was about to leave that place on some important assignment and would return to the investigation the following day.

There was a village called Rainagar which was a few miles away from Santoshpur. There was a room (*phnaarighar*) for visiting police officers in that village. Whenever any *daroga*s came into that area for any work, they would stay in that room.

Shyamacharan rode his horse and reached that *phnaarighar* in Rainagar all alone. After alighting from his horse, he entered the room and when he found a figure recumbent on a charpoy inside, exclaimed, "Is that you Bansiram *Dada*?! Are you asleep?"

Bansiram: "Who is it? Is that you Shyamacharan? I'm so glad you are here. I fell asleep waiting for you. Have you been able to find any leads that'll help the case?"

Shyamacharan: "This case is actually not my responsibility, *Dada*! It's yours. I am merely holding the fort and waiting to see how my *Dada* solves the case."

Bansiram: "After a long time, it's looking like this case might actually get solved. Earlier in the evening today I visited Santoshpur in disguise and hid near that dying river. After a while, some women of that village had come to the river to fill their vessels. From what I could hear of their conversation, I am fairly certain now that Nabakumar's wife knows more than she's letting on. It's impossible for a Hindu woman of these parts to remain silent if she knows anything about her husband's murder, but for an unchaste wife anything's possible. If what I have heard is true—if indeed Nabakumar's wife was involved in an illicit relationship with a fellow named Hari, and if that Hari went missing right after the day of the murder, then this case should not take long to be resolved. Who is this Hari? Whose son is he? Where does he live and did he actually have an affair with Promoda? I want you to investigate properly and meet me tomorrow with proper answers to these questions. You'll find me in this very place tomorrow night. Based on what you find, we'll then decide what our next step is going to be."

After listening to Bansiram, Shyamacharan sat there with him discussing the case for some time and then, after a while, took his leave.

The next day, Shyamacharan met Bansiram at the appointed hour. Bansiram got to know from him that Promoda had indeed been having an affair with Hari and that the young man had disappeared from the village the day after the murder. Nobody in the village or even in his family seemed to know where he had gone. And even if someone did have information about his whereabouts, they refused to breathe a word to the *daroga*.

IV

How very tough it is to predict the workings of an unchaste woman's twisted mind! They can wreak such havoc with the lies that come tripping off their tongues! It was for this very reason that Bansiram didn't dare to interview Promoda by himself. He decided that he would seek the help of a few people in that village, before he talked to her. Early one morning Bansiram went back to the village with some other police officers in tow. Shyamacharan was already there. Taking along a few important men of the village, they then went to Nabakumar's house. Promoda was not at home at that time; she had gone to visit someone in the neighbourhood. But she came soon after being summoned. Having heard that the police had come to her house again, she came accompanied by some elderly women from the neighbouring houses.

Her plan was to use one of them again as a mediator in her interview with the police. But this time Bansiram didn't agree to this arrangement and said, "Previously when I had taken Promoda's statement, I had used a mediator for the interview since I was under the impression that I was talking to a respectable Hindu woman, the wife of Nabakumar Basu. I had no reason to be dissatisfied with the answers that the woman speaking on her behalf had provided at the time. But today we are not here to take the statement of a respectable and virtuous Hindu woman, the widow of Nabakumar; today we have come here to unravel the horrific mystery behind Promoda's pernicious perfidy. So today I don't need anyone else's help. I request all you respectable ladies who have come here to return to your homes. Today it won't be necessary for someone to speak on Promoda's behalf and explain her side of the story to us. Promoda is more than capable of answering our questions herself."

The gentlemen from the village who had accompanied Bansiram to Nabakumar's house bristled inwardly upon hearing this. They had taken special care to ensure that nothing about Promoda's affair would reach the *daroga*'s ears. It was due to their instructions that no one in the village had uttered a single word about the matter to the police. None of the people who gave their statement to the police had uttered a word about it, and even the village *chaukidar*s had kept quiet about the matter despite knowing everything about it.

Even though Bansiram could sense the villagers' displeasure, he ignored them and pressed on. He focused on the work for which he had been sent to the village.

At first, he asked Promoda a couple of questions but when she refused to give any answers, he said, "Look Promoda, we are investigating a murder. When we ask you questions, you are bound by law to provide us with correct answers. If in fact we were to act upon the kind of information that we have collected about you, we wouldn't be obliged to treat you in a respectable manner in front of all these people in the village. We could simply arrest you and drag you from here to the police station and conduct the rest of the interview over there. The reason why we are treating you with a modicum of respect, despite knowing that you are unchaste, is because all said and done, you are the wife of a respectable person. But if you refuse to give us truthful answers, we'll have to take you to our *thhana* for the rest of the interrogation."

After listening to Bansiram, Promoda said in a very soft voice, "Please ask me what you need to. I'll answer your questions to the best of my abilities. There's no need to take me to the *thhana.*"

Bansiram then said to her, "That's good. Why did you, a Hindu woman, behave in the way that you did towards your husband?"

Promoda: "What do you mean? What behaviour are you talking about? I have never behaved badly towards my husband."

"Isn't it true that you have never loved your husband?"

"That's a lie."

"Why is it then that everyone in this village says that your husband suspected you of being unfaithful to him?"

"That's also a lie."

"I have heard that one night your husband had caught you with another man in your room and there had been quite an uproar. Isn't that true?"

"Neither did my husband catch me with another man in the house, nor was there any uproar."

"Are you saying that all the things that people say about your character are false?"

By then Promoda was no longer speaking in the soft tones that she had begun with. Her voice had gradually become quite loud. And the veil that had been covering her face when she began speaking had slowly slipped and her entire face was visible to everyone who was gathered there. Upon hearing Bansiram's last question she cried, "These are all lies. Blatant lies! My enemies are conspiring against me. Tell me who, amongst all these people who have come here with you to watch the fun, is a gentleman?! There's nothing that they won't say or do to harm me."

Bansiram: "I hear you. Well, if these people are your enemies, what about Hari? Surely he's not your enemy. Where's Hari?"

"Hari? Who is Hari? I don't know any Hari so how can I tell you where he is?"

"The Hari for whom your heart yearns all the time. The same Hari whose departure from the village made you so agitated and anxious that you forgot to grieve for your dead husband Nabakumar. Are you saying you don't know that Hari?"

"No, I don't know any such person. Do I have to say I know him, even though I don't?"

Bansiram went on, "Just a few days ago, Nabakumar had returned home at an unexpected time and seen Hari inside your room. Seeing him, Hari had scurried away to save his life. And later, when Nabakumar vowed to kill both of you, even you ran away from the house and took refuge elsewhere. And now you say you don't know Hari?"

"Yes! I'll say it again. I don't know any Hari."

"Well, we'll find out in a little while whether you recognize him or not. And that's when you'll also find out that an ordinary woman like you can never outwit *daroga* Bansiram. You'll find out that Bansiram *daroga* never leaves a job assigned to him unfinished. Look here Promoda, you are just a woman. Whether you committed this miurder because you were overcome by your feminine impulsures, or because you didn't know any better, or because you were acting upon someone's advice, it's best that you don't hide anything from me. Consider this my final warning, in front of all these gentlemen as witnesses: if Bansiram wants, he can save you and if he wishes he can also see you hang."

"You are police officers and I know that you have the power to twist things around and make them appear completely different from what they actually are. But why should I lie? Why should I admit to something that I don't know and ruin my reputation? I know nothing and if I had known something I would definitely have told you right now and avoided all this humiliation in front of this audience."

Bansiram listened to what she said and realised that Promoda was not like the women that he usually met in his line of duty. Special plans would have to be devised in order to make her spill the beans. Ruminating in this manner, he left the place along with all the other gentlemen who had gone there with him. Promoda was left alone in the house. But a policeman was posted outside the house to keep an eye on her. As a result, it became difficult for visitors to go into the house and it was almost impossible for Promoda to go out as and when she pleased.

The following day, Bansiram disappeared from the village. No one knew where he had gone or when he would be returning. Perhaps Shyamacharan had some information about his whereabouts, but we are not certain about this. He didn't say anything to anyone about it.

V

Ramlochan Ghosh's house was in Santoshpur. He had built the house when he had immense wealth but as his wealth declined, the house had also gradually fell into a state of disrepair and at present most of the rooms seemed to be in a run-down condition.

After about twenty days of the discovery of Nabakumar's corpse, four or five people were gathered in Ramlochan's old, decrepit house. One of the men sitting there said to another, "Hari! Is everything that you've told me so far, the truth? If there's anything false in what you've said, tell me right now."

The other person answered, "Believe me, everything that I have told you is completely true. Not one word is false."

"True or false, I have heard all that you have said. But I am giving you a very serious warning. Don't try to lie to us. Talk to us only if you're interested in telling us the truth. I'm leaving this room now but the others who are here will take your statement. Rest assured that when they hear you speak, they'll have no problem in discerning whether you are lying and deceiving them or telling the truth."

After saying all this, the first person left the room. Dear readers, have you guessed who the person might be? He's none other than the old *daroga* Bansiram whom you have all got to know so well.

Once Bansiram exited from the room, one of the men sitting inside took out a pen and a piece of paper and asked, "What's your name?"

"My name is Harimohan Ghosh and I stay in this village."

"Would you like to volunteer any information about the murder of Nabakumar Bose?"

"Yes, I would."

"What would you like to tell us? Go ahead."

The man called Hari then said, "Sir, my house is in this very village of Santoshpur. My father is still alive. I used to know the deceased Nabakumar very well. He had great affection for me and as a result I would go to his house quite often. Nabakumar's wife Promoda would not seem bashful when I visited the house, nor was she embarrassed about coming out in front of me. Without bothering about whether it was morning or evening, I would visit their house as and when I felt like it.

But whenever I went, I would find Nabakumar at home. At first, when he fell ill, he couldn't leave the house or move about too much. Subsequently, as his disease started to become incurable, he couldn't leave the house to go anywhere far. All he could manage to do was to visit people in the neighbourhood in the evenings.

Oh Sir! My tongue begins to fall silent and my entire body trembles as I begin to recount that terrible day when the poison tree was planted. That day I had visited Nabakumar's house at exactly seven in the evening. I couldn't see Nabakumar anywhere after stepping into the courtyard and there was no answer from him even when I called out his name. Promoda was doing some work inside the house and when she heard my voice she said, 'Please wait for a while! I'm coming in a moment.' I sat in the courtyard after hearing her words. But Promoda asked me to wait inside. I thought that she might be in the habit of cleaning the courtyard in the evening and therefore wanted me to move from there. So I got up and went indoors and sat on a mattress. At that time, dusk had just begun to fall and the inside of the house was turning quite dark. When I sat in the dark room, Promoda stepped into the room with an earthen lamp in her hand but the lamp was extinguished as soon as she came in. I have no idea whether it was *Pavan*, the wind god, being mischievous, or Promoda herself who was responsible for the lamp being put out. Promoda then went out of the room with the lamp and returned after a while, having lit it again. As soon as she entered the room, she exclaimed, 'Goodness! Will the wretched wind not leave the lamp in peace?!' With these words she locked the room from inside. There were now only two people in that lamp-lit room—Promoda and me!

That day, I completely lost my head thanks to the havoc wreaked by Promoda, whom till then I had never looked at with evil intentions or suspected of being anything but a virtuous woman. I threw off all sense of right and wrong and allowed myself to go along with her nefarious wishes. I kicked away all good morals that I had accumulated over the years, and plunged headlong into the sea of pleasures that Promoda had opened up for me. Alas! From that very day I forgot everything else and became detached from all my other emotional attachments, be it my mother's love or my father's affection. I began to feel the opposite of the regard and love, that I had earlier felt for Nabakumar. In fact, I looked for opportunities when Nabakumar would not be present in the house. I wanted nothing else but to have Promoda before my eyes all the time. She was also madly in love with me. If for some reason I failed to go to her house even on a single day or get delayed due to work, she would find some excuse for arriving at my house and departing only after she had got news about me. Gradually things came to such a pass that our secret affair didn't remain a secret; word about it began to spread from one to the other, and soon it reached almost everyone's ears. Before long, even Nabakumar heard about it. Every little thing made him suspect his wife. He also started despising me and soon after, he prohibited me from visiting their house. But then if the mistress of the house decides to favour someone, can that person be barred from the house? Promoda always managed to send me a message when Nabakumar stepped out of the house. Late in the night, when Nabakumar had fallen asleep and was dead to the world, I would get my message. Indeed, whenever she got the opportunity, Promoda would call me to the house.

A few days passed in this manner. Our sins overflowed all bounds of propriety and began to acquire terrifying forms. Nabakumar refused to tolerate this ignominy for too long. He had just recovered from his illness and was regaining his strength. As such, there was no reason why he should have gone on tolerating any of this. He started keeping a strict vigil. He would enter the house unannounced, or would suddenly wake up at odd hours from what had seemed like deep sleep. At times, he would feign sleep and watch Promoda's activities covertly. He even caught me a couple of times in his house at an unconventional time. And then one day, when he caught me with Promoda in the same room, he tried to kill me. But he didn't succeed. Both Promoda and I managed to escape from the house and save our lives. But everyone in the village came to know about this. Most of the villagers supported Nabakumar and even tried to help him catch me. In the midst of all this, I somehow succeeded in meeting Promoda one day with great difficulty. She begged me to elope with her from the village. But I didn't pay heed to her pleas and instead said to her, 'Since everyone in the village is against me, how and where will I survive after running away with you? We'll be caught sooner rather than later. And then we'll be humiliated in every possible manner and who knows, we might even be sent to jail.' Promoda agreed with this and then said, 'We'll need to think of some other way. Unless we find a way to be free of Nabakumar, we will have no hope left of being able to savour the pleasures that we have been enjoying till now.' She further added that she would think about it, come up with a solution and find a way to convey it to me and then we would act accordingly.

After this exchange, I just couldn't get a chance to talk to Promoda for the next seven or eight days. We only saw each other from afar and conversed through signs.

Finally, one day we decided that we would meet in the copse near Promoda's house. Promoda would often go there whenever she needed to answer nature's call. That evening I sought shelter in that place and soon enough Promoda also came to the spot where I was hiding. We sat together in the dark for a while.

VI

After we had sat for some time in that silent copse, Promoda gradually revealed the plan that she had come up with, to free us from Nabakumar's clutches. Given that women are known for their tender hearts, I could never dream, let alone expect to hear a woman come up with something like that! There were goosebumps all over my body and I felt dizzy when I heard what she had to say; in fact, I even fainted for a while. This is what Promoda had to say: 'Hari! I've thought about this long and hard and I have decided that till such time as this wretched man is not eliminated from our lives, we will not be able to fulfil our wishes. I know that I'll be a widow when he dies, but I feel that for me widowhood is a welcome thing. How can a woman want the long life of a husband whom she loathes with all her heart and whose very sight fills her with burning rage? I know that it's only in his absence that our road to lifelong joy will be clear and I'll be able to spend the rest of my days with you in great happiness. Nowadays the wretched man goes out quite often in the evenings. If he's killed at the time when he is making his way back home in the night, then all our problems will be solved. For if he's murdered in the dark, no one will know the killer's identity. And no police officer will believe that a Hindu woman could kill her husband or aid and abet the murder. You don't have to worry in the least, for they'll never suspect you. I'll make all the necessary arrangements and all you need to do is wait near the small gate at the back. As soon as you see him, strike a hard blow from the back and end his life. I'll be nearby, so don't worry."

After telling me all this, Promoda left the place and before she left, it was decided that the deed would be done that very night while Nabakumar was on his way back home.

Perhaps it's a little difficult for everyone to understand how hard it is for a man to disregard the wishes of his beloved, especially if it's one with whom he is utterly infatuated. Only those who have been in my situation might understand what I'm talking about. Even though I wasn't convinced about Promoda's plan, I simply couldn't say no to her. It was almost as if some inexplicable force drew me to the back gate of her house that night and I found myself sitting next to the pond in the dark. I can't describe to you the kind of thoughts that were racing through my mind, as I sat there. I had abandoned all sense of good and evil, and perhaps had even lost my mind. And just then, Promoda got a very sharp axe from somewhere, placed it in my hand and then sat quietly next to me.

After a while we saw Nabakumar returning home. As soon as he crossed the spot where we were hiding, I began to follow him with the axe. I even tried to hit him with all my strength but I failed and the axe fell from my shaking hands. Nabakumar turned around at the sound that the axe made when it dropped to the ground. He saw two figures in the dark, but couldn't see who we were. To begin with, his suspicions weren't aroused, and he simply asked, 'Who are you?' Before I could gather my wits, the answer, 'It's me, Hari!' slipped out of my mouth inadvertently. Upon hearing my name, Nabakumar was beside himself with anger and advanced towards me in an attacking manner. When he was almost about to catch hold of me, the witch couldn't bear it any longer and, picking up the axe from where it had fallen, aimed a powerful blow at his head. Immediately after that, Nabakumar's blood-drenched corpse fell to the ground. Unable to watch anything more than this, I fled from that place as fast as I could.

After this, I lost all desire to stay a moment longer in the village. After collecting some clothes and a bit of money from home, I left the village that night and ran away to save my life. Eventually I was caught by Bansiram *daroga* and brought here. After that incident I have not set eyes on Promoda. So I don't really know what happened after the murder that night."

Hari then became silent.

Questioner: "Is all that you have told me completely true?"

"Everything that I have said is true. Not one word is false."

"You can tell me if there's anything that's not entirely true in all that you have said so far. For I am not a police officer; I am the District Magistrate of this area and the case comes to me for its first trial."

"It doesn't matter whether you are the Magistrate or someone else. My statement will remain the same, for it's the truth. I will not tell lies whatever be the consequences."

At this point Bansiram entered the room again. He wasn't alone. With him was the sinful wretch Promoda! After entering the room, he addressed the Magistrate and said, "Sir! Promoda was sitting outside and has heard every single thing that Hari has just said. If you wish, you could ask her a few questions as well and see what she has to say for herself."

Magistrate: (to Promoda) "You have heard all that Hari has said about you. Now, is there anything that you would like to say to me?"

Promoda: "All that Hari has said is completely untrue. I don't know him and I don't know anything about the things that he has talked of. Do you really believe that a Bengali woman could kill her husband with her own hands? This is completely impossible and could never happen. Why would I murder my husband?"

After hearing her words, the Magistrate didn't say anything more and made her stand as an accused in the case and the trial began right there and then. Since no appropriate place could be found in the village to put up a tent for the trial, the court proceedings were held at Ramlochan Ghosh's house.

For the next seven days, the officers involved in the case stayed in the village and carried out their investigation. On the basis of several witness statements, it was decided that Promoda was responsible for her husband's death. As such, she became the prime accused in the case and was found guilty of her husband's murder. Ultimately the case was transferred to a higher court for the final judgment. Hari, who had assisted Promoda in this hellish affair, was seen as telling the truth and became the primary witness in the case. Even though he had seen everything happen with his own eyes and was unpardonable for the part that he had played in the entire episode, Promoda was adjudged as a far greater sinner than him. As such she was given the punishment that she deserved. Since her sentencing would have been impossible without Hari's testimony, the judge took Bansiram's advice and allowed Hari to be granted reprieve from being seen as an accused in this case.

In the court, the jury sat down to listen to Promoda's trial. All the witnesses who had given statements in the lower court were summoned yet again and their statements were duly recorded. Each of them repeated what they had said in the lower court. But for some reason, that worthless wretch Hari had a change of heart and, acting either out of love or compassion, began to look for ways in which he could save Promoda. All that he had said earlier against Promoda remained unchanged in his final testimony. But at the same time, he refused to say who had administered the fatal blow that night and killed Nabakumar. Instead, he asserted, "After giving me the murder weapon, Promoda had left that place and later when the weapon dropped from my hands and I fainted, she was nowhere around. So I can't really say who it was that finally killed Nabakumar. But I know that she wasn't there at the time."

However, even though a lovelorn Hari changed his earlier statement and framed a set of lies about not having seen the real killer, neither the members of the jury nor the judge believed what he said. Treating the statement that he had given in the lower court as the truth, the jury pronounced Promoda to be guilty. The judge agreed with their verdict, and punished Promoda accordingly by giving her the death penalty.

Since he had turned into a witness for the case in the lower court, with the help of police officers, Hari was not tried as an accessory to the murder. But in the end, even Hari couldn't escape divine justice and the judge in the High Court issued an order that a case be filed against him for giving false statements in the lower court. When the case was tried in the High court, Hari was sentenced for seven years of rigorous imprisonment. What a shocking end to the tale of the two lovers! And how fine are workings of divine justice!

Priyanath Mukhopadhyay

Notes

1 A *dao* would be similar to a machete.

2 *Boishnobi/Vaishnavi* refers to female practitioners of Vaishnavism in Bengal which is indelibly connected to the figure of Chaitanya—a devotee, mystic and teacher who lived from 1486 to 1533. Vaishnavism has a long and complex history both outside and in Bengal. Associated with the worship of Radha and Krishna, in Bengal it has also been significant for enabling the social mobility of non-Brahmin trading groups. In the nineteenth century it was hugely popular amongst many prominent Hindu houses as well as among so-called 'lower' classes and castes. According to Baptist missionary William Ward, at least one-third of the population of Bengal professed some form of Vaishnavism in 1815. For many Vaishnava women and men, renunciation was used as an option to leave normative caste, class, and gender roles and lead a wandering life. *Boishnobi* women were often literate and were even hired as teachers in elite households (like the Jorasanko Tagores) for educating the female members. From the nineteenth century, sexuality emerged (amongst certain sections of the *bhadralok*) as the key feature of disdain for the Vaishnavas. Terms such as "bawdy," "obscene," and "sexually explicit" were used to describe Vaishnava lyrics of the *padabali kirtan*. Similarly, the terms "prostitute" and "lax morals or virtues" were deployed as adjectives for *Boishnobis/Vaishnavi* who did not clearly belong to conservative and wealthy Vaishnava families and led unconventional lives.

11

'WHY! WHAT'S THIS?!'

'(Suicide or homicide)' Darogar Daftar, Jyeshth (mid-May–mid-June), 1896

I

This is an incident that took place quite recently. One evening, not many months ago, I was informed that an old woman had been brought to the Keoratala *ghat* for her last rites.[1] But since her forehead was showing signs of a wound, the sub registrar on that *ghat* suspected that the death may have been caused by someone administering a blow to the head. As a result, he stopped the cremation from going through, informed the local *thhana* and even prevented the men who had carried the corpse to that place from leaving the premises till the arrival of the police.

Officers of the *thhana* reached the *ghat* soon after they received this information. But when they couldn't decide on what had actually happened in that place even after listening to the accounts of the people gathered there, they requested us to help them with further investigation. At the time when this request came in, only I was present in our *thhana*. No other official was around. So the responsibility for helping them out fell on me.

I stepped out of the *thhana* and reached the Keoratala *ghat* as soon as I could. I think all my readers know that Keoratala *ghat* is very close to Kalighat. Most corpses are brought here for their last rites.

Upon going there, I found that an old woman's lifeless body was lying on a ramshackle bier. Looking at her I guessed that she was not less than eighty years old. Her body looked frail and worn out and it seemed as if she had died after a prolonged illness. However, despite the state of her body, the wound on the left side of her forehead was clearly visible. It didn't seem like a minor wound either. The cut was at least three inches long and one and a half inches wide. It also looked like she had received the wound and had bled that very day, for there were dried flecks of blood visible around it and the skin had yet to heal. What was also visible near the wound were marks which suggested that someone had tried to cover it with some wet mud.

After seeing all this, the first thing I wanted to find out was who had brought the corpse to that place. I asked the sub registrar and he said, "Today at around one in the afternoon, two men, Rameshwar and Bhavataran, and a woman, Bilashi, together brought this body here for cremation. When the official posted here went to check the corpse, he found signs of a large wound on the forehead. Then when he asked the people who had brought in the body about the injury and how she had received it, he felt that they were unable to give him a satisfactory answer. His suspicions were thus aroused and he decided he had no choice but to report the matter to the nearby *thhana*."

After hearing all this, I sent for Rameshwar and Bhavataran. I questioned them separately but both said, "We are Bilashi's neighbours. Today at around eleven o'clock Bilashi came to us and said that her mother-in-law had died and that since she didn't have any other family members, she needed help to take her to the cremation ground. Bilashi is our neighbour and we know that she has no other family to talk of. We had also known for a while that her mother-in-law was unwell. As such, we didn't hesitate to go down to help her. We felt sorry for her and merely wanted to fulfil our duties as a neighbour, that's all. When we went to her house, we found that the old woman's corpse was placed on the terrace and had been covered with a white cloth. We then got a bier and placed the shrouded body on it and later we brought it here to the cremation ground. Bilashi also accompanied us when we came here. Now we have told you everything about the circumstances in which we ended up bringing the old woman's corpse here; we really don't know anything more than this. It seems to us that nowadays it's a crime to even help anyone. For if we hadn't come here to help Bilashi, this crisis wouldn't have befallen us."

II

After listening to Rameshwar and Bhavataran's account carefully, I sent for Bilashi. When questioned about the circumstances in which the death had occurred, she said, "The old woman is my mother-in-law. I became a widow several years ago. And since then my mother-in-law and I have been staying in this house by ourselves. We don't have any other family. The old lady had some money and that's what helped us eke out a living. Besides that, my husband used to own a *hookah* shop in the Burra bazaar area that, after his death, was given to one of his employees to run. He too gives us some money every month which we use for our household expenses. I have heard that my mother-in-law possessed some cash and ornaments, but I have never clapped eyes on them. She never showed them to me. But if they ever came up in a conversation, she would say that all her possessions would be left to me after her demise. Since we were not together at the time of her death, she wasn't able to tell me or give me anything. So I have no idea about what she has left behind.

My mother-in-law was fairly old; she would have been close to eighty or thereabouts. And yet despite her advanced years, she was neither terribly frail nor indisposed. She used to do a great deal of household chores and also roamed around in the neighbourhood to her heart's content, visiting whoever she wanted. Before this, I have never really seen her falling ill even for a day.

It was around a month ago that she started running a fever. After four or five days, the fever subsided but then her limbs began to appear bloated and subsequently she had a fever again. She never quite recovered from it and gradually started becoming extremely feeble. A few days ago, her condition worsened considerably and she stopped moving altogether and became confined to her bed.

The house that we stay in is our own. It's built on three *bighas* of land. Most of the land is taken up by the trees on it, so the house is quite tiny. There are just two rooms in it, built of mud; I stayed in one of the rooms and the other was hers. When my mother-in-law's pain became intolerable, she decided to have her bed moved to the terrace and that's where she lay all day and night. It became her last resting place; while she was alive, she never moved from there. When she became too weak to leave her bed, I tended to all her needs. After completing all my household chores, I took care of her, lifted her up or lay her down and even cleaned her after she had relieved herself. But in the last two days the work had increased to such an extent that I was finding it nigh on impossible to do it all by myself.

Today, I was with her till eight o'clock in the morning. By then I had lost count of the number of times I had to lift her from her bed and clean her. Feeling at the end of my tether, I began to realise I would just not be able to take care of her by myself any longer. And yet I couldn't think of a single person in the neighbourhood who would come to my aid.

And then it struck me all of a sudden that Tarala, who lives in Bhowanipore, might be able to help me. She used to live near our house in the recent past and we had grown quite close to each other. She was so fond of me that if I asked her for something, even if it were inconvenient, she would go to any lengths to fulfil my wishes. When her husband found work in Bhowanipore, she had to leave this neighbourhood and accompany him. But even after moving to Bhowanipore she had visited us on several occasions and spent the night in our house. I would also go and visit her often.

When I saw the state that my mother-in-law was in, I decided I had no choice but to seek Tarala's help. I would have been terribly grateful if she could come to us in this hour of need. With this in mind, I left my mother-in-law alone in the house and set off for Bhowanipore to talk to Tarala. But unfortunately, I couldn't meet Tarala. I was told that she had gone off to visit her sister and would not be returning anytime soon. Feeling despondent at the failure to meet Tarala, I returned home and found my mother-in-law lying in exactly the same place and manner on the terrace as I had left her. I also noticed that a small part of her forehead appeared to be wounded and that the wound was bleeding. When I saw this, I got terribly scared, but I didn't tell anyone about this.

I asked my mother-in-law several times how she had got that injury but she seemed to have become completely incapable of speech. A few hours later, she died. And then with the help of two men from my neighbourhood, I brought the corpse to the cremation ground for the last rites. You already know what happened after that."

III

Even after hearing the accounts of Rameshwar, Bhavataran and Bilashi, I remained none the wiser as to what might have happened and how the old woman had been hurt. Our investigations in Keoratala ended at that point. We sent the body off for post-mortem and then paid a visit to the old woman's house. The house was exactly how Bilashi had described it. She then showed us the place on the terrace where the old woman used to rest, while she was sick. I saw that the spot was about four feet above the floor of the terrace. I also noticed that the low wall that abutted the terrace had some bricks placed in a row on top of it. When I asked Bilashi about the bricks she said that it was to prevent rainwater from flooding and washing away the mud floor of the terrace. However, I saw that the area around the bricks looked like it had been scoured and mopped very recently. Bilashi explained that she cleaned that area every day in a thorough manner after giving her mother-in-law a bath. That was the reason why it looked so spotless.

I asked her, "How many hours before going to Bhowanipore did you clean this place?"

"I left for Bhowanipore right after swabbing this place."

"How long did it take you to get back from Bhowanipore?"

"Not more than an hour, I think."

"And did you clean this place again after coming back?"

"Oh yes, of course I did."

"But why did you clean it all over again?"

"Well, upon my return from Bhowanipore, I saw that my mother-in-law had wet herself again and soiled her clothes. Since I do the cleaning myself, I always clean the entire place including the floor every time I wash her."

"And when you were cleaning the floor, did you see anything in particular that grabbed your attention?"

"No, I don't remember seeing anything out of the ordinary. But yes, there were a few drops of blood on the floor and I cleaned that up."

"Was the floor where you saw the bloodstains a little damp or was it entirely dry?"

"It was slightly damp, not totally dry."

"Did you see any marks on the damp floor?"

"I think I saw a biggish mark on the floor near the spot that was blood-stained. It looked like the kind of mark that would be made if something heavy was placed there."

"Did you notice any other marks besides that?"

"I feel I did notice some other marks."

"What kind of marks?"

"If I were to guess, I would say they looked like footprints."

"Can you point out to us the exact place where you saw them?"

"I doubt I'll be able to show you the exact spot. But I can give you a rough idea of where I'd seen the marks."

Saying this, she pointed out some spot on the floor.

Then I asked her, "Where are all the old lady's ornaments and her money?"

Bilashi replied, "I really don't know anything about her belongings. Even if she did have anything, I have absolutely no idea where she might have kept them."

"What about your own belongings?"

"I don't have any money."

"Any ornaments?"

"Don't have that either."

"I would imagine you had some jewellery when your husband was alive, didn't you? What's happened to it?"

"I've had to sell it all, one by one."

"If you did sell everything, where has all the money gone?"

"It went into feeding us."

"I think you told me earlier that your mother-in-law's savings were used to meet the household expenses and that what little was earned from the *hookah* shop also helped. Why then would you need to sell your ornaments?"

"Well, what can I say! They got sold."

While this conversation was taking place between the two of us, some of Bilashi's neighbours had gathered near us and were listening to our exchange. Suddenly, one of them spoke up, "Have you told him that all this while you were also feeding your paramour with your money?"

I asked Bilashi, "Did you hear what this man just said? Who's your paramour?"

"Please ignore him. He's my enemy. He's lying through his teeth to make me look bad. I don't have any paramours."

IV

After listening to Bilashi and taking stock of the house carefully, I wondered: what kind of death might this be? Was it suicide or murder? Or had the old woman simply died of natural causes?

But how could I call it suicide? There was no sign anywhere of the hard object with which the old woman had hit herself on the head, and yet we had seen blood stains on the floor of the terrace. Given all this, how could we rule this a suicide?

But how could we think of it as a death due to natural causes either? If there had been no signs of a serious injury on her head, we would have had no difficulty declaring it a natural death. Besides, when Bilashi had gone to meet Tarala, there was no one at home except for the old mother-in-law. Is it possible that at that time the old woman had started tossing and turning in a feverish state, fallen down from her bed which was on that raised place and hurt her head badly? Is that the reason we could see traces of blood so clearly on the floor? And when she felt a bit better, she had got up and gone back to her bed? Subsequently when Bilashi returned from Bhowanipore, she discovered that the old woman had died?

But if this conjecture were correct, then I struggled with yet another suspicion. Could the same old woman who had toppled on to the floor due to her illness have then climbed back into her bed all by herself moments before her death? And if she was able to manage this, then she would have had to use the steps leading to her bed. In which case whose were the footprints near the courtyard? After hearing all this, dear readers, you are now free to make your own conjectures.

For us the main conundrum was—was this a murder? If the old woman had not fallen from her bed and hit her head on a brick then how could we regard it as anything else but murder? Were the footprints that Bilashi was referring to, those of the killer? And if we were to rule this a murder, then who could have committed it and why?

There could have been two reasons for wanting to kill the old woman. One could be some sort of a dispute. But no one had talked of any dispute till now. The other reason could have been the desire to rob the old woman of all her possessions. But then, given that even Bilashi didn't know whether the old woman actually had any money, how could an outsider have had the information? At the same time, who knew if Bilashi was telling us the truth?

At any rate, the following questions began to surface in my mind at that time:

1. To what extent was it plausible that Bilashi knew nothing about the wealth of the person with whom she had lived for so many years?
2. How was it that Bilashi had no ornaments to call her own? If the *hookah* shop took care of their daily expenses, then what made her sell off her jewels and spend all the money?
3. Who was Bilashi's paramour? It was true that Bilashi had denied it all. But if the neighbours were insisting on the truth of their claims, then was she to be believed?
4. Was it possible that Bilashi's lover, or perhaps Bilashi herself, acting upon her lover's advice, had killed the old woman and cleared the path for fulfilling their own desires?

5 If Bilashi wasn't harbouring any sinful feelings of guilt, then why did she choose not to raise an alarm, when she saw the signs of injury on her mother-in-law's head and keep it a secret? What was even more surprising was that she decided to keep mum about the wound even when her neighbours were taking the body to the cremation ground for the last rites.

With these thoughts swirling about in my head, the officers accompanying me and I entered the rooms that Bilashi and her mother-in-law used to sleep in. The state of the rooms suggested that things had been either moved around or removed from it. I opened all the chests and boxes that were stored in the room, but couldn't find any ornaments or cash anywhere. When I talked to Bilashi's neighbours, they claimed that the two women were not particularly poor and that between them they owned a fair amount of ornaments. Bilashi however continued to deny having anything besides the house to call her own.

V

We left Bilashi's house after we finished questioning her and all her neighbours. Bilashi stayed on in that house and we placed a guard outside for the night, to allay her fears.

After leaving her house, our first job was to ascertain the truth of the claims about Bilashi having a lover and to find out his identity. Our search within the neighbourhood eventually bore fruit. Firstly, we got to know that she did indeed have a lover. And then we found out his name as well. He was called Gagan Chandra Ghosh. Bilashi was a Suvarna Banik, but her lover was a Goyala.[2] Once we unearthed his name, it didn't take us long to locate his address. We then went to his house but couldn't find him there. Apparently, he had left the house early in the morning after finishing breakfast and had said he would be visiting some relatives. He hadn't returned from there as yet.

However, it wasn't as though we came away after gathering this information about Gagan. We made every effort to collect as much information about the man as we could from his family.

One of Gagan's neighbours was a gentleman called Lakhhan Chandra. When he heard about the nature of our investigation, he came out and stood near us. As I started talking to him, he struck me as being amenable to being questioned and willing to help us in every way possible. It was also fairly evident that he knew Gagan's family quite well and that even the women in Gagan's house talked quite freely with him.

At our request, Lakhhan Chandra entered Gagan's house, asked the women who were inside the questions that we had given him and then transmitted to us the answers that they gave him.

I: "At what time did Gagan leave the house?"

Lakhhan Chandra: "He left the house around ten or eleven."

"Where has he gone?"

"He has gone to visit a relative."

"Where does this relative stay?"

"He didn't tell us that."

"Did you know the daughter-in-law of the old woman who died recently?"

"Do you mean Bilashi? We all know her."

"How did you get to know her?"

"Gagan and she are lovers and so she keeps coming to this house. Besides, about two months ago, Bilashi and her mother-in-law had come and stayed here for close to four or five months. Gagan had even made arrangements for them to stay in the two rooms that are situated outside the main area of the house. Two months ago, when the old lady started feeling extremely unwell, Bilashi left this house along with her and went back to her own house. After that neither of them came back here."

"Did you see any ornaments in their possession at the time that they were living in this house?"

"We had all heard that the old woman had some money and jewels, but we never saw anything. But many of us saw Bilashi's ornaments and they were definitely not a small amount."

"When did you last see her ornaments?"

"When they left this house two months ago, we had all seen them in her possession."

"Besides jewels, did she have any other valuables?"

"They had two chests full of brass and copper vessels."

"Where did they keep those chests?"

"In this house. They kept them in the rooms that they stayed in while they were here. The two chests are still lying there."

"So the copper and brass vessels have been kept in those rooms. But do you have any inkling about where they might have kept their ornaments?"

"The women of this household have no idea as to where the ornaments might be kept. We really don't know whether they gave them to someone for safekeeping or kept them with themselves."

"Would you have known if they had kept the ornaments with Gagan?"

"Yes, quite likely. For if he had kept the stuff, then either we would have seen it or he would have talked about it to us."

"What about the keys to Gagan's own trunk? Where are they kept?"

"They stay with him all the time. He never parts with them."

"And where is the trunk kept?"

"In the room where he sleeps."

VI

With the help of Lakhhan Chandra's mediation, we completed the conversation and then I thought to myself:

1 When everyone knew that Bilashi and Gagan were involved in an illicit relationship, and she had even left her home for a while to come and live in his house, then why did she deny this?
2 If, as these women had averred, she might have kept her valuables with Gagan and those were still somewhere in this house, why did she deny having any ornaments or money?
3 Was it that Gagan and she were accomplices in the committing of the sinful act (of murder)? And had Gagan then kept all the valuables with himself? Was that why Bilashi didn't want to mention his name at all? Was she terrified about our finding out the truth?

Once these thoughts surfaced in my mind, I also wondered whether, given the evidence that had come to light, one shouldn't search Gagan's trunk. But then we had not even ascertained whether we were in fact investigating a murder. Under such circumstances, wouldn't it be illegal to barge into Gagan's room in his absence and search the contents of his locked trunk? And yet, if he was involved in the murder of the old woman, surely he would move all the stolen valuables elsewhere once he returned home and got to know that the police had visited the house and were asking questions. How then could I refrain from conducting a thorough search of his room before his return?

I then said to Lakkhan *babu*, "Since Gagan is not here and we have come here to investigate an extremely complicated case, we have to search his room and his possessions. Please explain this to the women of this house and ask them to show us where everything is kept."

Lakhhan *babu* followed my instructions and even though the women in Gagan's house were very reluctant, they had no choice but to lead us to his room. Lakhhan *babu* accompanied us and some other gentlemen from the neighbourhood also decided to be present there. Since the keys to the trunk were with Gagan, we tried to open it with a different set of keys. But when nothing worked, we had to break the lock in front of the gathered audience.

We were all quite shocked to see the things that lay inside the chest. For inside it, there were gold and silver ornaments kept in an earthen box. I took it out and placed it on the floor in front of everyone. Everyone exclaimed, "How could Gagan have so many ornaments in his possession?" The women of that household had been watching everything from the next room. They were also taken aback by the discovery of all the ornaments and cried out, "So Bilashi's jewels are in this trunk! We have seen these earlier when she was here." I overheard their comments but did not say anything; in fact, I took the ornaments, quietly drew up a list of all that I took, and left the place.

On our way back, instead of going elsewhere, we decided to pay Bilashi's house another visit along with those ornaments. Upon reaching her house, we found her sitting in the courtyard and chatting with the constable who had been posted there for her safety. She seemed to become quite nervous when she saw us. It seemed as though our return had really terrified her.

We entered the house and asked her to come and sit with us. She got up from where she had been sitting in the courtyard and came and stood next to us. We placed all the ornaments that we had seized from Gagan's house in front of her and said, "Take a look at these ornaments. Do you know to whom these belong?" She looked fairly shocked and then glanced all around in a furtive manner. I realised she wanted to make sure that Gagan was not with us. Eventually she scanned the ornaments once again and said quite casually, "No sir! I have absolutely no idea as to whom these might belong to! I have never clapped eyes on them before this moment." We were all stunned when we heard what she had to say.

VII

After seeing Bilashi's reaction to the ornaments, our suspicions increased manifold. Someone even went on to say, "Now we are completely convinced. This was not a suicide, nor was it an injury due to an accidental fall. Everything that Bilashi has told us so far has been a pack of lies. It was she who killed her mother-in-law and then stole all her ornaments. And she then gave them, along with her own valuables, to her lover Gagan so that he could hide them. Why else would she refuse to recognise her own ornaments?"

When Bilashi heard this she began to wail loudly and said, "O my lords and masters! I haven't uttered a single lie. I can take any oath that you want me to. Please believe me, I haven't killed my mother-in-law, nor have I helped or seen anyone murder her. It's not right that you should be accusing a helpless woman. How can you accuse a poor woman facing such a terrible crisis in this manner? This is not right."

Hearing her words, a few of our officers abused her roundly while some even made to strike her with their fists. Seeing their aggression, a frightened Bilashi skulked off to one corner of the courtyard and sat down without uttering another word.

We then began to treat Bilashi a little differently, for she considered her a prime suspect in the murder of her mother-in-law. So an officer was now specially posted at her place, to keep an eye on her and ensure that she would not try to escape. In short, Bilashi was placed under house arrest, for all intents and purposes.

And yet we were beginning to realise that it would not be easy to extract any further information out of her. As such, I decided to investigate her thoroughly. But then I thought that it might be better to first find out a few things about Gagan Ghosh. Surely once we found him, we could get him to explain why the jewels had been in his custody. Thinking in this manner, we left her with the police officer who was meant to guard her and set off to investigate Gagan Ghosh.

Since we couldn't decide where to begin our investigation of Gagan, we decided to go back to his house. We found out from his family where all his relatives were staying and then set off to find Gagan in one of these places. But eventually, unable to find any trace of him anywhere, we returned to Bilashi's house in low spirits.

What we found upon reaching Bilashi's house confirmed the suspicions based on which we had begun our investigation. At the same time, what we saw also filled us with rage and shame in equal measure. I started blaming myself for the inadequate security arrangements I had made before leaving the house. For the officer who had been posted there to guard Bilashi was lying on one side of the courtyard fast asleep. Indeed, so deep was his slumber that he didn't even realise that we had returned to the house. After taking in the state of the guard, I began to look for Bilashi. I soon realised that Bilashi was nowhere to be seen. I awakened the officer and asked him, "What's happened to the woman you were supposed to guard?" Without answering my question, he began to look around as though searching for her. I realised that, taking advantage of his carelessness, Bilashi had escaped. Feeling desperate, I scoured the house and the garden once again but to no avail. There was no sign of Bilashi anywhere. Then I went into every house in the neighbourhood to look for her but I got no information whatsoever. Finally, I just sat down in one place and began to think of ways to find her.

At that time, I suddenly thought to myself that all said and done, there was no one in the neighbourhood who would feel sympathetic towards her. That was the reason why she had to go all the way to Bhowanipore to find her friend Tarala to help her with taking care of the old woman. One could safely surmise that it was Tarala, more than anyone else, that she trusted and depended on. We rushed to Bhowanipore that very night and after a great deal of searching, we were able to locate Tarala's house. But then we got to know that Tarala was indeed not at home and that she had gone out of town. We also found out that Bilashi had been telling the truth when she said that she had visited Tarala's house to meet her.

VIII

Almost the entire night was spent looking for Bilashi and her lover, and yet we were unable to locate either their whereabouts or get any sort of information about where they might have gone.

As I said to my readers earlier, the old woman's corpse had been sent to Bhowanipore for an autopsy. At around eleven o'clock we received news of the autopsy and saw that the medical report had arrived. When we read it, our investigation had to be concluded right then and there. It didn't matter anymore whether Gagan or Bilashi were at home. For it seemed that all our tireless efforts to investigate the case over days spent without much food or sleep had been in vain. The search for Bilashi and Gagan was also dropped.

In his report the doctor had written, "The dead woman was quite old and she had many of the diseases that are commonly associated with old age. Besides this, she had very high fever. As far as I can tell, she died due to natural causes related to old age. It's true that she had a wound on her forehead, but the injury was one that she would have had a few minutes before her death. At a cursory glance, the wound seems extremely severe but a closer examination reveals that despite being fairly long, the cut wasn't very deep. It had only scratched the skin and not impacted the bone in any way. The wound had no bearing on the old woman's death. Both the disease that caused her death and the time of death would have remained unchanged even in the absence of the wound."

The investigative methods that we had adopted and had been working on till then were abandoned entirely. We had to forget about those whom we had been treating as suspects as well as all our grave concerns at not being able to arrest them. Our elaborate plans for catching them also had to be forgotten. In short, right after this report we stopped the investigation and went off to our respective *thhanas*.

It's true that this investigation was over with immediate effect, but my mind refused to rest without solving the puzzle. How did the old woman get that wound on her forehead? I simply could not relax till I had found the exact truth of the matter.

Once the case was closed, I went back to my office. But not having been able to trace either Gagan or Bilashi, I didn't feel comfortable about handing over the old woman's ornaments to anyone else. As a result, I felt I had no choice but to keep them with me. And despite the investigation being over, I would make enquiries almost every day to find out if Gagan or Bilashi had returned home. After a while, I heard that Gagan was still missing but Bilashi was back in her house.

IX

When I heard about her return, I sent a message to her asking her to pay me a visit. Bilashi came to see me soon after receiving my message. I asked her, "So where have you been all these days?"

She said, "I did not have a fixed address. I ate wherever I could and slept in any house where someone was willing to help me out by giving me shelter for the night."

"But why did you leave everything and scarper off like that?"

"What else could I have done? When I heard all of you saying in unison that I must have killed my mother-in-law, I realised I had no choice but to run away. After all, who would willingly want to be arrested by you people, especially when one is innocent? Who wants to feel the hangman's rope tighten around their necks? When I realised that all of you had set yourselves against me, I had to think of saving myself by planning to escape from there."

"But there was a guard positioned in your house. How did you manage to hoodwink him?"

"When I saw that there was no one in the house except him, I spread out a mat for him in the courtyard and invited him to come and sit down on it. Then I spread another mat near it and lay down saying, 'I feel dead tired after a day's hard work. It's quite late in the night; I feel my body becoming numb with sleep. I am going to doze off. You sit here and do your duty.' When I pretended that I'd fallen asleep, I saw that he too began nodding with sleep. Even as he was about to drop off, he called me once or twice but then, on not getting any response, he felt certain that I was asleep and that's when he lay down and was soon lost to this world. I found the opportunity that I had been looking for quite easily. I slowly crept out of there and then, in the dark, tiptoed to the garden outside and eventually escaped through it."

"So if you ran away because you were afraid of us, why did you come back? How did you manage to overcome your fears?"

"When I got to know that my mother-in-law had not been killed by anyone and that it had been decided that her death was a natural one, I had no reason to fear you all, did I? Since it's not a murder, then how could you arrest me for anything?"

"Who gave you this information about your mother-in-law's death?"

"Never mind that. The only reason I have returned is because I have got this information. Else you would have never got to see me."

"Have you considered the fact that we might have tricked you into showing up? Since we needed to question Gagan and you for our investigation, don't you think we might have resorted to this minor trickery to make sure that the two of you land up in your own houses? After all, very few people outside the police get to know the truth about the doctor's report. What if we had decided to conceal the actual findings of the report and spread the news of a natural death in order to draw you out of your hiding place? And that is exactly what has happened. You had gone into hiding in order to be rid of us, and yet, here you are, caught in the trap that we laid for you. Sit and think about that now. I am convinced that we'll be able to capture Gagan as well in the same manner."

"I don't have the slightest doubt that you are all quite capable of the kind of trickery that you have described, in order to get your work done. But I know that in this case, whatever you might say now, it was declared a natural death. I have come to know through very reliable sources that my mother-in-law died of her illness."

"How can you be so sure that there is no deceit involved?"

"The family with whom I had last sought refuge while I was hiding, was one that read newspapers regularly. I overheard them discussing something after reading about it in the newspaper. I could hear them quite clearly and I realised that they were discussing the case related to me. I thought at the time that you people must have come up with this plan to spread lies with the help of newspapers and deceive me into returning home. Anyway, I asked the lady of the house to talk to her husband and get me some information about the case from him. I didn't however let on that I was Bilashi, and that it was my mother-in-law whose death had caused such a furore. The master of the house had his suspicions, but he promised me that he would dig out the truth about all that was going on in the case. Maybe he was acquainted with the doctor who had examined my mother-in-law's body. Anyhow, he did find out the truth and then said to me, 'The news about the old woman's death in the papers is true. There's no deception in what has been published.' It was only after he said all this that I decided to return home. Otherwise I would have continued to remain untraceable."

I was deeply astonished to hear Bilashi's account and thought to myself, "How fantastically clever this shameless hussy is!"

Then I asked Bilashi once again about the jewellery. She then admitted that those ornaments were indeed hers and that she had given them to Gagan for safekeeping. But she refused to concede even at that point that Gagan was her lover. I realised that it was her feminine bashfulness that was primarily responsible for her denying the truth. After talking to her for a while, I let Bilashi leave that day. I told her as she was going away, "When Gagan returns, why don't the two of you come here one day and collect the ornaments that are with us?" She heard what I said and then left.

X

A few days after this incident, both Gagan and Bilashi came to meet me and asked me for the ornaments. I said to them, "I do have all the ornaments that you want and I am more than willing to hand them over to you right now. But before I do that, I wanted to ask Gagan a couple of questions."

Gagan said, "You may ask me whatever you wish."

"You may have heard that at present you have no cause to be afraid of anything."

"I have heard everything. Why should we be afraid if we are not guilty of anything?"

"Well, in that case, perhaps you'll answer my questions truthfully, won't you?"

"Why would I lie? I'll answer all your questions truthfully, based on whatever I know."

"Do you know Bilashi?"

"If I didn't know her, would I have come here with her to meet you sir?"

"Is she related to you?"

"No, she's not. She's a Suvarna Banik's daughter and I belong to the caste of Goyalas."

"I know that the two of you don't belong to the same caste. But tell me, are you involved in an illicit relationship with her?"

"Sir, you have found out all about that already. What more do you want me to say?"

"Did Bilashi's mother-in-law know about it?"

"Yes, she did. The two of them came and stayed in my house for quite some time and the old lady saw everything with her own eyes."

"And to whom do these ornaments belong? The ones that you are here to take?"

"All of them are Bilashi's."

"How did they end up with you?"

"The two of them had given the ornaments to me for safekeeping."

"Can you tell me why, on previous occasions, had Bilashi completely denied the fact that the jewellery was hers?"

"Perhaps because she's a woman and felt frightened about admitting to the truth."

"Anyhow, when did you last see the old woman?"

"I had seen her even on the day that I later got to know she had died on."

"Can you recall what time you saw her, that day?"

"I think I saw her for the last time around ten or eleven in the morning."

"Where did you see her?"

"I saw her in her own house."

"Where was Bilashi at that time?"

"I didn't see Bilashi that day. I really don't know where she was at that time. I had to go out of town that day on some work and that's why I had set off from home quite early. I'd heard that the old woman had been down with a high fever the last few days and so I decided to drop in at their house, meet Bilashi and see the old lady before leaving, for I wasn't sure when I would be returning. As soon as I entered their house, I saw that the old woman was writhing in a feverish state and trying to get up from her bed which was on a raised level. No one else was at home that time. Before I could reach her, she had rolled out of her bed and fallen on the ground below. There were some bricks kept there and the poor woman hit her head on them and was badly hurt. I even saw her bleeding a little bit from where she had got wounded. I got very scared when I saw all this and started calling Bilashi in a loud voice. Not getting any response, I lifted the old woman from the ground and then placed her on her bed very gently. She had fainted by then. When I tried asking her something, I realised that she was completely incapable of answering my questions. It seemed to me that her end was near. I waited there for a while, hoping to meet Bilashi before I left. Then I decided that I couldn't wait any longer. The steamer would be leaving soon. Besides, quite often when one is very old, death doesn't come very easily. It could very well be two to three days before she finally died. Thinking in this manner, I departed from that place and began my journey towards my destination. I returned yesterday. It was only once I returned that I got to know that the old woman was dead and that Bilashi had been through terrible times ever since. I learnt that the finger of suspicion had been pointed at me as well. Now that the entire mess has been cleared up and you people have no reason to suspect us of anything, we are here to collect what's ours. After that we'll be on our way."

After listening to Gagan's account, the questions that had lingered in my mind even after the dismissal of the case were finally answered. Without another word I returned the jewellery to them. They made sure that they had got back everything and then went away from there and I turned my attention to other things.

Postscript

Dear readers, now you know how the case began and ended. But don't you want to find out what happened to Bilashi after all this was over?

A few months after this episode, I had to pay a visit to the place where Bilashi used to stay. When I went to the place where her house was located, I found it was no longer there. I became extremely curious to know what had happened and how her house had been completely destroyed. Upon a bit of digging around, I found out that following Gagan's advice, the sinful wretch had sold off everything that she had inherited from the old woman. She had then given all her earnings to her dearest friend Gagan for safe-keeping. Her ornaments were already entrusted to him; now all her remaining wealth that came from her inheritance also fell into his hands. At first Gagan made every effort to look after Bilashi. He brought her to his own house and treated her with greater love and affection than even his own family.

But this love didn't last for very long. Bilashi had thoughtlessly given away her most priceless possession (her virtue) to Gagan Ghosh and committed the greatest of sins; she soon had to start paying dearly for her sins. To begin with, Gagan resorted to all sorts of deception to throw her out of his house. He also told everyone in the neighbourhood that Bilashi had left his place with all her belongings. Even though he spread such rumours, no one believed him. But then no one did anything to help Bilashi retrieve her lost things, either. Bilashi couldn't get a penny of her own wealth. She went from door to door crying and pleading for help and even fell at Gagan's feet begging him for mercy. But all of this was in vain. She failed to get even a single coin out of him. After starving for a few days, she then decided she would start working as a housemaid. But those who got to know about her character refused to let her stay in their houses for very long. The heady days of youth that had filled her with reckless pride and made her commit shameful acts soon deserted her, and because of her reputation she was unable to find sanctuary in any genteel household. As such, she was left with the only option that fallen women of her kind often turn to, as their last resort. The raging fires of hunger compelled her to start begging for alms.

Priyanath Mukhopadhyay

Notes

1 *Ghat* refers to the landing-stage on the bank of a river/pond. Keoratala is a place in Kolkata where the *ghat* is used as a crematory.

2 Both Suvarna Banik and Goyala refer to caste groups in Bengal. While Suvarna Banik is associated with the mercantile group with dealings in gold and silver, Goyala is a caste group associated with pastoral activities. Refer to footnote 23 of the Introduction.

12

'IMPRUDENCE'

'(The terrible misjudgments of a foolish woman)' Darogar Daftar, Poush (mid-December–mid-January), 1902

Part I

I

It was the month of *Aashaadh* (approx. mid-June to mid-July of the *Saka* calendar). There had been a steady drizzling the entire night, and roads had become frightfully slushy. I had spent the night getting soaked inside a bullock cart that was equipped with just a thatch for protection from rain. I'd been sent to Cuttack on a Government assignment.[1] On my way to Cuttack, I had travelled on a ferry, but on the way back I had to take the road. With only a constable as my companion, I was returning to Kolkata in a cart and we were on the highway that is often taken by people when they visit Puri. Both the constable and I were sitting in the cart and the cart-driver was going ever so slowly on that wet, sludgy road. It was almost around dawn that I suddenly got the feeling that I could hear the distant sound of someone weeping. As we moved forward, the sound seemed to become louder. I was able to make out quite clearly that it was a woman crying and became extremely curious to see who it was. Taking along that constable who was accompanying me, I alighted from the cart. The sun had not as yet started to brighten the skies at that time and the world around us was still enfolded in the remnants of last night's darkness.

After getting out of the cart, we followed the sound of crying and moved in the direction from which it seemed to be coming. Soon we came upon a woman hidden by leaves and creepers on the side of the road, sitting and weeping all by herself. She was wearing a soiled sari that was completely drenched in the rain. We couldn't see anyone else near her. Looking at her one could guess that her age would not be more than thirty years and even though she wasn't particularly beautiful, she seemed to belong to a respectable family. Her clothes suggested that she was a married woman but there were no jewels whatsoever on her person, nor was there any *sindoor* on her forehead.

I approached her and asked, "Who are you?"

I didn't get any reply to my question, but her crying stopped. She remained silent. I then said, "Please don't be afraid. We are not thieves or dacoits and we don't have any kind of evil intentions. We have come here because we heard you crying and wondered if we might be able to help you in any way. We can guess that you're in some kind of trouble and we want to help. Please don't worry and if you wish, you can tell me quite freely whatever's going on in your mind."

The woman: "Who are you?"

I: "I am a police officer, but I am not from these parts. I stay in Kolkata. I had come here for reasons related to my official work. What about you?"

"I'm also from Kolkata."

"So how did you end up here?"

"That's a long, sad and shameful tale."

"Do you want to return to Kolkata now?"

"How am I going to go back there? I can't show my face to anyone over there."

"That can be decided later. Whether you are in a position to show your face to people there or not is not a matter of immediate concern. The question is whether you wish to return to Kolkata."

"No, I don't."

"But why?"

"I am not going back there."

"Well, where will you go instead"

"Nowhere. I don't have anywhere to go."

"Is there anyone with you?"

"No."

"There's no one at all? Do you mean to say you are completely alone?"

"Yes. Right now I'm totally by myself."

"Do you have any money with you?"

"I did have a great deal of money but at the moment I don't even have a paisa."

"And what about clothes?"

"Whatever you can see on my person right now."

"In that case, what are you going to do sitting here? Come with me. I'll make arrangements for sending you wherever you wish to go."

"Sir, you are extremely kind, but I don't think I deserve your compassion. If you wish, you could leave me here and go. I know only too well what awaits me in the near future."

"And what is that?"

"I have no other choice but to end my life."

"But that's a great sin."

"I know that and yet I'll have to commit that great sin."

"But why do you say that?"

"Telling you why will also be impossible."

"Well, do whatever you need to do, later on. Right now I insist that you come with me."

"Where will you take me?"

"I'm going back to Kolkata at the moment. So if you wish, I can take you there or if you decide you want to go somewhere else, then I'll make arrangements for your travel. I simply cannot leave you sitting here on the road like this. And you seem to have neither any companions nor any money or even any change of clothes with you."

"I just don't want to go anywhere and I don't wish to show my face in public."

"Why is there no one with you?"

"There's no one right now."

"Was there someone with you earlier?"

"Yes, there was."

"Where has that person gone?"

"I have no idea."

"Did the person not tell you where they were going?"

"No, they didn't."

"When did they leave?"

"I don't know that either."

"Is there any likelihood of their return?"

"I don't think so."

"So then there's no need for any further delay. Please come with me. It won't be wise to remain on this road any longer. I have a cart with me and you can travel in that quite easily. As long as I'm not able to get another cart, I can walk alongside without any difficulty at all."

This time the young woman did not protest. She slowly got up from where she was sitting and then began to follow me. When I stopped, she stood at some distance from me. I opened my portmanteau, took out a piece of clothing and gave it to her saying, "The clothes that you are wearing have become completely wet. Please get rid of them and wear this dry *dhoti*." Without any demur, she took it from me and changed out of her wet clothes at the back of the cart. I realised that her mental state was beginning to improve from what it had been earlier. It didn't seem any more like she wanted to kill herself. Rather, she seemed all set to go to Kolkata with me. When she had changed her clothes, I asked her to sit in the cart with me. Once again without any protest she climbed in and sat down. By then it was morning and the sun was out in the eastern skies.

After sitting down in the cart, she said, "Now that I've taken your place in the cart, how're you going to travel?"

"Don't worry. I'll hire another cart soon."

"But what will you do till you find another one?"

"I'll walk till then. An early morning walk is good for one's health in any case."

"After all that you have done for me, I would hate it if you had to walk like this because of me. Why don't you climb into the cart as well? I'll sit in one corner. Since I've decided to take your help, it would be pointless to feel embarrassed in front of you. You have saved my life after all."

When I heard these words, I felt as though the woman who was talking to me was not the same woman that I had met earlier in the day. The one whom I had met earlier was so shy that she could barely bring herself to utter a word while this one was asking me to sit in the same cart as her! The earlier one had talked of wanting to end her life. This one was sitting quite comfortably in the cart, having discarded her wet clothes and wearing the dry stuff I had given to her. Seeing all this, a few suspicions arose in my mind. I had helped the young woman thinking that she belonged to a respectable household. But listening to her now, I wondered if I had been wrong. Is she not a respectable woman, I asked myself. Or could it be that she'd been born into a respectable family but has subsequently lost her virtue and her reputation? Anyhow, if she travels to Kolkata with me, the two of us would have to spend at least two or three days sitting in the cart together. And since she was prepared to travel in this manner, I would be able to find out soon enough what she was like, where she lived, why she was in this place or in the situation that I had found her. Having thought all this, I climbed into the cart and then asked the cart-driver to drive on. The cart began to move. The constable who was with me walked behind the moving cart.

II

Dear readers, have you ever seen the kind of carts that travel on the roads to Cuttack? If you haven't, then there are still some that ply on that route from time to time. You could go and check them out if you wish. Those carts are called "Oriya" carts.

They are quite high and the thatched covers on top of them are also fairly high and broad. They are, in fact, so high that if one were to spread a mattress in the cart and sit on it, there would still be more than a foot's space overhead. They are not like the carts that are made here, where either one's head strikes the roof when one sits inside or there's no elbow space on either side. In the Oriya carts, there's so much overhead space as well as room on the sides, in the front and even at the back. The thatched roof is also fairly strong and is bound to the cart in such a way that it doesn't move, sway or sag easily. The semi-circular opening under the thatch towards the rear of the cart, that are usually left open in the carts found in Kolkata, are always closed in the Oriya carts. This means that no one can steal anything from the back of the Oriya cart and, in fact, no one can even peer in to see what's inside. A small part of the thatch protrudes onto the front half of the cart where the driver sits and it protects him from the elements. In fact, not just the cart-driver but even the person sitting near him is protected from the sun, or from being sprayed by rain in the front. Besides this, the semi-circular entrance to the cart has two straw curtains covering it and passengers can lift one part of the flap or both as they wish. If a passenger wants, he can close the flap and create a makeshift room for himself within which to lie down and sleep.

The Oriya cart that I was travelling in was also built in that fashion. Inside the cart, a thick layer of straw had been spread and on top of that lay a blanket and a mattress which was covered neatly with a sheet of cloth. In one corner there was space for keeping my portmanteau and other belongings. The constable who was travelling with me spent most of the day on foot. But in the evening when he was exhausted, I would ask him to climb into the cart and he would then rest near my luggage. Other than that, the entire space inside the cart was mine and I spent my time either sitting or lying down as I wished. I had one Bangla novel for company and I would read it from time to time. It mostly lay next to my pillow inside the cart.

When the young woman got into the cart, she sat on the spot where I had been sitting till then. But when upon her request I climbed into the cart, she relinquished that spot for me and sat where my constable had sat earlier, with her face completely veiled.

III

I became extremely curious to know who she was, where she lived and how she happened to be in that place. I thought to myself that I would definitely extricate all this information from her. But I also wondered whether I might get into trouble for travelling alone in a cart with a woman whom I had never seen before in my life. If the girl had run away from her home with someone and was being pursued by her kin, then if they chanced upon the two of us in this cart, they would surely assume that I was the one who had persuaded her to elope from home. How terrifying would the consequences be for me, in that case! Who would believe me in those circumstances? Should I then be taking this young woman along with me? And yet if she did indeed belong to a respectable family and was in distress, how could I simply abandon her and move on? Many such thoughts flitted through my mind, at that point. For a long while I sat quietly in the cart and thought of these things and yet I couldn't decide what I ought to do. Finally, I said to myself that whatever be the consequences or the disgrace that might befall me, I couldn't possibly leave a helpless girl alone on the road.

While I sat and brooded in this manner, the cart kept advancing on the road and the day progressed. From where I sat in the cart I couldn't see the young woman. For I was facing the front of the cart while she was sitting behind me.

At one point I turned around to see what she was doing. I found that her face was no longer covered in the way that it had been a little while ago; the cloth had travelled up, beyond her forehead and most of her face was now clearly visible. As soon as our eyes met when I turned around, she quickly pulled the cloth back over her face and covered it. I then started asking her several questions in order to find out who she was. At first, I asked her, "May I ask you a question?"

There was no answer.

I said again, "I want to ask you a question."

Even then there was no reply.

"You have talked to me previously so why are you refusing to speak now?" I persisted. "Especially since you'll be travelling with me the next three to four days, not talking to me isn't going to be possible. So please answer the questions that I ask you."

"What do you want to ask me?"

"What caste are you? Are you a Brahmin or a Shudra?"

"How is that going to help you?"

"It is important, which is why I want to know the answer."

"May I ask how it's important?"

"I have been sitting in this cart for very long and now I want to stretch my legs and lie down. That's the reason why I asked you."

"Why don't you then lie down?"

"I can't lie down till I find out your caste, you see. For if I were to lie down, my feet might end up touching you inadvertently and if you are a Brahmin girl then that'll surely make me a sinner."

"What's your caste?"

"I'm a Brahmin."

"Well in that case, you need have no worries. Rest assured, that you will not be sinning if your feet were to touch me accidentally inside the cart."

"You don't wish to reveal your caste to me?"

"No, I don't. In fact, I belong to an extremely low caste, lower than that of Bagdis."[2]

"I think you are lying. I'm fairly certain that you are either a Brahmin or a Kayasth or the daughter of a Sat-Shudra."

"Maybe I am a *bhadralok*'s daughter but I have lost the right to talk about myself as belonging to that family and so I won't talk about it."

After a while, I lay down in the cart. My head rested next to where the cart-driver was sitting and I had to keep my feet close to where the young woman sat. She moved away a little when she saw me lie down. Seeing her move, I thought that she had moved in order to avoid being struck by my feet. But she moved from her original place to sit at a point where the chances of being touched accidentally by my knee were higher. In fact, she was so close to me that as the cart moved in its usual jerky manner, my knee knocked against her quite frequently, but she didn't shift from that spot. Meanwhile, the cloth covering her face was also falling away.

Looking at her, I began to become ever more suspicious about her character; I was increasingly becoming convinced that she was a woman of loose morals. At any rate, I asked her again. "Why are you hiding your true identity from me? There's no one else here and I would never go against your wishes and publicise what you say to me. Please bear in mind that once you tell me everything, I might actually be able to help you. It's not as if confiding in me will ruin your future. Rest assured, I will only be of help to you."

"I do know that now. So please ask me whatever you want to and I'm prepared to answer you as well as I can. Ask me what you want to know."

"What's your name?"

"It's Usha."

"Where do you stay?"

"In Kolkata."

"Where in Kolkata?"

"Shyam bazaar."

"Is Shyam bazaar your natal home or your marital home?"

"My natal home."

"What is your father's name?"

"Suresh Chandra Adhikari"

"Adhikari? Is he a Brahmin?"

"Yes."

"I know one Suresh *babu*. But I'm not aware of his surname. I do know that he's very wealthy."

"Yes. That's my father."

"Good! Where's your marital home?"

"That I don't know. I've never been there. My husband used to live in my father's house."

"Your husband lived in your father's house? What's that supposed to mean? Where is he now? And how is it that you don't know where his parents live?"

"Well, his parents didn't belong to the city. But my husband Sharat used to live in a house very close to ours."

"Did he have other members of his family living there with him?"

"That I don't know. But I used to see a number of men in that house."

"Were they tenants living together in a hostel mess?"

"Yes."

"What sort of a hostel mess was it?"

"I think it was meant for students."

"And how did you get to know Sharat?"

"He used to visit our house very often with my brother, who is a student."

"Why did you elope with the young man if you didn't know him that well?"

"Since I've said that I won't conceal anything, I am not going to hold anything back from you. Soon after meeting him, I was completely transformed, as it were, and throughout the day I would keep thinking of ways to meet him, to get his attention, to talk to him and win his love. Sharat also realised what was going on in my mind and one day he sent a letter to me through the maid who worked in their hostel. When I read the letter, I was convinced that he felt the same way about me as I did about him. After reading his letter, I too wrote a letter for him and described in great detail the state that I was in. From that very day I constantly started looking for opportunities to spend time with him. Two or three months went by in this manner, but we just couldn't fulfil our wishes in the way that we wanted. Sharat couldn't come up with a way to enter the inner quarters of the house that I stayed in, and I was unable to go out of my house as and when I wanted. Whether it was to bathe in the Ganges, or to go to Kalighat or anywhere else, I had no means whatsoever of doing anything without a chaperone. Gradually it became clear to me that I would not be able to find a single opportunity to meet him secretly. As such, I agreed to his suggestion that I run away from my father's house with him and we find a place of our own. I started looking for opportunities to do that. One evening, I took all my jewels that I could gather together, as well as some cash, and left the house all alone through a small gate at the back.

As planned earlier, Sharat was waiting for me nearby and we escaped together in the dark. There was a carriage waiting for us on the main road and when I climbed in, I saw that another man was sitting inside. Sharat and I sat together in that carriage and it began moving after a while. After some time we got out of that carriage and took a different one, and then, after travelling some distance in it, we left that as well. In this way we kept changing carriages as we went on our journey.

Eventually the night was over and it was morning, but I had no idea where I had reached, or what our destination was. In the morning, when we alighted from our carriage, we couldn't get a new one. A bullock cart had to be hired at that point and all three of us got into it and continued our journey. We spent two or maybe three days in the cart, but I don't know what happened after that. I suddenly felt extremely sleepy in the cart and then I dozed off. When I woke up and opened my eyes, I found that I was lying on one side of the road. Except for the clothes that I was wearing, I had nothing else with me. The money and the jewels that I was carrying, or was wearing on my person, had all disappeared. The cart that we had been travelling in was nowhere to be seen, and I could neither find Sharat nor our travelling companion anywhere."

"Why didn't you tell me any of this earlier? If you had, I would have started investigating this whole matter from where we met and would have initiated the process of finding out where Sharat and his friend went off in that carriage."

"I felt too embarrassed to tell you all this."

"How much money were you carrying with you?"

"It would not have been less than at least a hundred rupees."

"And what about the jewellery?"

"That would also have been worth two or three hundred rupees."

"And what are your feelings about the entire thing now?"

"About what?"

"Who do you think has stolen your money and your jewellery?"

"I haven't a clue about what happened."

"Don't you think it was Sharat who ran away with all your belongings?"

"Why would he do such a thing?"

"Who else could have taken it?"

"What if he's also in the same situation as I am?"

"Well, it's not easy to suspect the person that one is in love with. At any rate we can't go any further now. It's true that Sharat was not anywhere on the road that we have covered so far. But what if we were to find him fallen by the wayside on the road before that? Although I doubt that very much, since before meeting you my cart was coming down that very road and we didn't see anyone. It's possible that we may have missed him in the dark. Whatever it is, all things considered, we can't go on. But let me tell you that I strongly fear you've been ruined by the very person whom you have loved with all your heart and trusted so much that you eloped with him and disgraced yourself. I know of course that you'll refuse to believe me."

"I'm quite sure Sharat is not that kind of a person."

"That's what you think now, but perhaps you'll get to know something different later on. Alright then, can you try to go over everything that's happened very carefully, and then answer all the questions that I'm about to ask you?"

"Yes, I will. Please ask your questions."

"Do you know where this road that we are on, will take us?"

"No, I have no idea."

"Try very hard to recollect the time when you got off the carriage and climbed into a bullock cart, and then answer the questions that I'll ask you now."

"Alright."

"What was the name of the place where you got into the bullock cart?"

"That I don't know."

"Can you not remember anything?"

"No. For I sat inside the horse-driven carriage till such time as Sharat and his friend fixed a bullock cart for our remaining journey. Then I alighted from the carriage and climbed into the bullock cart. So I didn't really get to see anything much of the place."

"Did you see any shops or houses where you stopped?"

"Yes, those I did see over there. It looked like a small town."

"Will you be able to recognise the place if we went back there?"

"Maybe I will."

"What kind of a bullock cart was the one that you had got into? Was it similar to the one that we are travelling in, at the moment? Or was it a different kind of cart?"

"It was like this one. It was being pulled by two big white bullocks and was driven by an Oriya man."

"Would you be able to recognise the driver if you were to see him now?"

"I'm not sure about that, for they all look the same to me. I don't think I'll be able to identify that man very easily. Maybe once I see him, I'll be able to say for sure whether I can identify him or not."

"Around what time do you think you got off the carriage and get into the cart?"

"It wasn't very late at night. It must have been around eight or nine."

"Where did you people eat that night?"

"After travelling for a while, we stopped near a bazaar. A room was taken on rent near that place and in the night we had our dinner there."

"Did someone cook the meal for you?"

"I did the cooking. Sharat and his friend had got all the raw stuff from the bazaar."

"And then what did you do?"

"After finishing our meal, we went back to the cart and continued our journey. Soon it was night and when we reached yet another bazaar on the way, we stopped to take another room on rent and spent the night there."

"Did you cook again in that place?"

"No, we didn't. We had some snacks and then went to bed."

"But where did you sleep? I'm sure you weren't carrying mattresses with you."

"No, we didn't have anything of the sort with us. The shopkeeper who had let out his room to us gave us a bamboo mat and a pillow and the three of us lay on that."

"All three of you?"

"Yes, we all lay our heads on that one pillow and spent the night."

"Would you able to recognise that shop keeper if you were to see him now?"

"I think I will."

"What happened after that?"

"We left that place at the crack of dawn."

"You took the same cart that you had taken till that point?"

"No, the cart-driver who had brought us till there didn't want to go any further. He was given his fare that night."

"So then you had to take a different cart in order to leave that place?"

"Yes."

"Where did you people get that cart?"

"The shopkeeper who had given us a room for spending the night helped us get a cart."

"And that cart was hired to go up till what point?"

"It was decided with the cart-driver that he would take us till Puri."

"Were you able to go up to Puri in that cart?"

"No."

"So till where did you travel?"

"Where you found me."

"Was a different cart hired at any point after that, or did you people travel in that same cart which the shopkeeper had arranged, till where I found you?"

"As far as I can recall, there weren't any other carts taken."

"That's good. So how did you travel once you left that place?"

"The three of us sat in the cart and we set off on our journey. Depending on our convenience, we stopped to rest and cook our meals either in the morning, or at times in the evening. Most nights we slept in the cart, though at times we slept in rooms given to us by shop owners. After spending four or five days like that, I was left in the manner that you found me."

"How did that happen?"

"I really can't say. All I can remember is that we had rested in a room inside a shop, the previous night. Then very early next morning, we left that place and set off once again on our journey in that cart. Soon it was close to mid-morning, but we didn't get off from the cart to get any food. When we passed a bazaar around ten or eleven in the morning, Sharat and his friend alighted from the cart and went in search of food, while I sat and waited for them. After almost half an hour, they returned carrying some sweets inside a paper bag and said to me, 'We couldn't find a proper place here to stop and cook. We'll cook later in the evening when we stop to rest somewhere. Let's just have these sweets and spend the remaining day.' Saying this, they gave me a paper packet and started eating out of another one themselves. The cart kept going and after a while I ate the food that they had given me. Soon I felt extremely drowsy and then fell asleep in the cart. I have no idea what happened after that. When I woke up from my sleep it was as if I couldn't quite recover consciousness and it felt as though I was half awake and half asleep. It was only after some time that I felt fully awake. And that's when I realised that I was lying at the side of the road all by myself and that my clothes had got completely drenched in the rain. I think it was quite late in the night when I came to."

"So what did you do when you saw what had happened?"

"At first I called in low tones, 'Sharat, Sharat!' But I got no reply."

"What did you do when you got no reply?"

"I tried to get up slowly from that spot, but I found I could barely stand since I felt terribly weak. But I forced myself to get up. It was pitch dark all around and I couldn't see anything. Except for the sounds of the forest close by and of the pouring rain, I couldn't hear anything either. I started feeling extremely scared and all kinds of terrible thoughts began to dart about in my mind. There was not a soul in sight anywhere. I couldn't hear the sounds of any vehicles either. I cried out 'Sharat' in a loud voice but got no response. But it seemed as if someone imitated my voice and shouted 'Sharat' in a similar way. Once again I shouted 'Sharat', and yet again there was a similar sound. I felt terrified when this happened and then I also noticed that all the jewels on my person had gone missing. Hoping to find some houses or people nearby, I wandered around for a bit in the dark, but there were neither any houses nor any people to be found anywhere. It felt as though I was in a forgotten land and after a while, I had no choice but to hide myself in the thicket next to the road. I sat there and began to spend the night getting wet and feeling utterly desolate and miserable. And then you appeared on the road. After waking up, you are the first person I have seen."

"Do you have any idea who is responsible for your sorrows?"

"No, I don't."

"Can you guess what might have happened?"

"I think a band of dacoits must have been responsible for our condition."

"'Our'? Or just your condition?"

"I know what condition I was in, and I feel that Sharat and his friend must also be in a similar state. I have somehow managed to survive but I have a strong suspicion that they may not have been able to escape death."

"But if your suspicions are true, wouldn't we have found them on the road somewhere? And where would that cart, in which you were all travelling, have gone?"

"Maybe they have been abducted by dacoits?"

"Dacoits are only interested in money and valuables. Why would they abduct the two of them?"

"The two of them may have run away somewhere in order to escape the dacoits."

"That's not impossible, but what is also possible is that they are the ones responsible for your ordeal."

"So your guess is that Sharat has stolen all my valuables and run away?"

"Isn't that quite plausible?"

"No, I don't think so."

"Why do you say that?"

"Sharat would never do something as deceitful as this. He loved me with all his heart."

"It is possible that he loved you with all his heart, but it's also possible that he loved your money and jewels a little bit more. How are you so sure that he couldn't have cheated you, given that you know next to nothing about him, his family and his background? The only reason you left everything to run away with him was because you became infatuated with his good looks, am I right? Cases of foolish young women ending up murdered for their money at the hands of those whom they trust blindly happen more frequently than you know. So how can you be confident that something of that sort hasn't happened with you? Aren't moths that are irresistibly drawn to the bright appearance of the fire reduced to ashes by that same fire? You became infatuated with physical beauty and then leapt into burning fire! So why do you feel that the fire could not have scalded you? Rest assured that the very person for whom you abandoned your family and household, whose looks you became so attracted to, that you forgot all scruples and began gadding about on unfamiliar streets, is the one who's responsible for your present condition. You are not the first to suffer in this manner. Many dim-witted women have had to suffer this kind of fate. Silly women do all this on an impulse and then they have to suffer the consequences of their actions for the rest of their lives. They have to spend the rest of their days and nights with a face that is continually drenched with streams of tears. Having lost their virtue and their family, as well as their community, they spend their days in utter misery. How can you say that something similar hasn't happened to you? Your sadness at the moment is merely the first step on the ladder of your sorrows and only god knows what the future holds in store for you."

"I am beginning to see the light after listening to you. I realise now that the person to whom I have revealed the very depths of my heart is the one who plotted my ruin. I don't really care about the loss of valuables and money, but I do want to be saved from social disgrace. I know that there's no way to atone for the sin that I have committed, and I'll never ever have peace of mind, but if I can somehow find a way to avoid losing my reputation, I'll consider myself lucky. If only no one were to find out that my very being has been sullied and that I lost the most important possession that a woman has—her virtue—after falling in love with someone, I'll count myself fortunate. I know that in my heart I'll never entirely be at peace, but if I can avoid being disgraced socially, then at least I won't have to hide myself forever from public gaze. Else I will have no other choice but to do what I have mentioned earlier. I'll have to kill myself in order to escape public humiliation."

"I think that now you have realised the nature of your mistake to a certain extent. At any rate, I will never let anyone else know what I've heard from you just now. I'll also try and protect you from public humiliation in every way possible. I'll see to it that no one gets to know that you've lost your virtue. You are indeed very lucky that you met me and told me all your secrets. Till now no one knows what you have gone through, but remember that after this you'll need to follow each and every instruction of mine in exactly the manner that I ask you to and you must not veer from the path that I set for you."

"Think of me as your obedient servant and rest assured that I'll follow your instructions in every way possible and won't do a single thing against your wishes. Please tell me what I should do now."

"I'll tell you what to do as and when the need arises, and you'll then follow those instructions."

IV

I could now see that Usha's attitude had changed quite a lot. But I also asked myself whether a woman who had lost her virtue and callously abandoned her parents, siblings and the rest of her family, along with all codes of conduct, in order to commit a sinful act, could reform herself and change her mind so easily. Anyhow, I was determined to make every possible effort to ensure that her reputation not be sullied in public. And besides, if it was Sharat and his friend who had committed the robbery then I would have to find a way to retrieve her money and valuables from them.

After taking this decision, I asked the cart-driver to stop the cart and when he stopped, I asked him, "Is there a post office anywhere nearby?"

The cart-driver: "I have no idea."

"And what about a bazaar?"

"That would be at least six miles or so."

"How far is the bazaar that we passed on our way here?"

"That would also be about four miles."

"Which of them would you call the main or better bazaar?"

"If you ask me, the one that we passed some time ago is probably the better one. But really good quality stuff is not available in either of them."

"Is there a police *thhana* near any of the two bazaars?"

"No, there isn't one in either of the places."

"In that case, where would the nearest *thhana* be?"

"Well, that would be the *thhana* close to the bazaar where we had stopped last night. There's a *daroga babu* who sits in that *thhana*."

"Is there a post office near that *thhana*?"

"I'm not sure but there might be one."

When I heard the cart-driver, I was quite certain that a post office would be situated somewhere close to it, for if a *thhana* is not located near a post office, official work gets delayed. With all this going on in my mind, I told him to turn the cart around and take us back to that bazaar—the one near a *thhana*—where we had stopped at night. The Oriya cart-driver heard my instructions and then began mumbling something to himself in the Oriya language, of which I couldn't follow a single word. But I could gauge from his mannerisms and his voice that he was extremely disgruntled at having to retrace his steps and go back to the place that we left behind long ago. Having discerned his mood, I said to him, "So you don't want to go to the place that I'm asking you to, is that right?"

"That place is way too far from here."

"How far?"

"Not less than ten miles."

"So what if it is that far?"

"This was not part of the deal when we discussed the fare."

"That's alright."

"So then why should I go?"

"What if I gave you extra money for it?"

"If I get extra money for it, then of course I can take you there."

"How much money do you want for it?"

"Definitely not less than a rupee."

"Well, why take less? Take more than that if you want. I'm willing to give you one and a half rupees for your troubles."

When the cart-driver heard this, he turned the cart around without another word and began taking us back to that bazaar. Seeing us turn around and retrace our steps, Usha asked me, "Why have we turned back? Why are we moving in the opposite direction?"

"For your sake."

"Why do you say that?"

"We are moving in that direction for three reasons."

"What reasons?"

"The first reason—finding a way to make sure that no one suspects you of anything."

"How will you do that?"

"Why, I'll send news of your crisis to either your father or your brothers."

"In which case, they'll know for sure that I have eloped from the house with someone."

"It's been a few days since you disappeared from the house in the dead of the night, and on that same night your neighbour Sharat and his friend also disappeared. Do you think your family hasn't drawn their conclusions yet and realised that you eloped with them? First and foremost, I'm making an effort to see if there's any way in which we can prevent the news of your disgrace from spreading all around."

"But how will you succeed in this impossible mission?"

"Let me show you what I plan to do."

Saying this, I opened the portmanteau that I was carrying with me in the cart, took out some paper and a pen and began to write a letter sitting in the cart. After I had finished writing it, I gave it to Usha and asked her, "Do you know how to read and write?"

"I do know how to read and write a little in Bangla."

"Will you be able to read my handwriting?"

"I think so."

"Well in that case why don't you read and see what I've written to your father?"

Usha then took the letter from my hand and began to read what I had written. It was as follows:

> Dear Sir,
>
> Even though we have never met, I know about you, but I can't claim that you might have heard about me. I have written my name under the letter. I am a police officer from Kolkata and I had traveled to Cuttack for work. On my way back, I found your daughter Usha in an extremely helpless state, on the road that leads to Puri. It's not that she was all alone in that situation. There were other women who had been travelling with her and who are also stuck like her. I have sent news about them to their relatives. An Oriya *panda* had gone to Kolkata, gathered some pilgrims with the promise of arranging for their travel to Puri and then set off from there with all of them.[3] Your daughter Usha also somehow got to know about the travel plans, and fearing that you wouldn't allow her to go with them, joined that group of travellers led by the Oriya *panda* and left Kolkata secretly with them. Since she couldn't ask any of you for help at the time, she simply took whatever money there was at hand and the few jewels that she could carry. At first the group that she was part of hired carriages and carts for their journey, but subsequently they all got together and began to walk on the road that leads to Puri.[4] It was during that time, while they were all asleep on the roadside at night, that dacoits robbed them of their belongings and fled. Fearing reprisals, the Oriya *panda* also abandoned the pilgrims in that spot and ran away. The women were completely at a loss and sat in that place feeling utterly helpless. None of them had any money with which they could have spent even a day there. Anyhow, almost all of those women have now been taken care of and have been sent off to their homes. Some have gone back with relatives who had come looking for them. Only Usha is now left, and I am looking after her as though she were my own family. I am returning to Kolkata and have decided to bring her with me and leave her with all of you in her house. If you or anyone from your family wishes to come here to take her, then you'll find us on the Cuttack road. This is the road

that I'm taking to return to Kolkata. But we are moving slowly and aren't able to cover more than ten or eleven miles in a day. Despite her crisis, Usha has not lost her virtue, and in fact she hopes to scrape up enough money and find the right travel companions so that she can continue on her journey to Puri, but I have told her not to do that and assured her that I would help her in her travel plans only after she goes back to meet her family. She has agreed to my proposal. If you believe what I say, please send someone whom you trust, along with some money to the Cuttack road and he can take her back home. If not, I'll make arrangements for her to go back to her family. What I've also heard recently is that at the time that she left her home along with her travel companions, they were followed by some men from the neighbourhood. It is quite possible that the robbery was committed by them. When I reach Kolkata, I'll begin investigating who they were and whether they were behind this entire disaster. I have written down everything for you. It is now up to you to decide what you want to do.

Yours sincerely

Shri Priyanath Mukhopadhyay, Cuttack Road

After reading the letter Usha said, "Now I know what I need to say to my parents, and with the solution that you have devised, I feel that the possibility of suspicions about my character arising in people's minds can be avoided. I have no idea how I'll ever repay you for this great favour that you have done for me. I will listen to whatever you say for as long as I live."

"I will remain the only person who knows anything about your character. And I have no desire to disclose anything of what I have found out to anyone. So you don't have to fear social disgrace and humiliation in any way. The only other people who know what you've done are Sharat and his friend. But even if they start talking about your character in public, no one is going to believe them. It's with the intention of proving that they are thieves that I have written those last few lines. From the very outset, we will try to prove that they are thieves so that whatever they might claim in their defence, no one will believe them. You must go back home with whoever comes to take you back. Don't make excuses or raise any objections. For if you refuse to go, your character will again be at risk of being judged adversely."

"I will not return home with anyone else but you."

"In that case, I'll take you to your house in Kolkata and explain the entire matter properly to him."

"Of the three reasons that you talked about, I have now followed the first. What's the second?"

"I think that you still believe quite firmly in Sharat's innocence. But let me tell you that I have no doubt that it was Sharat who has robbed you of your virtue and your wealth. At any rate, in order to open your eyes to the truth, I'll first try and find them in this place. I'll search for them as thoroughly as I can and if they are in some sort of trouble, we'll find them quite easily. Otherwise you'll know that my conjecture was correct."

"And what's your third reason?"

"My third reason would be to nab the person who's responsible for stealing your money and jewellery."

"I won't say anything against your wishes. Especially since I'm a woman. I am extremely impressionable, which is why this has happened to me. Please do whatever you think is necessary. From now on I'm prepared to follow whatever instructions you'll have for me."

"You are saying that now but I'm not very certain about your actual intentions. Maybe I'll have a better sense of what's on your mind once I've spent a few days with you. Well, I'm not sure that even then I would be able to gauge your mind completely. For I doubt that there's a single man on this earth who can claim to understand a woman's mind fully."

"You may think whatever you choose, but the truth is that I haven't concealed anything from you and I won't in the future either. Nor will I go against your wishes. I don't really care what kind of repercussions this will have on my future."

We conversed in this manner while the cart moved in the opposite direction and I lay down inside it, in the manner that I have described earlier. Usha kept sitting near my feet. My presence was no longer making her shy or awkward in any way.

Part II

V

In due course we reached the bazaar. By the time we reached the bazaar, it was nearly two in the afternoon. During my investigation, I got to know that there was a post office and a *thhana* very close to the bazaar. I went to the post office and posted the letter and then went to the *thhana*. Usha kept sitting inside the cart.

When I visited the *thhana*, I saw the *daroga* of that place sitting there. He was an Oriya Kayastha. I had made his acquaintance when I had travelled to that area while working on an investigation. He recognised me instantly and asked me what had brought me to the *thhana*.

"Do you know of any incident that has occurred in your area?"

Daroga: "What incident are you referring to?"

"A robbery."

"No, I'm sure I don't have any information about that? When and where did it happen?"

"On the road to Puri."

"What was it that was stolen?"

"Money and jewellery."

"And what would have been the value of the stolen goods?"

"Almost four to five hundred rupees."

"How is it that such a major robbery has happened, and yet I have absolutely no knowledge of it? Nobody's come to report it at the *thhana*. Who was it that lost so much jewellery and money?"

"That person is sitting in my cart."

"Has the person come to register a complaint?"

"I can't say that the person has come to file a complaint, but it's true that I have brought her here."

"Where did you find her?"

I: "I found her sitting by the road. Once I realised that she was completely alone and helpless, I brought her along with me. It is clear that she belongs to a respectable family in Kolkata. Besides, I have heard of her father and he's a well-known gentleman."

"How did she get robbed?"

"She had left her house in Kolkata in order to travel with a group of people who were on their way to Puri. The thieves must have somehow got to know that she was carrying a lot of money and jewels and that's why two men followed her all the way from Kolkata. At some point, they introduced themselves as travellers and then managed to insert themselves into the group and began moving with them. Eventually, they bought some foodstuff for the women and gave it to them. After a while, the girl lost consciousness and as a result she can't recall what happened at that time. Finally, when she opened her eyes, she found that she was lying on the side of the road and that there was no one else with her. All her belongings had disappeared, the jewellery she was wearing had gone and the only things that she was left with were the clothes that she was wearing. I noticed her lying next to the road as I was returning from Cuttack in a cart, and after I had taken her into the cart, I gradually found out about the circumstances in which she had ended up there. I have told you all that I could elicit from her."

"Was she on the road with all the other travellers?"

"All the others were on foot, but she had hired a cart and was going along with them."

"When she consumed the eatables, was she sitting in the cart or had she alighted and was standing with the others?"

"As far I know, she sat in the cart and ate the foodstuff and then fainted after a while."

"Where's the cart-driver?"

"He seems to have disappeared as well. I told you earlier that when the girl recovered her consciousness, she found that she was lying by the wayside. She never saw the cart-driver after waking up."

"This doesn't sound like a simple case of theft. For they were given poisonous food to make them lose consciousness and then all their possessions were looted. This being the case, what do you want me to do?"

"What would you want to do?"

"Do you think we'll be able to solve this case?"

"It's not as though the case can't be solved if it is investigated thoroughly. For if you can find out about the two men who had pursued them from Kolkata, trace their whereabouts and find out where they live, then it's quite possible that the case will get solved."

"Perhaps if I can find the cart-driver, that would really help me solve the case."

"I am not so sure about that."

"Why do you say that?"

"If the two men who were pursuing them had removed the girl from the cart as soon as she had fainted, paid the cart-driver his fare and sent him on his way, then it's unlikely that we'll get any kind of assistance from him. But if those two men are arrested then the witness statement of the cart-driver will become crucial."

"And what if the entire thing was perpetrated by the cart-driver?"

"I don't think so. For in that case why would she have been left in this manner on the roadside?"

"Well, if you are so convinced that this was committed by those two men and that they came following these people all the way from Kolkata, then why don't you get this case moved to that city and investigate it over there? And if you need any help in your investigations here, I'll be more than willing to provide it."

"Why do you feel so nervous about taking on this case?"

"You are an extremely experienced police officer so I don't think you need an answer to that question from me. If I take this case on, there is no way that I'll be able to complete the investigation in the way that I want. For as soon as the news spreads that I have started working on this case, the Inspector of the area will arrive. After that, the Jailor *sahib* and his assistant will also come and try to shove their respective oars into the investigation and, in short, wreak havoc on the case. And I'm sure you know only too well that once all the senior officials begin to gather for the solving of a case, the investigation is pretty much doomed. Such cases often remain unsolved, since every senior official has a different opinion on the matter and the officers are obliged to pursue every suggested manner of investigation. Besides, when senior officials are present, the junior officers are not responsible for the final solving of the case, and as such they don't feel very motivated to come up with their own views on the investigation. In fact, if you remember that adage which talks of too many cooks spoiling the broth, then you'll know what I'm talking about. That's why I feel that if you could get the case transferred to Kolkata and start investigating it by yourself, and we agree to help from the outside, then the case has far brighter chances of being solved successfully."

"What you are saying is completely true! I know this only too well. Even I don't want this case to be investigated here. I know that if this case is registered and investigated here, the young girl who hails from a respectable family will have to go through hell. Whichever officer arrives here to investigate this case will then want to summon the appellant and hear everything from her. I have heard her account of all that happened very carefully and I've even begun to think of ways in which her jewellery and money can be restored to her. But I have a very important reason for coming to you. I'm pretty sure that the theft was committed by none other than the two men whom I talked of suspecting. Besides, I also feel that since the robbery was committed yesterday, the two men couldn't have gone very far; there are no trains or any other fast means of transport that go on this route and so they would have had to either take a cart or walk. I am a stranger to these parts, and besides, I don't have too many people assisting me here. As such, I don't really have the wherewithal with which I can follow or investigate them and then place them under arrest. But if you were to take this on, I'm sure you'll be able to find them quite easily. That's the reason why I have paid you a visit."

"You have saved me from the terrible problems that I would have had to face, if the case were registered here. So of course I will do this for you. Why don't you wait here for a while and I'll make arrangements to begin this work."

With these words, the *daroga* sahib called all the junior officers who were present in the *thhana* at the time, and then, after gathering all the information about the physical appearance of the two men from me, he sent all his men in different directions along with all this information. Some went on foot, some on horseback and others in carriages. They were instructed to look for the two men in every bazaar and ask every shop-keeper, cart-driver and traveller whom they might meet on the road whether they had seen anyone who fitted the description. Needless to say, I paid for the expenses that would be incurred on these journeys from my own pocket. All the various officers collected their money and then set off, one by one.

After bidding them farewell, the *daroga* fixed an accommodation for me and requested me to remain in that place till the officers returned. I accepted his offer and stayed in that house along with Usha and the constable who had been travelling with me. From time to time I would leave the house along with the *daroga* and ask various people whom we saw on the road about the two men.

The next day was meant to be the day when the *chaukidars* of the various villages that came under the jurisdiction of the *thhana* were supposed to come and report to the senior officer of the *thhana*. By noon, all the *chaukidars* of the nearby villages had gathered over there.

The *daroga* then called all of them to one place and addressed them in this manner: "Two men, who look like this, have gone missing in since the last few days. They have a great deal of jewellery and money with them. The *chaukidar* who's able to locate them and bring them to us, or bring information about them for us, will be duly awarded by the govt. when the case is over. And we'll pay the person Rupees two hundred from our side as soon as he gets us any news."

Upon hearing of a prize money which they could get from the govt. at a later point, along with the sum of Rupees two hundred that they would get from us immediately, the poor, underpaid *chaukidars* rushed off to investigate the whereabouts of the two men in their respective villages. The *thhana* had villages that spread up to forty miles under its jurisdiction. There was therefore no doubt in my mind that if those two men were anywhere in any of the villages in that forty-mile radius, they would surely be found and arrested by one of the *chaukidars*.

After those men, who were greatly excited at the prospect of the prize money, had left in search of the two offenders, I began to feel a little concerned about something. It was true that we had promised to pay the *chaukidars* two hundred rupees for capturing the men and retrieving the stolen goods, but the men they would be arresting had a lot of valuables with them and could easily bribe their potential captors with far greater money. As such, I began to worry as to whether the low-born, poor *chaukidars* would be able to resist the temptation of far greater money than what we would be able to give them and bring the culprits back to us. Such thoughts did arise in my mind, but not having any way of preventing such an eventuality, I was forced to trust the *chaukidars*.

VI

Usha, my constable and I continued to stay in the house that the *daroga* had fixed for us. The house was situated in the bazaar, near the *thaana* that I have mentioned earlier. It belonged to a shopkeeper of the area and he had built the rooms for travellers to stay or/and have their meals in. The owner of the place also owned a shop nearby which had most things that are needed in order to cook meals. Even though the stuff that he had was not of great quality, he stocked most of what would be considered essentials in those regions, for instance utensils, wood for lighting a fire, coarse rice, oil, salt and vegetables. Puffed rice and sweets were also available most of the time in his shop. Once we started living near that shop, the Brahmin constable brought all the necessary stuff from there and cooked a meal for all of us. He kept his food separately and then presented the rest to Usha and me. By the time he had finished cooking, it was fairly late in the evening and, not having had a morsel to eat all day, it felt as if a fire was raging in our bellies. As soon as the food was served, I sat down to eat and urged Usha to begin eating as well. It was evident that Usha was also terribly hungry for without further ado, she shed all her feminine inhibitions and sat down promptly at some distance to eat her food. Even though I was no longer a complete stranger to Usha, by now she had started treating me as though I were a member of her family or a very close friend and as such there were no traces of shyness or embarrassment in her behaviour. We spent two days in this manner in that place.

Of the various *chaukidars* who had gone off in search of the two men, several returned after two days without having found any traces of the suspects. Many of them who had left for their respective villages in order to look for the suspects said they had been unable to get any kind of news of the two men. Another day thus passed while all this happened. I began to feel that it would be nigh on impossible to get any further information about Sharat and his friend in these parts. We then decided to leave that place and return to Kolkata. The cart that we had come in was still waiting for us nearby. But as we were preparing to get into the cart, two *chaukidars* and a constable of another local *thhana* came and stood before us. Looking at them I got the feeling that they were carrying some news for us. I asked the constable, "Do you have any information for us?"

Constable: "I think I have relevant information for you but I'm not entirely sure."

"Well, what is the news?"

"There's a bazaar located about ten or twelve miles away from here on the road to Puri."

"Yes, I know about that. I have been through it."

"There are some prostitutes who live in one of the houses in that bazaar."

"Go on."

"There were two men, matching the description that you gave us, who spent a day and a night in that house. They apparently had a fair amount of money with them. While they were there, they saw an empty carriage that was on its way from Puri and they quickly hired it and set off for Kolkata."

"I don't see any horse-drawn carriages on this road. How did they manage to find one?"

"It's true that horse-drawn carriages on this route are rare, but there are times that one finds one or two. This happens especially if there's a wealthy person who comes this way from Kolkata and hires a horse-drawn carriage and then lets it go after reaching Puri. Such carriages are often empty on their way back. I think they must have found a carriage of that kind returning from Puri and hired it to go back to Kolkata."

"In that case we won't be able to find them easily, will we? If they left this place two days ago in a horse-drawn carriage, then there's no way we can follow them now in a cart and hope to catch them. Perhaps if we try to chase them on a very swift horse, we might be able to get hold of them."

At the time that I was talking to the constable, the *daroga* was also standing nearby. Hearing my words, he said, "There's no one who has a horse in a radius of eight or ten miles in this area. The only person with a horse here is me. And at the moment, a junior officer has taken that horse for investigating some matter and hasn't returned as yet. If he returns after a while, I'll send someone on that road or go myself to catch your culprits. If you decide to return to Kolkata on this road, you'll surely see a horse rider passing you."

I agreed to the *daroga*'s suggestion and went back to our cart. Usha didn't waste any words either and silently climbed into it even before I got in. Our cart resumed its journey towards Kolkata. The constable who had accompanied me began to walk behind the cart. While inside the cart, I kept turning around to see if a horse rider was coming down the road, but no such person followed us.

VII

Eventually we reached Kolkata, after travelling on the Puri road for quite some time. It's not as though I was spared the troubles that one usually faces when one travels with a female travel companion. But if I were to describe them, I would have to write a separate book devoted to that topic alone. Anyway, we managed to overcome all those problems and reached Kolkata. We travelled in the same cart till a point where we could hire a horse-drawn carriage. We reached Kolkata in the carriage. On the way we didn't meet anyone who had been sent by Usha's father.

Upon reaching Kolkata, I said to Usha, "What do you wish to do now? Do you want to go to your father's house by yourself?"

"Do you think my father has received the letter that you sent him?"

"I don't really see any reason for him not to have received it. I'm fairly certain that he has got it by now."

"Hasn't he then believed what you wrote about me?"

"Why do you think that?"

"Wouldn't he have sent someone to look for me, if he had?"

"How do you know he hasn't sent anyone?"

"Wouldn't we have seen him on the road?"

"Well, I can't say for certain that we would have seen him on the road. For it wasn't as if we were on the road all the time. At night we would stop and sleep in rooms that we hired from inn keepers in bazaars, wouldn't we? It would have been quite easy for anyone sent by your father to have missed us at that time and go on ahead. So it's hard to say whether he sent someone or not."

"Do you think I should go back immediately to my father's house?"

"In my opinion, it would be your duty to do so."

"I'll do whatever you think is my duty. But think about this scenario: what if my father hasn't believed what you said about me, decided that I had disgraced myself and therefore didn't send anyone to find me? In that case when he sees me and says, 'I don't want to see your face. You've brought shame to our family. Get out of here!'—what am I going to do? Can you imagine how I'll feel? At that time, I'll have no other choice but to commit suicide. And yet where will I get the stuff to kill myself with?"

"How will your father know that you had eloped with someone? I got to know about all that had happened because you told me everything in detail. But how would he know all the things that happened?"

"Do you really think the news about my elopement with Sharat hasn't spread yet? Around the time that my parents realised that I was missing from home, the news about Sharat's disappearance must also have spread. What do you think are the conclusions that everyone would draw in these circumstances? For everyone knew that Sharat visited our house frequently and so our disappearance at the same time would surely lead them to believe that we had eloped. I therefore don't wish to return to my father. Please take me elsewhere. I am even willing to work as a maid in your house to earn my livelihood."

"I think I know all that's going through your mind. If your father doesn't take you back, but Sharat wants to marry you, will you be willing to go to him?"

"Oh no Sir! How can you speak of Sharat! Just think of what he did, of how he ruined my life despite my having loved him with all my heart and even committing the great sin of elopement for his sake. Please don't take his name in front of me. I'm prepared to kill myself if you ask me to. But I'm never ever going to take his name again for the rest of my life, let alone going back to him. Whether you wish to give me refuge or not, I'm never going to leave your side. For as long as I live, I'm going to stay close to wherever you are."

"I can understand your feelings. To begin with, I am going to take you to your father's place and not to my house. But I won't take you into the house as soon we get there. You can keep sitting in the carriage with the doors closed while I go into the house by myself and meet your father. Once I meet him, I'll have no difficulty in gauging how he feels about the entire thing. I'll then decide what to do based on what I see. If I feel that he has believed everything that I have said in my letter about you and has no suspicions whatsoever, then I'll take you inside and hand you over to him. Else I'll take you to my house."

After assuring Usha in this manner, I took her to her house. I asked the carriage to stop and wait at some distance and, leaving Usha sitting inside it, I went into her house alone. When I walked in, her father was sitting with some other gentlemen in the outer room of their house. I introduced myself and felt that my name wasn't entirely unfamiliar to him even though he probably couldn't place me immediately. He asked me, "How can I help you?"

"I wish to make your acquaintance."

"Please tell me what you want."

"The reason why I'm here is something that I can't discuss in front of everyone. Is it possible to talk to you in private?"

Upon hearing my words, he got up from his chair and after leading me to the veranda said, "What is it that you want to tell me?"

"I had written a letter to you and sent it some time ago. Did you get the letter?"

"You have written a letter to me? Where from? And why?"

"I wrote it on my way back from Puri."

"Is that the one that contained news about Usha?"

"Yes."

"I did receive it and even sent one of my sons to that place to fetch her. Why, didn't you meet him on the road?"

"No Sir, we didn't."

"Then where is Usha, at the moment?"

"I have brought her with me."

"You had written that robbers had stolen all the valuables that she had taken with her. What all did they take?"

"They took all the jewels that she had on her person and besides that they also robbed her of all the money that she was carrying with her."

"How did the robbers get hold of the jewels on her person?"

"They had mixed some poisonous things with her food that made her lose consciousness after a while. After that it wasn't difficult for them to steal her jewellery."

"The poison could even have killed her, couldn't it?"

"Yes, very much so. She was saved by a hair's breadth if you ask me. It was god's grace that kept her alive. If I hadn't reached the place where she was lying, quite by chance at exactly that moment, then nothing could have prevented her from falling right into the jaws of death."

"You had written in your letter that it was two men from Kolkata who had pursued her and then finally robbed her of her valuables?"

"My investigations of the matter suggest that that's what must have happened."

"Have you got any idea who these two might be?"

"I haven't been able to find out their names since my investigation is not yet complete. I have reached Kolkata just now."

"I think I have some information on the matter. If you wish, I can tell you what I have heard."

"What is it that you can tell me?"

"There is a hostel very close to our house."

"What about it?"

"Two men suddenly went missing from that hostel the very night that Usha left the house."

"Does anyone know where those two might have gone?"

"No, no one has been able to say anything. But at that time many of my enemies began to spread the rumour that Usha had eloped with one of the two men."

"Can you tell me what their names are?"

"One of them is called Sharat. About the other one I have no idea."

"So it seems that it was these two fellows who followed Usha that day when she left the house, and then robbed her of all her belongings when they got the opportunity. What I have learned from my initial investigation of the matter was that the two men who robbed the travellers had followed them all the way from Kolkata. Anyway, have you tried to find out if Sharat and his friend have returned to Kolkata?"

"No, I haven't got any information about that and truth be told, I wasn't particularly interested in finding out either."

"One should try and find out whether they have come back. If I can catch them at this point, then we can easily retrieve all the stolen goods."

"I have no idea what all Usha had taken with her and what then got stolen. Where is Usha now? Has she gone into the house?"

"No, she hasn't entered the house yet. I asked her to wait in the carriage while I came here to see you and asked you a few questions. She is still waiting in the carriage. If you permit it, I'll bring her to you now."

"You could bring her here or if you tell me where the carriage is waiting, I could send a maid who'll get the carriage to come inside."

"I'll go and bring her here."

Saying this, I left that place.

VIII

When I reached the place where Usha was waiting in the carriage, she saw me and asked immediately, "So what's the news?"

"The news is good."

"What kind of good news is it?"

"Your father had believed everything that I wrote in my letter and had in fact sent your brother to the Cuttack road to get you back."

"Do you mean to say he didn't doubt my character in the slightest bit?"

"He did. To begin with, everyone thought that you had ruined your family's name and run away with Sharat, but my letter laid their fears to rest. Now everyone believes that Sharat is a thief and that he followed you and then returned after stealing all your valuables."

"So what do you suggest should I do?"

"Come with me. I want to take you to your father and be relieved of my responsibility."

"So I have to go back to the house and return to the life of a prisoner?"

"What's this that you're saying Usha? I can't understand what you mean. Are you saying that you don't wish to return to your father's house?"

"I do wish to go back but then once I go in, there'll be no way of being in touch with you. In case I feel tormented in that house for some reason, or if someone casts aspersions on my character and there are all kinds of whispers behind my back, I won't be able to bear it. I'll want to leave my father's house for certain. But if I know where your house is, then I wouldn't have to seek refuge elsewhere; I would come to you straight away. For having spent the last few days with you I have got to know you fairly well and I have come to believe whole-heartedly that I can trust you completely."

"There is absolutely no need for you to be this anxious. You won't have to do any such thing for I'm quite sure that once you go back, you won't have to leave your father's house ever again and that your parents will look after you in every possible way. But despite everything, if you ever feel the need to reach out to me, then write a letter and I'll try to meet you. I have already told you what my address is. Besides, if I come to this side of the city for work, I won't forget to pay your house a visit and find out how you are."

"It's true that you'll get news about me but if you come to visit I'll never be able to talk freely to you in front of everyone else. So if I listen to you and go back to my father's house, then I beg you to show me where you live. If there's a crisis and I need to see you, I'll find a way of going to your house."

"There's no time to do that now. If you had thought of this earlier, I would have taken you there before coming here. Since we couldn't do this earlier, there's no way to do it now. But I can assure you that I'll have to keep visiting your house till such time as Sharat is arrested and your valuables are restored to you. And on one such day when I come to visit, I'll convince your father to allow you to accompany me to my house so that you know where I live. After that you'll able to come and visit me whenever you wish to."

"Alright. If you say so. Please bear in mind Sir, that I'm returning to my father's house at your insistence. But please don't forget your promise. Do take me with you some day soon to show me where you live. Else tell me now and I won't step into my father's house."

"Don't worry. I'll definitely find a way to take you to see my house very soon."

When Usha heard these words, she agreed to go into her house. I saw that Usha's mother and several other women from inside the house had come out and were waiting for her near the gate. As soon as Usha stepped out the carriage, her mother rushed to her, held her hand and then after showering kisses on her face took her inside the house. I went back to sit near Usha's father once again. After talking with him for a while, I said, "Sir, I have been on various roads for quite some time now and feel utterly exhausted as a result of this long journey. So if you allow me, I would like to take your leave and go back home and rest. I'll come back later and meet you."

"As you wish. But how do we get Usha's jewellery back?"

"Why don't you first talk to Usha, and hear all that she has to say? After that I would suggest you think about the entire thing calmly and decide what you want to do. You could also try and find out whether Sharat has returned to the neighbourhood. Meanwhile, after resting for a while, I'll apprise my senior officials of all that's happened and then we'll take the case forward in the way that we think would be best. I'll come and see you whenever it's convenient."

"Alright. Please do whatever you feel would be right. I'll find out if Sharat has returned. When will you be able to come and meet me?"

"I won't return today. But I'll come and meet you tomorrow in the evening and do my duty to the best of my abilities."

"Please keep this in mind and don't forget us. If you don't help, I'll end up losing a great deal of money."

"No, I won't forget. I'll come and meet you tomorrow evening."

With this I left the place.

IX

Soon after taking his leave, I returned home and then in due course, I met my senior officer and gave him a version of the developments in the Usha-related case—the way in which I had found her on the Cuttack road, how her possessions had been stolen etc. It was the same version of the events that I had given to her father. After hearing the account, my superior said, "If that's where Usha's valuables were stolen, then why didn't you file a case over there at the local police station? They would have investigated the case and if necessary, you could have assisted them."

"I had gone there and talked to the officers about this but then Usha was reluctant to file a case of theft in that place, so I brought her to Kolkata."

"Where is she now?"

"I have left her at her father's house."

"Is she willing to make a formal complaint now?"

"I can't quite answer that question without meeting her once, for who knows what she'll decide to do after talking to her parents."

"Even if she does, it might still be impossible to solve the case."

"That may not be true, since I do know who the culprits are."

"Who are they?"

"A man named Sharat, along with his friend, has committed the robbery."

"How were you able to find this out?"

"On my way back, I tried to investigate the matter a little and I came to know that at the time when Usha and the other women left their home and set off for the pilgrimage, two men began to follow them from Kolkata. Later, as soon as the two saw an opportunity, they robbed the women and made their escape. I have found out where Sharat and his friend used to live in Kolkata and I've also got to know that they escaped in the direction of Kolkata in a horse-drawn carriage with all the stolen goods. We came on the same road that they had taken, and I asked various people I met along the way whether they had seen anyone matching their description. I have got news that the carriage has entered Kolkata."

"Well, if you feel that this case can be solved, shouldn't we then take it on and begin investigation?"

"Let me meet and talk to Usha and her father one more time and find out what they have to say. I'll also try to find out where Sharat is at the moment and where he might have kept all the stolen stuff. Subsequently, if they lodge a formal complaint, then I'll decide whether to transfer the case to the place where the theft had taken place."

After talking to my superior officer in this manner, I went to Usha's father's house later in the evening. As soon as he saw me, Usha's father asked, "So have you been able to recover the stolen valuables?"

I: "Have you decided whether you'll be registering a formal complaint?"

"If you think that's what we should do then I'll do that. I'll never be able to repay you for all that you have done for me. And I also know that you'll never give us advice that can harm us in any way. So I'm willing to do whatever you ask me to. If you ask me to forget about all the stolen money and the extremely valuable jewellery, I can even do that."

"Have you found out about the things that I had asked you to?"

Usha's father: "Yes, I did."

"What did you find out?"

"We had found out earlier that Sharat and his friend had left the hostel the very night that Usha had left the house. We've now got to know that the two of them came back to the hostel about three days before you returned with Usha. They were in the hostel for a day and then they left and no one knows where they have gone. They apparently told the people who run the hostel that they were going back to their village."

"Do you have any idea where their village is?"

"I know the district they belong to, but not the village. I've heard that there are a few others living in the hostel who've come from the same village."

While I was conversing with Usha's father in this manner, there was no one else in the room, but after a while, I saw that Usha had come and was standing at some distance, almost hidden from view. I then said to her father, "I think Usha has come here. Have you asked her what all she has lost?"

Usha's father: "I have asked her that."

"So, what have you decided? Are you prepared to file a case against Sharat and his friend?"

"What other choice do I have? Not complaining will mean I'll lose all that money."

"If you decide to file a complaint, then Usha will need to meet my superior officer once and tell him everything that has happened."

"Isn't he an English *sahib*?"

"Yes."

"Then how will this be possible? How can Usha go to meet a *sahib* and talk to him?"

"She doesn't need to go and meet him. All she'll have to do is go to my house along with me. The officer will come over there and I'll give the answers to the two or three questions that he might want to ask her. Usha simply needs to be present."

"After all that you have done for us, I have no objection whatsoever to Usha going to your house. But I'll need to find out if Usha's willing to go there."

Usha was right there, and she said, "What reservations can I have about going to the house of the person, who saved my life? I'm prepared to go this very moment."

I'm sure readers have understood what the actual purpose of such a proposal was. I had promised Usha that I would arrange to take her to my house and make sure that she know its location. When Usha heard my proposal to her father, she understood immediately what I had in mind and was ready to accompany me. I took Usha along and went to my house. This time she was chaperoned by a maid. There was no proposal of any kind made by my superior officer, even though that's what I told Usha's father. So while Usha was in my house, neither did any *sahib* pay us a visit, nor was Usha asked any questions. She stayed in my house till ten at night and then I went back with her and made sure that she reached her home safely. After this incident, whenever Usha felt like it or had the opportunity, she would pay my house a visit. Her parents came to know about this but neither of them objected to it.

X

A case was filed against Sharat and his friend and I embarked on the investigation myself. I went to their hostel and found out that they had indeed been missing from there for quite a few days. And then they suddenly appeared one fine day, and after spending just a day in the hostel they informed everyone that they were going back to their village.

Then they left the premises yet again. No one knew where they had actually gone. I knew that a couple of men staying in that hostel had come from Sharat's village. Once I gathered Sharat's address from them and then asked one of them who knew what Sharat looked like to accompany me, it didn't take me long to locate the two culprits. The two men denied ever being on the road to Cuttack, knowing any girl called Usha or pursuing her anywhere.

Since I knew the inside story only too well, I didn't believe a single word they uttered. Their house was searched thoroughly and while I couldn't see any jewellery, I did see a great deal of cash in a box belonging to them. Given their circumstances, it was nigh on impossible for them to possess that much cash. As such, I turned a deaf ear to their protestations that the money was theirs and took both men along with the money and went to the nearby *thhana*. In the *thhana*, I handcuffed both of them and placed them in custody. They were in a cell that entire night.

Early next morning I brought them out of the cell and made them sit next to me and then said, "The two of you will go to prison even though you are innocent."

Sharat: "Why do you say that?"

"Because you are not telling the truth."

"But I am!"

"What truth is that?"

"What's it that you want to know?"

"I want to know from where you got all the money that we have recovered from you."

"Why, it's my own money!"

"That's a complete lie. I know only too well where that cash has come from. There's no point in trying to hide anything from me. By lying, the two of you are only widening the road that leads to a prison cell, whereas in my opinion, if you told me the truth, you would escape unscathed in the trial."

"What's the truth?"

"Look Sharat, it's one thing to steal from someone but it's a different thing altogether if a woman becomes infatuated with you and then decides, of her own will, to give you all her worldly belongings. That can't be considered a theft. Usha had been infatuated with you for many days and had obsessively thought about ways to meet you secretly. Her desire to leave her house by whatever means she could, seek refuge with you and then spend the rest of her life in your house, has clearly not been fulfilled. As soon as she found the opportunity, she eloped with you and then out of love, she gave all her valuables to you. And because of your own foolishness, you are now being termed a villain for having accepted all that she gave you, of her own free will! Tell me, is there anyone more stupid than you in this whole wide world?"

"How do you know all this? Did Usha tell you this?"

"Do you think I can't figure all of this out on my own, without Usha telling me anything? You were on the Cuttack road traveling to Puri. We have spoken to the drivers of the various horse-drawn carriages and bullock carts that you hired and that the three of you travelled in. So now you can decide whether I succeeded in unearthing the truth about everything that happened, or not. Don't you think it would be utter foolishness on your part to go to prison on charges of theft whereas the truth is that Usha gave everything to you of her own accord?

After hearing my words, Sharat drew his friend to a corner and the two of them confabulated for some time. Finally, they approached me and said, "Whatever you have found out till now through your investigation, is absolutely true. None of it is false. But please tell us, what we should do now? Has Usha accused us of theft?"

"I haven't met or talked to Usha yet. It is her brother and father who have accused the two of you of theft. I don't know what Usha herself would say. But why don't you tell me what the truth is?"

"All that you have heard is the truth."

"So it was Usha who gave you all the money and her ornaments?"

"Yes Sir, she gave it to us."

"So then what have you done with her ornaments?"

"Since I needed some cash, I have pawned the jewels."

"Where did you pawn them?"

"In Kolkata."

"Can you show me the place?"

"If you take me to Kolkata, I can show you the place."

Through such means, I was able to elicit information from Sharat about what he had done with Usha's jewels.

I brought Sharat and his friend to Kolkata after this. They directed me to the place where they had pawned Usha's jewellery. Once that happened, I arranged for its retrieval.

Soon after this, Sharat abandoned all sense of shame and began announcing to the world, even to Usha's father and brother, that he had not stolen Usha's jewels. He claimed that long before Usha had left her house, she had become infatuated with him and had gradually started giving him her jewellery. Eventually she discarded all sense of shame and concern for her family's honour and decided to elope with him. He said he would be able to get several shopkeepers from the Cuttack road as witnesses and their testimonies would prove whether he had followed her like a thief or Usha had accompanied him like a wife. Usha, he said, was a depraved woman, which is why she had eloped with him but after a few days, she grew tired of him. She set her sights on someone else and that's the reason why he had left her on the road all by herself. After all, how could he stay with a woman who, soon after eloping with him, began making overtures to someone else? That was the reason why he had abandoned her on the road and gone away.

Sharat thus began to malign Usha's character. However, in the given circumstances, no one believed what he said. He had been arrested on charges of theft so who, after all, was going to believe him? Once a man is arrested for a crime, no judge will believe what he says, unless he can produce evidence to support his claims. Sharat and his friend said very many things of the kind mentioned earlier, and tried very hard to tarnish Usha's name, but since they weren't able to furnish any proof, no one believed their accusations. On the other hand, the testimonies of various shopkeepers and cart-drivers from the Cuttack road brought to light the manner in which Sharat and his friend had bought food for Usha which had rendered her unconscious in the cart, and how they had then fled with her jewellery. Thanks to our efforts and the money spent by the govt., all of them were able to come to Kolkata and give statements freely in court about everything they had seen and heard. The statement of one cart-driver in particular convinced everyone that Usha had fainted after eating food given to her by Sharat and his friend. He said that after hiring the cart, all three had travelled in it and that at one particular point in the journey, instead of making any arrangements to cook, the two men went and bought some food and then divided it into two different packets. They gave one of those to Usha while they ate from the other. Usha began to lose consciousness upon eating that food and once she had passed out completely, they carried her out of the cart and placed her on the roadside. Then they took out all their luggage from the cart and asked him to leave. The place where they left Usha had nothing but wilderness for miles around. After leaving them there, the cart-driver had gone to the nearest bazaar to have a meal and rest, and while he was sitting there, he had seen the two men going off with all their belongings in a different vehicle. Usha was not with them. He had gone up to them and asked them about Usha's whereabouts, but the men had ignored him and left hurriedly. There's no gainsaying that I behaved immorally in concealing quite a few truths while presenting the case against Sharat in court. Having made a reprehensible promise to a gentlewoman that I would do everything possible to protect her reputation, I had no choice but to be true to my word. As a result, even though I knew a great deal more about Usha, I did not make anything public.

When Sharat and his friend were produced in front of the judge and Usha was also brought in to give her statement, Sharat asked her several questions to make her reveal everything that had happened, but she held her own counsel. The judge became convinced that it was in order to save his own skin that the convict was harassing Usha with false accusations. The two men were punished accordingly. Only those two men and I were truly aware of the whole truth about Usha. Usha is still alive but she seems to have aged a fair bit. Till date, she comes to our house at regular intervals and spends time with all of us.

Priyanath Mukhopadhyay

Notes

1 Cuttack is a town in Odisha, a neighbouring state to Bengal. Puri, another town in Odisha, is known for the famous Jagannath temple that draws several pilgrims from all over India. Oriya is a word used to refer to the inhabitants of Odisha.
2 The *bagdis* are a "scheduled caste" today. Variously described as "indigenous", "aboriginal" and "tribal", they are wood-cutters, fishermen, litter carriers, and agricultural wage labourers/share-croppers. Three sub-castes—Tentule, Kushmete and Mal—form this caste group. I am deeply indebted to Saswati Sengupta for the detailed information and history of caste groups in Bengal.
3 *Panda* refers to a network of men who operate within Puri and convince devotees visiting the Jagannath temple that they will be given a faster and smoother entry into the temple sanctum in exchange for money.
4 Often women from respectable and elite families travelled in groups (that were not necessarily segregated in terms of caste) to visit places of pilgrimage like Puri.

INDEX

For Product Safety Concerns and Information please contact our EU representative GPSR@taylorandfrancis.com
Taylor & Francis Verlag GmbH, Kaufingerstraße 24, 80331 München, Germany

www.ingramcontent.com/pod-product-compliance
Lightning Source LLC
Chambersburg PA
CBHW071109100726
47908CB00008B/2324
9780367540999